# FINLAND: PEOPLE, NATION, STATE

# FINLAND

## PEOPLE · NATION · STATE

*Edited by*

## MAX ENGMAN & DAVID KIRBY

HURST & COMPANY, LONDON

INDIANA UNIVERSITY PRESS, BLOOMINGTON AND INDIANAPOLIS

The essays in this collection, excepting
that by David Arter, were originally published
in Swedish in *Historisk Tidskrift för Finland*, 3 (1987)

First published in the United Kingdom by
C. Hurst & Co. (Publishers) Ltd.,
38 King Street, London WC2E 8JT
© Historiska föreningen, Helsingfors, 1989
ISBN 1-85065-055-1
Printed in England on long-life paper

Distributed in North America by Indiana University Press,
Bloomington, Indiana 47405

**Library of Congress Cataloging-in-Publication Data**

Finland : people, nation, state / edited by Max Engman and David Kirby.
    p. cm.
    ''All the essays in this collection, excepting that by David Arter,
were originally published in Swedish in Historisk tidskrift
for Finland, 3 (1987).'' T.p. verso.
    Includes bibliographies and index.
    ISBN 0-253-32067-4
    1. Finland—History.    I. Engman, Max.    II. Kirby, D. G.
III. Historisk tidskrift för Finland.
DL1032.F56    1989
948.97—dc 19                                                    88-33057

1 2 3 4 5    93 92 91 90 89

# CONTENTS

# THE AUTHORS

*Risto Alapuro* is professor of sociology at the University of Jyväskylä. He has published a study of the Academic Karelian Society (*Akateeminen Karjala-Seura*, Porvoo-Helsinki 1973), and his most recent work is *State and Revolution in Finland*, Berkeley 1988.

*David Arter* teaches government and politics at Leeds Polytechnic, England. His recent works include *The Nordic Parliaments*, London 1985, and *Politics and Policy-making in Finland*, Brighton 1987.

*Erik Allardt* is professor of sociology at the University of Helsinki, and currently chairman of the Finnish Academy. He has written extensively on many aspects of contemporary Finnish society, and has collaborated with scholars in Eastern and Western Europe in a number of joint publications.

*Max Engman* is professor of general history at Åbo Akademi, and has published a major study of Finnish migration to St Petersburg (*St. Petersburg och Finland*, Helsingfors 1983). He is currently working on a comparative study of the successor states.

*Osmo Jussila*, professor of history at the University of Helsinki, has done more than most in recent years to revise the image of the Finnish-Russian relationship. His works include *Venäläinen Suomi*, Porvoo-Helsinki 1983, and *Terijoen hallitus*, Porvoo-Helsinki 1985.

*Eino Jutikkala*, professor emeritus of the University of Helsinki and an academician of the Finnish Academy, is one of the most eminent Finnish historians of his generation. His many publications include *Suomen talonpojan historia*, Helsinki 1958, and (with K. Pirinen) *A History of Finland*, revised edition, London 1979.

*David Kirby* teaches history at the University of London. He is the author of *Finland in the Twentieth Century*, 2nd impression, London 1984, and numerous articles on European socialism.

*Matti Klinge*, professor of history at the University of Helsinki, is writing the official history of the University, and has published a history of the student corps. His many collections of essays include *Bernadotten ja Leninin välissä*, Helsinki 1975, and *Kaksi Suomea*, Helsinki 1982.

*W. R. Mead* is professor emeritus of the University of London. A distinguished geographer and long-time friend of Finland, his publications include *Farming in Finland*, London 1953, and *Finland*, London 1968.

*Jukka Nevakivi*, professor of political history at the University of Helsinki, has specialised in twentieth-century international relations. His study of the proposed Allied intervention in the Winter War was translated as *The Appeal That Was Never Made*, London 1976, and a further study of Anglo-Finnish relations during the war years appeared as *Ystävistä vihollisiksi. Suomi Englannin politiikassa*, Helsinki 1976. He is currently writing the history of the Finnish foreign ministry.

*Aarne Reunala*, of the Institute of Forest Research and a *docent* at the University of Helsinki, has written numerous articles on the forest industry in Finland.

*Hannes Sihvo*, professor of Finnish literature at the University of Joensuu, is a leading expert on Karelia and Karelianism in art and literature. His publications include *Karjalan löytäjät*, Helsinki 1969, and *Karjalan kuva*, Helsinki 1973.

*Irma Sulkunen* is a senior research scholar attached to the Finnish Academy. Her study of the origins and development of the temperance movement in Finland was published as *Raittius kansalaisuskontona*, Helsinki 1986.

*Heikki Ylikangas* is professor of the history of jurisprudence and Roman law at the University of Helsinki. He has a special interest in the violent behaviour of the Ostrobothnians, and has written on the peasants' revolt of 1596–7 and the mayhem and disorder of the period of the knife-fighters. A general overview is given in his article 'Major Fluctuations in Crimes of Violence in Finland', *Scandinavian Journal of History*, 1 (1976), pp. 81–103.

INTRODUCTION

# FINLAND THROUGH THE LOOKING-GLASS

In northern latitudes, December is the darkest month; hardly the most propitious time for celebrating national independence. Thursday 6 December 1917 was a particularly gloomy day; the clear, cold weather of the previous week gave way to gusty flurries of sleet and rain, and the snow in the streets of Helsinki rapidly turned to slush as the day advanced. Galoshes and wet feet were thus much in evidence as the members of the Finnish parliament prepared in the gathering gloom of the early afternoon to take the momentous step towards a declaration of Finnish independence. The decision was not unanimous: a socialist motion calling for a negotiated agreement on independence with Russia was defeated by the non-socialist majority, which authorised the government to take what measures it deemed necessary to gain recognition of Finland's independence.

The sixth of December 1917 has greatly influenced Finnish thinking about the nation's past: but at the time, the launching of the ship of state upon the storm-tossed international waters was a perilous venture. On 26 November, General Ludendorff had urged Finnish representatives in Germany to declare their country independent as soon as possible, and had promised German support. Addressing the Finnish Social Democratic Party congress in Helsinki one day later, the commissar for the nationalities of the new Soviet government, J.V. Stalin, promised fraternal aid for the revolutionary cause. Finland's future as an independent state was in fact very much at the mercy of the shifting currents of international politics. Finland was not the only one of the borderlands of the former Russian empire to declare independence in 1917–18: it was Finland's good fortune however that the decision of the sixth of December also fitted in well with the war aims of the German high command. Of the new states of eastern Europe which came into existence after the First World War, only Finland was able to achieve independence before the final collapse of the Central Powers in November 1918.

At the end of 1917, there were still a number of Russian soldiers and sailors in Finland. One of the first actions of the White troops in the civil war which broke out at the end of January 1918 was to disarm Russian soldiers in Ostrobothnia (thereby permitting the Whites to speak of the war as one of liberation). The assistance given by some Russian troops to the Red side in the civil war, and the subsequent curious state of undeclared hostility between Finland and Soviet Russia, made the recognition of Finnish independence by the Bolshevik government at the end of 1917 largely nugatory. Finland's relationship with Russia was not placed on a formal basis until 1920, when the two countries signed a peace treaty in the Estonian town of Dorpat (Tartu). The pro-German course of the Finnish government in 1918, which imposed serious limitations upon the new state's political, military and economic rights of self-determination, persuaded the French to withdraw their recognition of Finland's independence (granted on 6 January 1918) and the British and Americans to withhold theirs until the spring of 1919.

As on many previous occasions, Finland's fate was determined more by the shifts of international politics than by the actions of the Finns themselves, even if these were not entirely without significance. The declaration of independence was the expression of a desire which was to be realised by virtue of events outside Finland's boundaries. The country's independence is not therefore simply a matter of what happened on that slushy Thursday in December 1917, but is also tied up with the chain of events and international upheavals which occurred between 1917 and 1920.

Even though the declaration of independence was seen in the young republic as the key moment in Finnish history, and the sixth of December is the most important day in the calendar of official celebrations, historians have long debated which other decisive moments have made Finland what it is today. For some, the sixth of December has acted as a kind of looking-glass through which to view the past in search of events presaging independence. Other historians have adopted a more structural perspective, looking at circumstances and events within and outside the country which have exercised a decisive influence on the area which later became Finland, without necessarily regarding these events as pointing the way to independence. The overwhelming concern of Finnish historiography with the state has tended to mean that most of these turning-points have been sought in the area of political history, though they have also been looked for in social and cultural history.

During the interwar years, Finland was commonly regarded as a bastion of the West and Western values against those of the East, whether in the form of the Orthodox church, the Russian state and culture, or Bolshevism. It was therefore natural for nationalist-minded historians of the period to seek to establish when Finland was brought within the Western sphere of culture. The twelfth- and thirteenth-century Crusades thus became important moments of history, though occasionally difficult to pin down to one particular date or even year. Christianity and Swedish colonisation in Finland do in fact predate the Crusades, whose main significance is that they brought much of the land under the influence of the Swedish crown and the Catholic church.

The conquered areas were not however treated as colonies, but soon acquired equal status with the other parts of the Swedish kingdom. A momentous occasion in this respect was the first recorded instance of representatives from Finland taking part in the election of the king of Sweden in 1362. From that time on, Finns continued to participate regularly in meetings of the estates of the realm. The medieval land and town laws, embracing the entire realm, were also important features of this process of integration. The great law code of 1734, which even today contitutes the basis for much Finnish legislation, is in some ways the culmination of this process.

Integration into the Swedish realm also took place in economic and social spheres. There were Finns in Stockholm from the earliest days of the city, and the regions across the sea from the Swedish capital played an important role in the trade and provisioning of the city. From the seventeenth century onwards, Stockholm developed into a true capital in the modern sense, a royal residence and the centre of government, and its influence over the surrounding area, on both sides of the Baltic, was greatly enhanced.

Although Finland was thus drawn more closely within the ambit of the Swedish capital, it was by no means a clearly defined or united area. The very term 'Finland' applied to different areas at different periods. Moreover, there was no linguistic homogeneity in what is the present-day republic of Finland, for although the majority of the inhabitants were Finnish-speaking, there was a sizeable Swedish-speaking population along the coastline. There were also Finnish-speaking communities west of the Gulf of Bothnia. The grand duchy of Finland was not so much a clearly-defined territorial entity as a titular creation of the sixteenth-century kings of Sweden, and the areas administered at various times by specially-appointed governors-general of Finland were never identical.

As a great power in the seventeenth century and as a shrunken remnant of its former glory in the eighteenth, the Swedish realm consisted of territories strung along the coast of the Baltic, and the most integrated parts of the kingdom were those nearest the capital. The peripheral areas, such as the lands wrested from Denmark between 1645 and 1660 and hinterland Finland, were less well integrated, in spite of the growing influence of the Swedish language and the centralist policies of the absolutist kings.

The socio-economic process of integration into the Swedish kingdom was thus uneven, and it is important to stress that there were many parts of what later become known as the grand duchy of Finland after 1809 which fell outside this sphere of influence, but were affected by political and cultural influences from the east. Although these have not traditionally been seen as great moments of history to be compared with the Crusades, such events as the founding of Valamo monastery on Lake Ladoga may be seen as cultural milestones.

The Western and Eastern powers, represented in the Middle Ages by Sweden and Novgorod, soon came into conflict. In 1323, a peace treaty was concluded at Nöteborg, and this established the first eastern frontier of the Swedish kingdom. Whether this frontier ran into the Gulf of Bothnia or further north has occasioned much debate amongst Finnish historians. The southern course of the frontier from the Karelian isthmus to central Finland is however not a matter of dispute, and what is certain is that this frontier irrevocably divided the territory inhabited by the Karelian people between east and west.

The frontier established at Nöteborg was but the first in a long and complicated line of eastern borders. The eastward expansion of the Swedish state in subsequent centuries brought significant new accretions of territory, especially in 1595 and 1617. At the peace of Stolbova in 1617, Sweden succeeded in excluding Russia from the Baltic through the acquisition of the provinces of Kexholm, Ingria and Estonia. These areas were not incorporated into the Swedish kingdom, but were administered separately as conquered provinces.

Finland's position was not only affected by this eastward expansion; the acquisition from Denmark between 1645 and 1660 of territory which now constitutes southern Sweden also meant that the centre of gravity of the kingdom shifted southwards and westwards. With the rise of Russia in the eighteenth century and the loss of territory on the eastern border in 1721 and again in 1743, Finland became an exposed frontier zone once more. Finally, in 1809, after the fourth Russo-Swedish war in less than a century, the 700 years' association with Sweden came to an end. By the terms of the treaty of Fredrikshamn, the frontier was shifted to the Tornio river, the present-day boundary between Sweden and Finland, splitting the Finnish-speaking population in the north.

A major milestone in Russia's westward expansion was the foundation of the new capital of St Petersburg in 1703. Peter the Great's bold decision to site his new capital on territory only recently conquered from the Swedes, in the midst of a war which was to drag on for almost two more

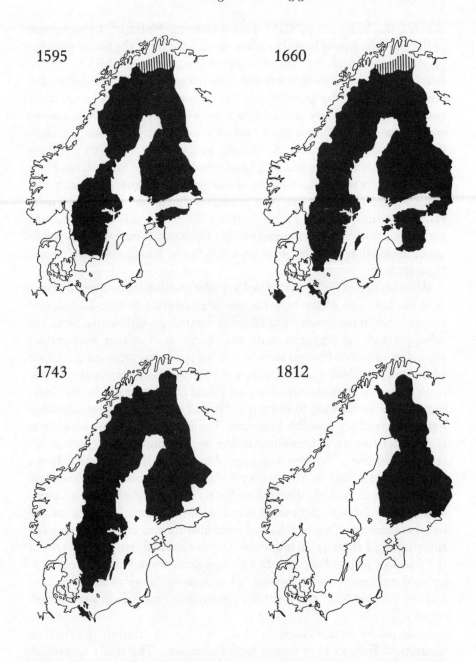

1595

1660

1743

1812

Sweden's rise and decline, 1595–1743. The last map of the sequence shows the Finnish provinces separated from Sweden in 1809, with the addition of the territory taken by Russia in 1721 and 1743.

decades, was to have significant consequences for Finland. The protection of the city which now bears the name of the founder of the Soviet state has played a central and often decisive role in the nine wars which have been fought on Finland's eastern frontier since the beginning of the eighteenth century. St Petersburg grew rapidly and soon extended its influence westwards into the territory acquired by Russia in 1721 and 1743, organised administratively as the province (*guberniya*) of Viborg, but known familiarly as Old Finland. Like Stockholm in an earlier age, St Petersburg became in time an important social and economic centre for Finland. Finns and Swedes are to be found among the earliest inhabitants of the city, and in subsequent decades St Petersburg continued to attract immigrants from eastern Finland and the Finnish towns. The influence of the Russian metropolis was even more apparent after the Russian conquest and subsequent acquisition in 1809 of the area which the Russians briefly termed New Finland.

Whether or not Finland occupied a special position in the Swedish kingdom has been one of the major bones of contention in Finnish historiography. Administratively, Finland was treated no differently from the other parts of the kingdom, with the exception of certain brief periods when large parts of Finland were placed for special reasons under separate administration. Nevertheless, nationalist historians have sought to discover particular features, even a consciousness of a specifically Finnish identity, in their endeavours to show that Finland was indeed a distinctive and separate part of the Swedish kingdom. The Finnish language, which was the mother tongue of four-fifths of the population, is one such feature. (Finnish became a written language during the Reformation, thanks largely to the efforts of Michael Agricola, whose translation of the New Testament into Finnish appeared in 1548.) On the other hand, a knowledge of Swedish was commonly perceived to be essential for a career and social advancement, and this has led some historians to argue that, far from enjoying equal rights, Finland was in fact in a subordinate position within the Swedish realm. Even the fact that soldiers from Finland were conscripted and sent to distant battlefields to fight for the glory and honour of Sweden has been seen as a form of oppression on the part of the Swedish crown.

Attempts by certain elements of the nobility to promote the separate interests of Finland have also attracted attention. The father of Finnish nationalist historiography, G.Z. Yrjö-Koskinen, claimed in the nineteenth century that the support of the Finnish nobility for the Catholic king Sigismund against his uncle, duke Karl, at the end of the sixteenth century was motivated by national interests, a claim which has not gone unchallenged. The strong Finnish involvement in the officers' conspiracy against Gustav III during the war against Russia in 1788–90, when there was talk of detaching Finland from Sweden and attaching it to Russia, has also claimed attention, as have the special Finnish groupings in the diet (*riksdag*) during the eighteenth century.

An opposite viewpoint, which has gained ground in the last few decades, maintains that it is not possible to juxtapose a united Finland with a united Sweden, since these separate entities only came into existence in 1809. According to this view, Sweden as a great power was a multi-national empire, with a variety of linguistic minorities. Whereas some historians have attached great importance to the founding of a university in Finland in 1640, and to the interest in things Finnish shown by scholars at the university in the eighteenth century, others have seen this simply as an expression of *Landespartikularismus* of the kind which flourished elsewhere in Europe and other parts of the Swedish kingdom. Many of the students at the university came from Småland, in Sweden, and there were also many Ostrobothnians studying in Uppsala university. The activities of the nobility are also seen more as an expression of their particularist interests than as the pursuit of specifically 'Finnish' policies.

Both lines of interpretation are agreed that there are features which distinguished large parts of the area which in 1809 became the grand duchy of Finland from other parts of the Swedish kingdom: disagreement occurs over how these differences are to be interpreted. The debate is by no means concluded, and probably never will be, but the different interpretations of Finland's past do lead to conflicting views on Finland's union with Russia in 1809, one of the most important dates in the country's history. If there is a separate Finland and a separate Finnish identity — as the nationalist historians of earlier generations were inclined to believe — then 1809 acquires a significance as a fulfilment of a development already begun, for which 6 December 1917 is the logical conclusion. If not, then 1809 is a decisive break with past development, when a part of the kingdom of Sweden suddenly found itself attached to the Russian empire and having to create something entirely new. Seen in this light, the history of Finland begins in 1809, as the nineteenth-century historian Zachris Topelius observed in his youth.

The Russian conquest of Finland in 1808–9, the diet convened by the emperor Alexander I in the small Finnish town of Borgå/Porvoo, and the subsequent creation of an autonomous grand duchy of Finland constitute a decisive sequence of events. Alexander I's intentions and the nature of

Finland's autonomy have been the subjects of debate ever since. Nine-teenth-century Finnish constitutionalists developed a line of argument that a kind of state treaty based on Swedish fundamental law was concluded at Borgå between two almost equal parties: this was rejected by their Russian opponents, who maintained that the emperor, who had after all conquered Finland, had merely issued a decree consonant with his autocratic powers, which surrendered nothing to the claims of alien fundamental laws. Both interpretations, however, agreed that the fact that Finland was allowed to keep its legal system, religion and social structure, and for the first time in its history was given its own central administration, laid the foundations upon which a modern Finland was built. Finland was given a separate exis-tence within the Russian empire which had been inconceivable while it remained an integral part of the Swedish kingdom. Furthermore, the emperor took the remarkable decision in 1811 that the territories separated from the kingdom of Sweden a hundred years earlier should be united with the grand duchy. This decision was to give Finland a territorial definition which, with the exception of minor adjustments on the Arctic coast in 1920, was to remain until 1940.

With its Swedish legal system and its new central administration, which the Russians showed no sign of wanting to dismantle in favour of greater central control, loyal Finland forged ahead along its own course. Upon the foundations laid down in 1809 there developed a process of state- and nation-building, a civil society and a national identity, a domestic market, and a parliamentary life in the form of the four-estate diet which was given a regular existence after 1863.

In the long-established states of Western Europe, nationalism led to integration, the more or less continuous assimilation of ethnic minorities and colonial expansion. The multinational empires of Central and Eastern Europe sought to follow suit, but were dogged by the problems of the small nations, which sought to create their own culture, their own institu-tions and to press for autonomy or independence. In this division between Western European state nationalism and Central and Eastern European cultural nationalism, Finland lies somewhere in between. Though lacking historical antecedents, the political contours of the state were created in 1809 by Alexander I. It was within that embryonic state that the nation was formed.

This harmonious development, characterised by a strong sense of loyalty to the throne, was finally broken by the constitutional conflict of the late nineteenth century. The manifesto issued by the emperor Nicholas II in February 1899, and the legislation introduced in subsequent years to bring

Finland more closely under the control of the imperial government, helped to politicise a large number of Finns, whose support was solicited by the passive resistance to Russian measures. The revolution of 1905, which found expression in a patriotic national strike in Finland, led to major parliamentary reform, with the antiquated four-estate diet being replaced by the most democratic parliament in Europe at that time: but the renewal of Russian pressure meant that it was not allowed to function effectively. The conflict between Finland and Russia opened up a serious divide, though there was still a residual loyalty to the emperor, and there were very few who even dared contemplate the idea of an independent Finland. In this respect, 1917 did represent a sharp break with the past, for the option of independence was only seriously taken up with revolution and the collapse of imperial authority in Russia.

Nevertheless, the looking-glass of December 1917 seems to offer a very unsatisfactory, even a false view of Finland's history, a kind of searching for one's roots at any price. But this is not to underestimate the importance of independence, the seventieth anniversary of which was celebrated in 1987. During the jubilee year, the historical journal *Historisk Tidskrift för Finland* invited a number of Finnish and British scholars from different disciplines to look at important questions in Finnish history, drawing comparisons from the experience of other countries where necessary, in order to see in broader perspective what it is that makes up the Finland we know today. The resulting essays were published in a special jubilee issue, and have been revised and translated for publication in English. An additional essay, covering the present-day Finnish economy and political scene, has been written by David Arter. The work of translation of the original articles from Finnish and Swedish has been done by Eva Buchwald, John Desborough, Thomas Munch-Petersen, John Screen and David Kirby. The task of editing has been shared by Max Engman and David Kirby, and was considerably eased by the genial assistance and encouragement of Tom Söderman.

*Editors' note*

Finland has two official languages, Finnish and Swedish. In this book, we have adopted the following usage: the Swedish names of historic events such as the Treaty of Nystad, and of the historic provinces of Finland (unless there is a generally accepted English version) are used. The names of towns and geographical features (such as rivers) are given in the Finnish form where there is no English equivalent.

*Acknowledgements*

The illustrations have been kindly supplied from a number of sources, which are indicated by a capital letter following the relative caption, as follows:

The Ateneum national art collection, Helsinki, *A*; Museovirasto, Helsinki, *B*; Risto Kamunen, *Suomen rakennustaiteen museo*, Helsinki, *C*; Sota-arkisto, Helsinki, *D*; Kaupunginmuseo, Helsinki, *E*; Imperial War Museum, London, *F*; Lehtikuva Oy, Helsinki, *G*; Pressfoto, Helsinki, *H*; Kaupunginmuseo, Tampere, *I*; Marttaliitto, Helsinki, *J*; Työväenarkisto, Helsinki, *K*.

# PERCEPTIONS OF FINLAND

*W. R. Mead*

In the opinion of the French historian Jacques le Goff, the questions asked by history cannot be posed 'without reference to the lessons of our geographical masters'. Lessons in geography range from the elementary to the advanced. The elementary call for constant reference to simple facts such as area, location and physical circumstance. The advanced introduce theoretical and technical considerations. Nineteenth-century historians such as Henry Thomas Buckle in Britain and Zachris Topelius in Finland adopted a determinist approach to historical development. And Finland has experienced the pressure of the Nietzschean 'iron hand of necessity' too often for geographical determinism to be entirely dismissed by theorists. Those who seek escape from causally-determined explanations turn their attention to the opportunities offered by the environment — favouring a theory of possibilism or probablism. But whatever the approach employed for interpreting the historical evolution of Finland, it must pay regard to location — location in time as well as in space. For the significance of location changes materially through advance or decline in the technical milieu and mentally through changes in human perception.

This essay is concerned with perception. It is an exploration of some of the ways in which outsiders have perceived and (in certain cases) continue to perceive Finland and the Finns. In it, perceptions of past and present myth and reality are mingled. The themes of the frontier and peripherality are recurrent, but the approach and the selected illustrations are inescapably personal. 'We see things as we are, not as they are,' warned the American geographer Preston James.

All countries are interested in the ways that others perceive them. A contributor to *Åbo Tidning* in 1800 believed that 'nothing is more pleasurable and instructive than to see one's own land through the eyes of foreigners', but it was not until a generation later that a serious attempt was made to assemble information about the Finns and their country. Carl Christian Böcker, the most enterprising of the early officers of Finska Hushållningssällskapet (a society for promoting economic knowledge), sought in items 11 and 76 of his *Utkast til plan för en statistik över Finland* to gather information about Finland 'as depicted by outsiders'. Böcker's questionnaire did not yield a very rewarding harvest because, independently of the problem of access to information, there was little to be gleaned.

'A Journey round Europe': a not untypical foreign image of nineteenth-century Finland as a kind of nature reserve, here presented in a children's board game from around 1855 (detail).

Robert Burns, the Scottish poet, was still writing his appealing verses when Böcker was a boy. Their humble wisdom and wit have made them a happy hunting-ground for social scientists. In his poem *To a mouse*, Burns sought the gift to see ourselves as others see us. In most countries, Finland included, gathering information about the perceptions of outsiders has become a professional pursuit. In general, the results perplex more than they please and are more likely to be material for amusement than for socio-scientific analysis.

Nevertheless the image of Finland and the Finns as it has evolved abroad is a part of history and has a history in its own right. It may appear to be like Isis — all things to all men — but certain common features can be detected at the international level. Thus, from the beginning of their acquaintance with Finland, West Europeans have tended to emphasise two characteristics. The first is the frontier location and the stresses that it generates. The second is the maritime and lacustrine relationship and the ameliorating influence that it provides.

The frontier location has been subject to varying interpretations, but in the eyes of outsiders the frontier as a political feature has always taken precedence over the frontier as an ecological concept. And, while the frontier location has been treated as an incubus, the maritime relationship has been regarded as a stimulus. Foreigners looking at Finland have focused attention on the strains born of a European boundary zone rather than upon the physically hazardous frontier zone of settlement. For them, the military exposure of 'the cockpit of the north' has prevailed over the high-latitude exposure to the failures or famines of a hard-pressed farming community. Accordingly, the attention paid to Finland has waxed in time of war and waned in time of peace. Furthermore, the degree of concern has been measured by the value of Finland, sometimes in moral as well as in material terms, to the outside world.

The frontier is associated with two points of the compass. Long before Renaissance cartographers designed their frameworks of latitude and longitude, outsiders had linked Finland with the north and the east. Through the years, poet and geographer alike have verbally strengthened the impression. While Franz Michael Franzén applied the epithet *Östens son* (son of the East) to his native land, the first English-language geography of the country, written by the American Eugene van Cleef, underscored Finland as *The Republic Farthest North* (1929). The scientific fact that Finland is in the East European time zone and that the sun rises correspondingly earlier than along the Atlantic seaboard are less important to literature than the decorative metaphors that elaborate Finland's location as the easternmost (and therefore the most alien) part of Western Europe. As for the north, while it attracts the compass needle, it is presumed to repulse mankind. For the poet W.H. Auden, it cried 'Reject'. North implies nadir in contrast to the zenith of the south: darkness in contrast to light. Well might a Finn tire of the impressions of outsiders and challenge a midsummer visitor with the rhetorical questions of Esaias Tegnér:

> *Hvar är öster nu och väster?*
> *Hvar är söder? Hvar är nord?*\*

\*Where is the east now and the west?
Where is the south? Where is the north?

The compass-point has a different meaning for the mariner. It has been by way of the sea that Finland has come to know the outer world and by way of the sea that the outside world has come to know Finland. Furthermore, as L.W. Lyde expressed it when writing of Finland in 1909, 'the sea is the greatest of all geographical civilisers.' For Western Europe, the Baltic Sea is the Eastsea: for Finland, the Eastsea is the way to the west. But the Eastsea, upon the freedom of which Finland depends, is an enclosed sea and subject to the control of whichever littoral state is powerful enough to claim dominion over it. It is also subject to closure by ice for a shorter or longer period in winter. Accordingly, the maritime relationship itself can be an additional cause of stress. The outside world has been most conscious of Finland when maritime access has been or is most subject to physical or political constraint. Thomas Mann may have dismissed the Baltic Sea as 'a provincial body of water', but for generations it has been a cynosure of the naval authorities of Western and Northern Europe.

In Great Britain, the conceptualisation of Finland begins with the mariner and the map. Sources for the appreciation of the country and its people are gradually multiplied through travel literature and the somewhat repetitive accounts of atlases and encyclopaedias. Intermittently, when war

The icebreaker *Murtaja* at work in the frozen Baltic. (From *Finland i 19de seklet*, Helsingfors 1893)

casts a spotlight upon the country, they are more precisely illumined by documentary materials. Finally, given the contemporary means of communication, the information knows no bounds. It follows that the possibilities of misrepresentation are correspondingly enhanced.

The earliest British reference to Finland — Femelandiam — sprang from its frontier location. In *Leges anglorum Londoniis* (1210) it was grouped with Estlandiam and Wirilandiam as lying on the frontiers of Scantiam and at the outer limits of Christendom. The reference is of obscure origin and probably echoes the Baltic Crusades.

More precisely, the concept of Finland first emerged from the map — the map as it was produced by the succession of Renaissance cartographers, and the chart as it was refined by generations of mariners. For Britain approached Finland from the standpoint of a maritime power, trading the critical products of the softwood forests and to a lesser extent of the mines. It is unlikely that the *Carta marina* of Olaus Magnus — Scandinavia's first significant publicist — was seen by many (if any) British, but J.B. Fickler's *Olai Magni, Historien der midnächtigen Länder* (Basel 1567) and the English translation of Olaus Magnus, *Compendious History* (London 1658), provided informative texts. Fickler's numerous woodcuts added a pictorial dimension to the text. From the work of Olaus Magnus three basic facts emerged — that Finland was an integral part of the Scandinavian world, a marchland country afflicted with the recurrent scourge of war and a hyperborean land in which winter took precedence over summer. It was, in effect, what the sixteenth-century poet Andrew Boorde called a 'kingdom of the night'.

The British and the Dutch rivalled each other in their endeavours to reduce the hazards of negotiating Finnish harbours, their charts known as 'waggoners' (after their Dutch originator, Wagenhaers) charts, based largely on the personal observations of sailors, gradually providing a more accurate representation of the intricate coastline. John Seller's *English Pilot*, William Faden's charts and Sir John Norris's *General Draught* of the Gulfs of Bothnia and Finland illustrate the progress.

Simultaneously, had they wished to indulge their curiosity in this northern land, a handful of wealthy bibliophiles might have acquired Moses Pitt's *Magnus Ducatus Finlandiae* (1680), the first important British representation of what its author chose to call 'the great principality'. The map recorded over 370 place-names. Among those to which it gave some prominence was 'Europae' (Ayräpää), as if to emphasise that Europe began (or ended) in the Karelian isthmus. Interestingly enough, the intensity of mountain symbols engraved upon Finland was as great as that upon the

Scandinavian peninsula. It was to be a long time before the cartographic image of Finland was to present a low-lying land.

Although the Dutch led the way cartographically, they produced nothing quite like the *Atlas maritimus et commercialis* (1725), bearing the name of the astronomer Edmond Halley, dedicated to Admiral Sir John Norris (who had attended the Nystad peace conference) and with an anonymous text attributed to Daniel Defoe. The significance of the text from the point of view of Finland is that it included the first lengthy and reasonably accurate geographical description of the country in English.

It was natural that there should be cartographical errors and that the time-lag in their correction should sometimes last for generations. 'Engravers unskilled in geography' were accused by Thomas Salmon in 1745 of copying foreign maps 'with all their errors'. The political outlines on maps of smaller scale were especially subject to misrepresentation. A.K. Johnson's *Russia in Europe* (1743) gave to the province of Uleåborg a coastline of some tens of miles along the Arctic Ocean beside Varangerfjord. The 1743 boundary continued to be reproduced on some British maps into the early nineteenth century, with the name of Sweden in some instances still firmly inscribed across the grand duchy. And, from the same period, strange place-names still appeared. Thus an agent of Lloyds of London wrote to *The Times* about the name of a navigational warning — *Här förvillas compassen* — which had been turned into the name of a place.

Finland was brought a little more into focus during the Napoleonic wars. The turn of the century yielded the lively accounts of Joseph Acerbi and Edward Clarke, both of whom journeyed overland and skirted interior Finland. Though the impact of their books must have been limited, they provided more factually accurate information about Finland than any English source down to their time. Readers would have been able to appreciate more fully than hitherto the course of a northern war, for regular despatches in 1808–9 claimed space in *The Times*. A climax came when Sir John Moore and his army were denied the opportunity of proceeding farther than Gothenburg, otherwise he might have gained immortality on the battlefield of Finland rather than at Corunna. During the campaign, public collections were made in the City of London for the Finnish refugees, while the British and Foreign Bible Society sent testaments to succour their souls. It is not easy to assess the criteria employed in Clark's *Chart of the World . . . exhibiting the state of civilisation* (1822), in which the Finns were given top listing as 'enlightened', while the Lapps were 'barbarous' and even the Norwegians were only 'civilised'. Is it possible that he was influenced by his namesake Edward Clarke's flattering account of Åbo uni-

The Finnish sauna has always attracted the prurient curiosity of the foreigner. The well-clad gentleman peeping in at the door is Giuseppe Acerbi, a late-eighteenth-century traveller through Finland, whose *Travels through Sweden, Finland and Lapland to the North Cape* appeared in 1802.

versity — written during the last years of H.G. Porthan but only published in 1810–23?

By the time that British and French sights were set on Finland during the next years of stress, 1854–5, the country had become more than a silhouette for the outside world. Visual images were offered, pictures were painted by official war artists, the *Illustrated London News* reproduced engravings, even Mr Punch provided a cartoon. In the context of the Crimean War, the naval campaigns in the Baltic may have been a sideshow for the British and French, but they brought the Finns more before the eyes of Western Europe than at any time in their history. In the process, considerable sympathy and understanding was generated for what R.G. Latham called these 'Ugrians in possession of a sea coast'. The *News of the World* (19 March 1854) praised the Finns as 'a noble race of seamen, second to none in the world'. Members of the peace party kept the name of

Finland unsullied and, through the compensation that they offered to those afflicted by the Allied naval assault, Finland remained a matter of concern after the cessation of hostilities. Even across the Atlantic, Quaker circles were alerted to the name of Finland. Nevertheless, for most of those who heard of the grand duchy in mid-Victorian Britain it signified the 'colonial' fringe of the continent and an antechamber of imperial Russia. Among the growing number of educational games for children, *A Journey round Europe* offered a picture of Finland filled exclusively with bears attacking cattle in the south and reindeer being savaged by wolves in the north.

After the campaigns of 1854–5, except for those who traded in softwood products, Finland slipped out of the consciousness of most West Europeans until the turn of the century. As late as 1902 (22 April), the editor of the *Daily Express* wrote: 'Until recently, most Englishmen vaguely conceived of Finland as a country inhabited by eskimoes and polar bears.' While this may have been the opinion of the popular press, elsewhere the stress created by Russian oppression was sufficient to give rise to widespread action. The image of Finland was sharpened by concerted publicity in Western Europe in general and Britain in particular. Liberal and intellectual publications produced a regular succession of articles, while the first flush of semi-popular travel books about Finland multiplied. The powerful quartet of contributors who wrote about Finland in the outstanding eleventh edition of the *Encyclopaedia Britannica* included Prince Kropotkin, who knew Finland personally, and the astute Secretary of the Royal Geographical Society, Sir John Scott Keltie. The pioneering first *Atlas of Finland* was reviewed. The music of Jean Sibelius entered concert programmes. The first tourist literature circulated. The first group of British journalists was formally invited to Finland. *Kalevala* — for John Crombie Brown 'precious flotsam' from Karelia and for McCallum Scott 'a swan song of paganism' — was at last translated fully by William Kirby. In brief, Finland had made a major impact.

The strategic concern of Britain and France in the Baltic area gradually diminished. For a short while following the First World War, Lord Balfour was able to speak of 'protecting the nascent nationalities with the help of our fleet'. Thereafter, 'Baltoscandia' was left to its own devices: it lay increasingly beyond the Allied sphere of geopolitical capability. In the most scintillating essay written on Finland during the inter-war years, Georges Duhamel reverted to the themes of remoteness and winter. It was indicative of the image held of Finland that an incipient inter-war tourist trade should advertise its principal attraction as being 'off the map'.

All too soon, Finland found itself very much on the map. In 1939, the horsemen of the apocalypse returned. In the black and white photographs of newspaper reporters there were more than echoes of Fickler's sixteenth-century woodcuts. And, whatever the adventures or misadventures others attributed to Finland in the Continuation War, it was the Winter War that struck the lasting picture — a latter-day Thermopylae for those without, a sacred myth for those within. Even James Joyce immortalised the situation in his own peculiar way. *Finnegan's Wake* is no more, no less than 'The Finn again wakes'. 'Poor little Finland', lamented Western sympathisers despairingly in a variety of languages. The perception was of a small country in which even the Finns themselves seemed reduced to the size of Davids confronting Goliaths.

If the epic struggle transformed the image of Finland and the Finns, the outcome transformed Finland itself in a way that foreigners could scarcely have expected and to which they responded but slowly. It took a long time for the outside world to realise that while Finland may have lost two wars, it won the peace. The years of resettlement, reconstruction, manpower shortage and capital deficiency were marked with an effort largely ignored by a world involved with its own problems. As Finland escaped from its treadmill existence, a much-neglected member of the European commu-

'Finland's secret weapon.' (*Daily Express*, 1940)

nity gradually began to create new impressions in the international arena.

The delay in this appreciation was inseparable from the fact that Finland has always been marginal to the issues that have stirred the European heartland. Most European nations have looked upon Finland as peripheral to their interests. The fact is underlined by the vocabulary applied by foreign observers — isolated, solitary, remote. 'Its remoteness has kept it greatly isolated,' wrote H.G. George in *The Relations of History and Geography* at the time of the Russian oppression. 'The desolation and isolation expressed by Sibelius in his Sixth Symphony spring out of Finland itself,' commented a radio announcer in 1987.

'Stern famine guards the solitary coast,' wrote a poet of wintry Bothnia, and echoes of famine throughout the nineteenth century made clear that the isolation of Finland itself was repeated in the isolation of its widely-scattered rural settlements. Down to the Second World War, Finland was presented in all accounts written by foreigners as a land of forest farmers. In the more discerning texts, it was described as a country across which were drawn the frontiers of occurrence of many familiar European plants and animals. The corollary of this was the restricted range of food crops and the limited period of outdoor grazing for animals. It was a part of the price paid for occupying the continental frontier of settlement. An additional consequence was the retarded diffusion of techniques and ideas. And even when the transformation began, the English-speaking world was slow to appreciate it for terminological reasons. The persistent translation of *talonpoika/bonde* into the word 'peasant', with its somewhat derogatory connotation, was scarcely calculated to convey the impression of a progressive rural husbandry.

In the past, foreigners have been well aware that peripherality has had a serious financial effect upon Finnish trade. Location is still expressed in terms of the tax of distance from markets. Air communication has eased matters, but Helsinki is very much a terminal point in Europe's air network and is some 1,500 km. from the commercial, financial and cultural hearts of Europe. Moreover, as Gunnar Andersson has put it, Finland's setting is on 'the cold periphery of Europe', and even air transport has to pay some regard to this.

The significance of location is inseparable from technological opportunities. It has become apparent to the outside world that technological change has fostered experiment in Finland — structurally, organisationally and physically. In the process, the tax of location has been modified. Three examples will suffice. First, as the export of low-priced raw materials has been replaced by higher-priced capital and consumer goods, the incidence of transport costs has diminished. Secondly, the toll exacted from Baltic navigation by winter icing cannot be treated independently of the rise in icebreaker technology. We cannot command nature except by obeying her, wrote Francis Bacon. A determinist might argue that had not Finland been forced to face the problem of the winter freeze, it might never have developed a world expertise in specialist shipping. Thirdly, Finland has produced model structures for rural management — a fact made manifest internationally through the conferences of agriculturalists and silviculturalists. Already in the inter-war years, Thorsten Odhe's book *Finland, a Nation of Cooperators* drew the attention of a modest circle of readers to a new area of enterprise and experiment.

Shifts in trading patterns have also run side by side with changes in the attitude to location, but the outside world has been slow to appreciate them. Thus, for generations, Britain was Finland's principal trading partner and Germany its major rival. The shift of primacy to the Soviet Union could scarcely have been forecast, though in theory both propinquity and the common problems of the 'cold periphery' favour the relationship.

Again, balancing cost and benefit, isolation can protect. 'The last refuge that Europe could afford them' was the graphic conclusion of the nineteenth-century ethnographer Max Müller of the land occupied by the Finns. Yet, in so far as they could eke out an existence in their isolated settlements and communities, it enabled them to preserve a highly distinctive ethnography. Its features were widely observed by travellers and gave rise to distinctive chains of adjectives in European encyclopaedias. Isolation also preserved the Finnish language, to the fascination of such British polyglots as the parliamentarian Sir John Bowring and the author George Borrow. Nevertheless, language no less than geography was to isolate Finns (or many of them) and confront them with a problem of communication of a different character. Ethnographical factors lay behind the frequent confusion of the Finn with the Lapp among foreign observers and his common appearance in literature as some kind of *lusus naturae*. Indeed, it is only in recent decades — to use the patronising observation by the nineteenth-century traveller A.M. Clive-Bayley — that Finns have been found to be 'not at all unlike ordinary Europeans'!

It has been said that the character of a country lies in its contradictions. Complementarily, Lionel Trilling has asserted that the essence of a culture lies in its central conflicts. Contradictions and conflicts have produced plenty of tensions in Finnish domestic affairs, but in so far as the problems springing from them are resolved, the result can be a new strength and tensility. Past visitors have been conscious of the linguistic, religious and political antitheses in Finnish society and the iconography associated with them. As long ago as 1800, Edward Clarke observed 'a nation . . . in all things given to excess, whether on the brighter or the darker side', yet 'a nation in which the extremities are surprisingly blended'. 'Blending' is the easier when there is material prosperity — and the outside world has yet to realise that Finland's living standard is high in the world league.

In *Bluebeard's Castle*, George Steiner expressed the view that the scientist looks to the future — 'time and light lie before' — while the humanist is drawn backwards to the past. Finland is a nation with a cadre of energetic scientists, engineers and technicians who look to the future and who are bent upon advancing the status that the country has already achieved. It is a far cry from the lamentation written by M.A. Castrén to A.E. Arppe in 1844 — 'A man who cultivates scientific thoughts in our country is isolated.' At least some outsiders may be accounted unfortunate if they are not aware of scientific developments in Finland itself.

Simultaneously, in the applied arts — and in the face of past social, economic and physical restraints — a handful of gifted people have demonstrated that (as Aldous Huxley once attested) creativity is not a gift of propitious circumstances. Limited natural resources, the need for economy, the threat of climatic uncertainty, the prospect of political instability have not prevented Finnish artists in the broadest sense of the word from taking the outside world by surprise with the originality of their products and ideas. For a limited period, the juxtaposition of a sophisticated minority and a relatively primitive rural majority served Finland well.

Meanwhile, the historian as humanist has been no less active in endeavouring to explain the past while the archaeologist has quested with increasing diligence for the artefacts that might identify the origins of his ancestors. It is something of a paradox that, while science carries the country forward, an increasing volume of literature is amassed about the past. For some of its authors, it is a case of refining interpretations in the light of new evidence: for some, it is a matter of retouching the backdrop — of creating a past more worthy of the present; for some, it is even a part of the image-making process. In fact, the gift to see ourselves as others see us is no longer enough. A corrective to misconceptions is sought so that we may have others see us as we would be seen.

Foreign observers, contemplating Finnish historical experiences, can appreciate that Finns are rather less given to nostalgia than most Europeans. Nostalgia is rooted in a traditionalist view of the past where, to quote the poet Stephen Spender, 'a happy geography was married to a happier history.' Finland's myths do not include a golden age. Until recently, even at the personal level, it can only have been a minority who have been able to identify a 'land of lost content'. Finns have rarely if ever had a happier history than during the last generation. And, thanks to the technology that has changed their relationship to the physical environment, they have never been aware of such an agreeable geography. They have demonstrated that the cold periphery of Europe is, in the words of Reimo Pietilä, capable of being transformed into a 'temperate zone of wellbeing'.

The current international impact of Finland, which is out of all proportion to the size of its population, is inseparable from such facts. Additionally, the time-lag in the difference between the actual state of affairs and the perceived image of Finland is reduced. Other facts must also be taken into account. First, the scale and intensity of commercial linkages east and west have enabled Finland to escape from the restrictions imposed by a limited home market. In the process, a large number of Finnish entrepreneurs have moved into the trading centres of the world. By their very presence, they diffuse new knowledge about their homeland: nor are they slow to sponsor the export of the arts, which contemporary Finland seems to develop in abundance. Secondly, because of its distinctive relationship to the Soviet Union (still the subject of considerable external misunderstanding), Finland can aspire to a bridge-building role. Thirdly, because of its historical connections, outsiders increasingly recognise Finland as an integral part of the Nordic community of nations — more popularly, as a part of the vague but widely admired concept of Scandinavia.

The company that Finland keeps attracts much attention. In many respects, neigbouring Sweden continues to offer models for international emulation. Iceland offers a constitutional example for smaller countries aspiring to self-government. More than one sociological survey has pronounced Denmark to be the world's most desirable state in which to live. Norway, always the most romantically projected of the five states, has acquired additional status on the score of its energy resources. With so much attention focused on its Nordic neighbours, Finland cannot escape attention. The features increasingly attributed to it by outsiders are those of the Scandinavian countries which, coupled with its increasingly successful projection of its national identity, are bringing it sharply into focus in the eyes of the international community.

Meanwhile, there seem to be few limits to the possibilities opened up by the technocrats. The options for action have been broadened: in detail, the manipulative capabilities have been refined. 'Our northern situation and very short season require brief and binding resolves,' ran a letter received by a Liverpool trading house from Hackman's Handelshuset in 1816. It is not only the environmental constraints that have been relaxed in the interim, for long-term credit and financial dealings add a new flexibility in trading. In all respects, flexibility is cumulative. '*La technique . . . l'exaltante danse de Dionyses*': Finns may not express it with such *brio* as the French author Jean Brun, but they can well appreciate his meaning.

The large number of visitors can bear witness to the compensations. Among them is the investment of Finland's superficially non-productive environment with new values. The wilderness areas, for example, have acquired a new attraction for the outside world. 'Nature worship is a product of good communications,' wrote Aldous Huxley. 'Untamed nature is exasperatingly obtrusive.' Finland has established good communications, so that visitor and native alike can worship nature in comfort. Protected by the carapace of the welfare state, extremes of activity and inactivity can be indulged. There is space for exercising (or exorcising) animal spirits: there is time to stand and stare at the infinite detail of the Finnish scene. Natural scientists have discovered variety in a landscape which nineteenth-century travellers regarded as monotonous. Artists have discovered the rainbow of colours in the black and white of the dead season. Sportsmen have learned to play with winter, carrying their prowess to Olympic heights and presenting the image of an athletic homeland with its cult of the sauna.

Of course, the so-called progress machine generates its own problems. They are manifest in the different types of risk that have arisen as the old familiar hazards have declined. A peripheral location in Europe is no protection against the instabilities of the world's economic and financial systems. At the same time, integration into world systems increases the understanding of Finland abroad, while the rise of Finland from post-war penury to late twentieth-century affluence excuses its occasional over-optimism in the face of international economic volatility. For long, the image of Finland was of a country beset with misfortune. Today the observer would have to declare it *Finlandia Felix* — Finland the fortunate.

In the course of his history lectures to students in 1854, Zachris Topelius declared that his ambition was 'to win for Finland a name in Europe [in order that] the dark myths about it might disappear and the victory of light might be the greater and more honoured'. Myths, whether among outsiders looking in or among insiders themselves, tend to be tenacious. For better or for worse, they play a primary role in establishing the perceived image of a country. H.G. Porthan must have been one of the first Finns to be disturbed by what he called the 'false and preposterous accounts' written about Finland by foreigners. Today, public relations officers spend their lives trying to dispel, correct or modify false ideas that prevail about their home countries. And they know that it is the curiosities rather than the commonplaces that attract attention, that it is conflict rather than consensus which creates headlines. Thus, Finland's economic miracle has been in its way no less remarkable than that of West Germany, but it has always been the subject of subsidised newspaper supplements rather than of the columns by accredited reporters. Contrastingly, because outside observers traditionally associate tension with Finland, harmonious relations, especially at the international level, are either disregarded or viewed with scepticism. One of the continuing images of Finland as an entity in political geography is symbolised in the title of the novel by Desmond Bagley, *The Tightrope Man*. The same attitudes lie behind the coinage of the word 'Finlandisation'.

The existence of myths is perhaps less important than an understanding of why and how they emerge. As Birgitta Odén declared in her 1987 retirement address at Lund, the task of the historian is not only to evaluate myths, but to seek to replace them with empirical generalisations. Myths affect behaviour at the personal and at the national level, while the messages that they transmit are frequently crucial.

Messages are best stated in simple terms, free from the ambiguities that accompany myths. In spite of the misrepresentations both old and new that surround the image of Finland in the eyes of foreigners, at least one message has come through with growing clarity to the international community as the twentieth century has advanced. It is a political objective which was originally proclaimed by Zachris Topelius in a lecture given in 1871 — 'To be neutral, to be self-sufficient, to have the freedom to look after one's own interests'.

# THE COLONISATION OF FINLAND AND THE
# ROOTS OF THE FINNISH PEOPLE

## Eino Jutikkala

### The population of Finland in an inter-disciplinary perspective

In 1980 an inter-disciplinary conference was held at Tvärminne research station to discuss whether the findings produced by different disciplines can be reconciled in order to provide a non-contradictory picture of the historical roots of the Finnish people. My task was to draft the summary, and I defined the problem as being to ascertain whether the process of colonisation in prehistoric and historical times as described by various disciplines leads to the present-day genetic composition of the Finnish people as revealed by medical research. The mixture of 'Western' and 'Eastern' genes is of particular interest in this context.

Medical scientists of today have a quite different concept of race from that to be found in old books of reference with their illustrations of typical representatives of various races. Such 'secondary' traits as height or the colour of skin, hair and eye are no longer regarded as durable racial characteristics. The Lapps of Finnmark are now taller than their Norwegian neighbours were at the beginning of the century, and the incidence of blond hair in northern Europe was increased by the damp climate with little sun which prevailed in that region during the first millennium BC. 'Primary' racial characteristics like the shape of the skull are more durable, but only blood groups are unchangeable. Nothing was known about blood groups, and they therefore played no role in the choice of partners. There cannot consequently be any question of a certain blood group becoming more common and another less common through conscious selection. If blood groups are used as a criterion for classification, we cannot really say that an individual belongs to one race or another, but only that the relative frequency of the different blood groups varies from one race to another.

Archaeology has become less important in the study of prehistoric settlement. An illuminating example is provided by the western bronze culture in Finland (ca. 1500–500 BC), which has left behind it — at the latest count — 5,000–6,000 cairns.[1] However, this figure includes cairns with few or no contents, which cannot therefore be dated and some of which were erected during the early Iron Age. These cairns consequently cover a period of at least 1,500 years. The archaeologist T. Seger bases his analysis

Building, by Akseli Gallen-Kallela (1903). A

on 3,000 cairns. In most of them only one person has been found buried, but in order to avoid arriving at an underestimate, Seger uses three burials per cairn as the basis for his calculations. This gives nine burials per year within the area of Finland's western bronze culture, and the number of people who died must have been much greater than that. When the archaeological evidence is insufficient, it is all the more necessary to look for other traces of settlement, and pollen analysis now provides us with that.

It was most difficult to reconcile the findings of different disciplines in relation to the first demonstrable migration into Finland. Philologists claim that the people who lived by the bend in the Volga around 2000–1500 BC spoke a language from which both the Baltic Finnish and the Volga Finnish languages developed. However, archaeological findings in Finland reveal traces of migration from the east only from around 3200 BC.

A possible explanation is offered by the extensive mobility of the nomadic peoples, and the source of disagreement has subsequently been removed. Even before the conference at Tvärminne, philologists had pushed back the period when a large number of proto-Germanic loan words entered the Baltic Finnish language to around 1500 BC. Koivulehto later demonstrated that the borrowing of Indo-European words occurred 'long before the Bronze Age'. The ancestors of the Baltic Finns must therefore have lived in their present homelands as early as the Stone Age.[2]

However, human beings had lived in Finland before the Finno-Ugric migration from the east, from as early as the late eighth millenium BC. These earliest inhabitants of Finland were not Finno-Ugric, but they seem to have passed on certain everyday words to the later Baltic Finnish peoples. This Arctic people may be assumed to have had 'eastern' blood group frequencies. The blood group frequencies of the Volga Finns have not been studied, but 'Mongolian' traits are strongly represented in the 'primary' racial characteristics of at least the Cheremis.[3]

Western genes were introduced into Finland with the people who sustained the boat-axe culture shortly before 200 BC. These immigrants are thought to have been among the ancestors of the Balts. They practised pasture-farming, but the traditional view that the boat-axe people introduced agriculture into Finland has recently been challenged. It has been pointed out that the land which we know to have been cleared in the Stone Age was intended for pasture, and that this does not prove that burn-beating was practised.[4] However, it is of no significance for our purposes whether grain-growing occurred in the Stone Age or not, since at all events it clearly occurred during the Bronze Age.

The boat-axe people spread over large parts of south-western Finland and were assimilated by the original inhabitants, who borrowed a number of words from proto-Baltic. There was no admixture of races or cultural changes north-east of the line Hamina-Kokkola, even though the population of this region also adopted some Baltic loan-words. The extensive influence of proto-Germanic on the Baltic Finnish languages was so strong that it must be assumed that people of Germanic origin lived side by side with the first Finns for a considerable time. This assumption is strengthened by the fact that the sparse Bronze-Age objects in the coastal tracts of western Finland are of Scandinavian type. The inhabitants of Finland inherited western genes from these Scandinavian settlers.

The theory propounded by the archaeologist Alfred Hackman, which has now been abandoned, sought to demonstrate that the ancestors of the

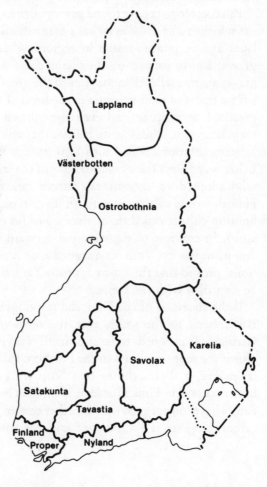

The historic provinces of Finland within the 1812 frontiers. Kexholm, the part of Karelia east of the dotted line, was acquired by Sweden in 1617, and never became an integrated part of the realm.

Finns began to move into Finland from the Baltic lands to the mouth of the Gulf of Finland around 100 AD, and assumed that Finland had been virtually uninhabited during the pre-Roman Iron Age. This theory also asserted that colonisation was a gradual process which began in the west and then moved eastwards, since the oldest Iron-Age graves are younger the further east one goes. However, since most families, even during the prosperous Bronze Age, could not have allowed themselves the luxury of a cairn grave, it is quite natural that when the climate deteriorated and all families became poor during the pre-Roman Iron Age, the tradition of placing artefacts in graves was discontinued and was only resumed as a cultural innovation after the birth of Christ. Without denying that migration within Finland occurred, it is possible to see the growing frequency of family graves containing burial goods as connected with the development of field cultivation, which forced people to live permanently in the same place.

Palaeoecologists have found grain pollen in many lakes and bogs in deposits which can be dated as far back as the second millennium BC. All of these lakes and bogs are located in regions where there are no Bronze-Age graves, and in some cases they lie in areas where even the first Iron-Age graves are no earlier than the time of the great migrations.[5] The Lapps have left no traces of their presence in the form of grain pollen, since they never practised agriculture, and even agricultural terminology is absent from their language. Philologists believe that the population of the country's western interior divided into two groups around 1000 BC and that the Baltic word *šämä* (land) was the origin of two different words: the people who adopted an agricultural culture called themselves *häme* (later the Finnish name of the province of Tavastia), while those who followed a hunting culture called themselves *sabme* (in modern Finnish and Swedish, *same*). In contrast to the view put forward by supporters of Hackman's dominant theory, Voionmaa argued as early as the 1940s that 'other indications' proved that there was a 'proto-Tavastian' population which cannot be identified with the Lapps.[6]

If the ancestors of the Finns did not migrate into the country from the Baltic lands to the south after the birth of Christ, how then are the Germanic loan-words to be explained? This is easily done: Germanic loan-words are more common in the northern than the southern Baltic Finnish languages, and this shows that borrowing from proto-Germanic must have occurred in Finland at least as often as in Estonia. Specialists on place-names have long argued over whether certain names are of proto-Germanic origin, but even if a number of cases are still in dispute, it is certain that there are a good many such names. Moreover, the survival of these names is further proof that settlement has been continuous.

The population of Finland obtained a further infusion of 'western' genes when Swedes moved into the Turku region during the Roman Iron Age, and probably Germanic peoples from the continent also moved into south-western Satakunta during the Merovingian period. Vahtola has assembled several hundred settlement names in the south-western provinces of Finland which 'probably or possibly' were derived from an Old Scandinavian or continental Germanic personal name.[7] I do not question his etymologies — and indeed am not competent to do so — , but I am suspicious of his dating. It is probably safe to assume that, in contrast to the nomadic people who supported a hunting culture, the farmers who migrated into Finland during the Iron Age built visible graves. However, there are no such graves from the early Iron Age in many of the villages included in Vahtola's lists or even sometimes in the parishes where these villages are located; indeed, in many cases there are not even graves from the late Iron Age. A more natural explanation of these place-names may therefore be that they bear witness to Swedish colonisation during the period of the Swedish Crusades in Finland. If so, Swedish colonisation originally penetrated much further into Finland than the area later inhabited by Swedish-speakers.

The Iron Age provides many controversial problems of detail. The prehistory of southern Ostrobothnia has long attracted the attention of scholars. The origins of Iron-Age settlement offer no difficulties, since in this case too it is possible to discern a direct continuation of the western Bronze-Age culture. However, the archaeological evidence almost totally ceases with the eighth century (see below). A new explanation which has been advanced for the desertion of southern Ostrobothnia is that the population, like that of Gotland, was decimated by plague, one of the after-effects of the epidemic in the time of the Emperor Justinian (542–3), but this theory is a controversial one.[8]

It has been argued that there was migration into what later became Finnish Karelia from the eastern and southern shores of Lake Ladoga during the Viking period. However, the form of burial on the Karelian isthmus is different from that on the eastern and southern shores of Lake Ladoga, and blood group frequencies among Karelians who lived on the isthmus before the Peace of Moscow in 1940 are the same as among other Finns. Philologists disagree among themselves about whether there was migration to the isthmus from the eastern shore of Lake Ladoga. There are therefore, as it were, two votes against and one abstention in relation to this suggestion. The conclusion must be that the graves in Karelia from the Viking and Crusade periods constituted a cultural innovation sustained by the original inhabitants of the area, who probably received reinforcements from the west.

It used to be believed that Swedes settled in the previously uninhabited Åland archipelago during the sixth century AD, but pollen analysis shows that agriculture was practised there as early as the fourth century, and the oldest objects found on the islands are in part Finnish, even if the form of burial is Swedish. Blood group frequencies in our time are the same as in Sweden. The philologist Hellberg has shown that the evidence provided by place-names suggests that the ancestors of the present population of Åland moved to the islands at about the same time as Swedes migrated to the Finnish mainland, and his conclusions have been generally accepted. It is therefore possible to regard the history of settlement on the Åland islands as a matter on which there is inter-disciplinary harmony.[9]

The place-name specialists of our own time are agreed that the substantial and well-known Swedish migration to the Finnish mainland did not occur earlier than the period of the conversion to Christianity. The earlier view was that Swedes settled in Finland Proper and western Nyland in the twelfth or perhaps already in the eleventh century, but C.F. Meinander has recently argued that they did not arrive until the thirteenth century and only reached eastern Nyland and Ostrobothnia after the middle of that century. There are many names of Finnish or partly Finnish origin in the coastal areas — for example, names with the suffixes *lax* (bay), *sar* and *sär* (island) —, but it was argued that they only prove that the Finnish inhabitants of the interior previously kept fishing huts on the coast, not that there was permanent Finnish settlement. Meinander has not only suggested that Swedish settlers arrived later than was formerly believed, but also emphasised that there was a Finnish population along the coast, especially in the Vaasa region.[10] Certain archaeological finds from the Viking period have now been discovered in southern Ostrobothnia, and even if they may be regarded as traces of short-lived new settlements, the grain and hemp pollen found in a number of marshes demonstrate weak but nonetheless continuous signs of human settlement in southern Ostrobothnia.[11] The greater the degree of continuous habitation which can be demonstrated in the province, the greater must have been the Finnish element in the blood of the mixed population created after the arrival of the Swedes. However, it should be emphasised that this mixed population emerged through intermarriage between the Swedish immigrants and people whose ancestors had lived in these areas since the Bronze Age, not Finns newly arrived from the valley of the Kokemäki river. Julku has suggested that the early inhabitants of the area stretching from Tavastia forest in the south-east around the Gulf of Bothnia to Bygde stone in Västerbotten were a people called the *Kainuulaiset* (in Swedish, *kväner*),[12] and this theory has received a certain measure of support from the Iron-Age grave-fields in northern Ostrobothnia excavated in recent years.

In historical times innumerable individuals transferred themselves from one linguistic group to another. This occurred in both directions so that such individuals largely cancelled each other out, although there may perhaps have been more Finnish-speakers who switched to Swedish than vice versa. The effect of this process was a continuing mixing of races, which further increased the number of 'western' genes in the Finnish population and to some extent introduced 'eastern' genes into the Swedish population.

I now return to the point with which I began this section. Geneticists have drawn our attention to two particular blood groups. One is unknown in Western Europe, but 6–10 per cent of the population of Northern Asia belong to it. 2 per cent of Finnish-speakers and 1 per cent of Swedish-speakers on the Finnish mainland also belong to this blood group. 40 per cent of West Europeans, but only 5–15 per cent of Lapps and the inhabitants of Northern Asia, belong to the second blood group in question. 32 per cent of Finnish-speakers and somewhere between 32 and 40 per cent of Swedish-speaking Finns belong to this blood group. The repeated migrations into Finland from the south and the west have in the course of time altered the original, presumably eastern, genetic stock of the country's inhabitants to such a degree that the western features have become dominant. The limited size of the population in prehistoric times contributed to these changes, since it meant that even a small number of immigrants could produce relatively large changes. This mixing of races took place over five millennia.

It must therefore be said that the findings of geneticists are in fairly close conformity with the findings of those disciplines which study the historical roots of the Finnish people. Another matter is that this harmony may perhaps have disappeared after a decade, when each of the disciplines involved may have revised the picture they each now give of Finland's prehistory. However, the level of disagreement has so far decreased because of the removal of the difficulties associated with dating the Finno-Ugric migration into the country.

## The population which cannot be counted

Lehtosalo-Hilander has attempted to calculate the size of the population in Viking times in the village of Kauttua in Eura, the site of one of the most extensive grave-fields in Finland. Using skeletal remains as a basis for calculation of mortality rates, she estimates the population of the village to have been between 23 and 37 persons. This is a wide margin, but the techniques of historical demography provide no basis for criticising her method. However, it is uncritical to check this result against the size of the population in 1540, which she places at _ca._ 85 using the oldest land-register as a source of information. The variations in the size of the population in earlier times cannot be presented as a line that rose more or less sharply but rather as a wave that sometimes rose and sometimes fell.[13]

The population of the whole country cannot be calculated in this way, even if one were prepared to undertake the time-consuming work involved in such micro-analyses. By no means all possible archaeological sites are known or, even if known, have been excavated. Moreover, as we have seen, not all settlement has left any traces behind it. Seger has introduced new statistical methods into archaeological research and tries to determine the growth and decline of settlement in each of the country's provinces during the various periods of the Iron Age. His tables and diagrams give a realistic picture of the chronological and geographical changes, provided the omissions are more or less equally great in relative terms for every province and every period.[14] However, this analysis tells us nothing about the absolute size of the population.

A quite different method of calculating the size of populations in prehistoric times, albeit with a very wide margin, has been suggested by anthropologists who have observed present-day primitive tribes which live by hunting. The density of population among such tribes naturally varies with climatic conditions, and it has been calculated that during the Stone Age not more than 0.01–0.04 persons per square kilometre could have supported themselves in northern Sweden and the whole of Finland.[15]

If the land surface of Finland is reduced by the area added after the Stone Age by the fall in the sea-level, these calculations produce a population of between 2,500 and 10,000 people. However, this method becomes impractical for periods after the introduction of agriculture: while virtually unlimited opportunities for working the soil remained unexploited, it is not meaningful to speak about a maximum density of population.

We are therefore obliged to move forward to the surviving bailiffs' records, which begin in the reign of Gustav Vasa. There is no reason to suspect that some farmsteads were excluded from the first land-registers. One reservation must, however, be made: the unit of taxation in Savolax was not one farmstead but the *arviokunta*, which was collectively responsible for the taxes due. Pirinen has calculated that the oldest land-register from 1541 shows that there were 1.7 peasant households per *arviokunta*.[16] Families which held no land were naturally also excluded, but since the crown did not tolerate people who paid no land tax, their number was probably fairly small in the middle of the sixteenth century. The later land-registers do not reflect reality as closely as the first ones, since farmsteads were divided and amalgamated, and these changes were not always taken into account when the taxation records were compiled.

However, even if we know the number of farmers' households and that families holding no land were still few, we need also to know the size of each household in order to calculate the size of the population. It used to be common to use a number of coefficients, but they were selected in an arbitary manner. It therefore seems much more scientific to base calculations on the records for church taxes or extraordinary taxes. The Swedish military historian Sundquist adopted this approach. He used primarily the accounts of the Elfsborg ransom tax from the second decade of the seventeenth century and a description of the *näbb*, a unit of taxation, which he found in the church tax accounts for the county of Borgå.[17] However, this description was rudimentary in character and was misunderstood by Sundquist, with the consequence that he counted each peasant and his wife twice. His 'probable minimum' for the population of Finland in the second decade of the seventeenth century must therefore be reduced to 175,000 — a figure that is so low in comparison with the number of inhabitants at the end of the century that it is of no value.[18] The accounts for the Elfsborg ransom contain too many gaps as a list of people to be of much use in this connection. Wallén's dissertation is in many respects a work of fundamental importance, but he used this source as a basis for estimating the number of Swedish-speakers in Finland at the beginning of the seventeenth century, and Wallén also accepted Sundquist's interpretation of the term *näbb*. The gaps in the accounts and this misinterpretation cancel each other out to some extent, but at all events the final figure is too high, and Wallén himself concedes that the figure produced by his analysis, 70–73,000, is 'a maximum figure'.[19]

The prehistoric period, as far as quantitative demography is concerned, thus lasts until 1634 in the case of Finland. Nonetheless, after examining the hopeless attempts to calculate the size of the country's population during this 'prehistoric' period, it is still reasonable to emphasise that we know a lot about the chronology and geography of settlement. As we have seen, our knowledge of medieval colonisation is not exclusively dependent on the sporadic sources left by the Middle Ages: we can also draw retrospective conclusions from the extensive taxation records of the sixteenth century. The expansion and contraction of settlement since the reign of Gustav Vasa can be followed even more closely.

The late Middle Ages were a time of decline and the sixteenth century of reconstruction in the whole of Europe and, where the Nordic region

Breaking new land for cultivation has played a crucial role in the colonisation of Finland from the earliest times up to the present day. An illustration from Börje Sandberg's *Finland och finnarna* (Helsingfors 1946).

was concerned, especially in Norway. The editors of the book summarising the findings of the Nordic research project into the desertion of farms felt able to entitle the chapter on the sixteenth century 'The Way Up'. In the 1520s 38–68 per cent of the original farm units were deserted in the areas of Norway selected for study; by around 1600 settlement had reached the same extent as in the early fourteenth century in large parts of the country and especially in areas that had been hardest hit by the crisis. 'Overpopulation' and a deterioration in the climate were previously suggested as the main factors in the contraction of settlement. If that were the case, then the growth in the number of farms and holdings during the sixteenth century should either have led to a crisis of overpopulation, as in the late Middle Ages, or been matched by a significant improvement in the climate. However, there are no signs of 'overpopulation', and indeed previously abandoned farms continued to be brought back into use after 1600. The climate may have been somewhat milder during the first half of the sixteenth century, but it certainly was not during the second half, and the seventeenth century witnessed the culmination of the little Ice Age. The main reason for the abandonment of farms must therefore have been plague epidemics.[20]

Like someone looking for a nail on the floor with the aid of a torch, Finnish scholars have also attempted to find signs of abandoned farms during the late Middle Ages. Some signs have been found, but not of contraction of any great scale.[21] The virtually complete absence of contraction in the case of Finland also supports the plague theory, since the same deterioration in the climate must have affected the whole Nordic region, whereas the plague did not reach remote villages in thinly-populated areas as easily as in more populous regions. On the other hand, there was no intensive reconstruction in Finland during the sixteenth century. Instead, there was new colonisation as the inhabitants of Savolax broke new soil on the lake plateau.

When settlement reached its height in the 1560s, the land register suggest there were 34,300 farmsteads in the rest of Finland and 2,200 taxable units of cultivation in Savolax. When the latter figure is multiplied by the coefficient of 1.7, a total figure of close to 36,000 farmsteads is produced.

As early as the 1550s the term 'deserted' (*öde*) was used to describe farmsteads unable to sustain all or some of the taxes they were due to pay. Historians regard such farmsteads as deserted in *cameral* terms: only some of them were unfarmed (i.e. *economically* deserted) or completely uninhabited (*demographically* deserted). On the other hand, there were farmsteads cultivated by the occupants of another farm who paid taxes on them, but which were uninhabited. The land-registers and the special lists of deserted farms only record farms deserted in the cameral sense, and the number of demographically deserted farms can only be established through laborious comparisons of different taxation lists. It is clear that the decline in the population was not as great as the number of demographically deserted farms might suggest, since many more families than before seem to have lived in the villages without holding any land during the seventeenth century. The number of farmers' households, which can be calculated from 1634 from the poll-tax lists (*mantalslängder*) instead of from the land-registers, fell to 28,000, though Savolax provided another 1,000 or so.[22]

*The size of the population according to sources available for statistical analysis*

The poll-tax lists began to be kept in 1634 or 1635. With the exception of certain small groups, every man and woman over the age of twelve (later fifteen) was meant to be included on these lists. In the 1650s the practice, which was already very widespread, of excluding old people was legalised. The division of the population into various age-groups in the agrarian society of the seventeenth century cannot have been fundamentally different from that in the following century, and we have exact information about the latter. If we add children under 15 and old people over 60 or 63 in the same proportions as can be deduced from the parish records of the late eighteenth century, we ought therefore to be able to arrive at a fairly accurate figure for the total population. This is the position in theory, but in practice the variations from year to year in the number of people included on the poll-tax lists is so great that these lists cannot possibly reflect the true size of the population. Eli Heckscher described the differing numbers included on the poll-tax lists as a measure of the material welfare of the Swedish nation, but this claim is highly exaggerated, since the same persons are excluded from the lists year after year. Moreover, Heckscher does not ascribe any decisive importance to the legislative and administrative changes which occurred. The earliest lists, and also the lists for 1654 and 1694, were compiled after new instructions had been issued and under especially close supervision. In the case of Finland at least, the lists for these years contain so many more names than those for the immediately preceding and succeeding years that they may be regarded as reasonably reliable.[23]

Church records provide another new source. The lists of baptisms and burials enable us to calculate backwards from the first census in 1749. We can get back to the 1680s in the case of so many parishes that this material must be regarded as representative. There are large gaps for the period of the Russian occupation between 1714 and 1721, but this material has survived almost completely in one form or another for the period after the Peace of Nystad (1721). However, there are some problems associated with using this material. Infants who died before or soon after baptism were often not listed among either the births or the deaths, but so long as their names were not included on either list, this had no effect on the overall population figures. What is worse is that the parish records for this period still did not note movement from one area to another, and Finland suffered a net loss of population in migration to and from Sweden proper.

Another means of calculating the size of the population is to combine the number of baptisms and burials with the number of people included in the poll-tax lists and in this way to estimate the possible margins involved. I have used all three methods to calculate the population of Tavastia and arrive at the figures 40–45,000 for 1634, 44–45,000 for 1654 and 60–70,000 for 1694.[24] Virrankoski has applied the same methods in northern Ostrobothnia and arrived at the figures 24–26,000 for 1654 and 40–44,000 for 1694.[25] Both estimates show a fairly rapid population growth during the second half of the seventeenth century before the famine years of 1695–7. This population growth produced not an increase in the number of farmsteads but an expanding group of cottagers and other landless families. The number of farmers' households only grew to 32,500 to which 1,000 or so crofter families should be added. A large proportion of the families who held no land were removed by malnutrition or disease during the famine years, while the remainder had a good chance of taking over farmsteads which had become demographically deserted after the death of their occupants.[26]

Åström has estimated that the approximate percentage of the population included on the poll-tax lists varied between 30 and 45, and concludes that the total population of Finland (excluding the province of Kexholm) in 1695 — that is to say, just before the radical decline during the famine years of 1696–7 — was 352,000. He concedes that this figure is both 'very open to criticism and a minimum'.[27] It can be added that it is a minimum which diverges quite significantly from the probable size of the population suggested by working backwards from the figures available for the late eighteenth century. Before the territorial losses of 1721, the population of Finland was just over 400,000.[28]

In a recent study, Lindegren has arrived at lower losses for the Finnish units in the Swedish army than the figures which have traditionally been accepted and which were mainly calculated by Hornborg. Lindeberg's estimate is based partly on the greater number of women than men in certain age-groups in 1750 and partly on an analysis of recruitment into certain units. He argues that the number of men lost in wartime was not the 50,000 previously suggested but 'at the most' 35,000.[29] However, Lindegren's calculations do not include civilians murdered by the Russians, deported to Russia or conscripted into the Russian army. Victims of this kind do not appear in the church records, which suggest, at least in the case of Tavastia, that there was significant growth in the population of the province during the Great Northern War. The figures for Tavastia are not entirely representative because this province was only affected to a limited degree by the bubonic plague in 1710–11, but it must be assumed, especially in view of Lindegren's new calculations, that the population of Finland grew somewhat between 1700 and 1721. It would therefore have been less than 400,000 when the Great Northern War began in 1700, including the province of Kexholm.

The lists of burials for the years 1695–7, which have survived for many parishes, show that the famine was a catastrophe which reduced the population by at least 100,000. The population ought therefore to have numbered about half a million before the years of famine. The province of Kexholm must, of course, be subtracted if this figure is to be compared with Åström's, and even if we assume that there was also no decline in population in this county during the war, its population cannot have exceeded 30,000 in 1700.[30]

## The colonisation of Finland

In geographical terms, Finland was colonised in the period following the incessant warfare of the years 1560–1721 and which ended with the breakthrough of the timber industry, that is to say 1721–1870. The population grew from *ca.* 400,000 to 1,769,000 during this century and a half or — if one takes 1865 as the terminal date instead of 1870 — to 1,843,000. That is to say that the population more than quadrupled.[31] The accompanying maps show that settlement was still fairly sparse in the interior of the country at the middle of the eighteenth century, and the existence of virtually unpopulated areas along the borders of the various historical provinces is very noticeable. In contrast, the whole country, with the exception of Lapland, was fairly evenly settled in 1865 — the small white spots on the map represent lakes. The natural population increase in Finland in the second half of the eighteenth century was five times as high as in Denmark and twice as high as in Norway and Sweden. Virtually the whole of this larger population was absorbed by the agricultural sector and much of it by clearing new land: the proportion of town-dwellers was only 5.6 per cent in 1727, 4.5 in 1810 and 6.7 in 1865.

At the beginning of this period the opportunities for clearing new land were virtually unlimited, and there seems to have been no pressure of over-population during the eighteenth century. A selective study of four areas in the south-west of the country between 1721 and 1850 showed that demographic crises occurred most often in the prosperous region surrounding the town of Turku, that these crises seldom followed years of crop failure, that the number of deaths in the spring was not greater than in 'normal' years and that the increase in mortality was mainly accounted for by children in the 1–9 age group. These findings are all definite signs that the main cause of the higher mortality-rate during the years of crisis was epidemics. Turpeinen's analysis of all deaths and of deaths caused by epidemics between 1751 and 1806 produces the same results for the country as a whole.[32] However, it is probable that there were recurring food shortages during the latter part of this period, at least in eastern Finland, and that rapid population growth ultimately proved too much for the primitive agricultural system, especially in the eastern burn-beating area, and led to the catastrophe of famine and disease of 1868.[33]

### The linguistic groups in a quantitative perspective

According to the earliest reliable figures, Swedish-speakers numbered 256,000 people or 13.9 per cent of the total population of Finland in 1865. Wallén has calculated that there were 87,000 Swedish-speakers in 1749, which corresponds to 20 per cent of the total population after subtracting the Swedish-speakers in the parish of Pyhtää in the part of Finland ceded to Russia.[34] If we compare these figures or attempt to work backwards from the time when censuses began to be taken, frontier changes must be taken into account. The areas which belonged to Russia between 1721 or 1743 and 1812 were almost entirely Finnish-speaking. It is therefore most meaningful to use figures for the whole period which relate to Finland within the frontiers of 1812 or, in the case of the seventeenth century, Finland plus the province of Kexholm. If this is done, the population in *ca.* 1750 comes to 540,000 of whom 16 per cent were Swedish-speakers, a somewhat higher figure than 100 years later. The decline is connected with the lower rate of population growth in coastal areas compared with the interior. Written sources, which are virtually all that we have for the eighteenth century, suggest that there was some movement of population from, for

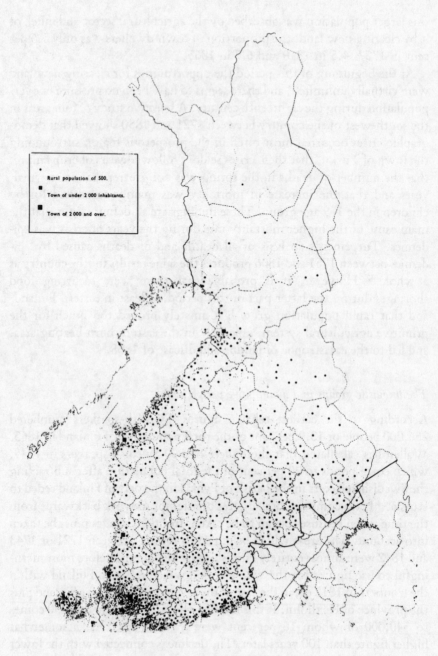

Distribution of population in 1749.

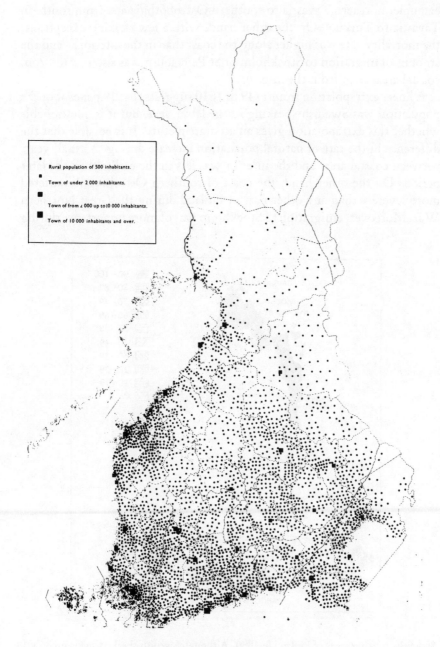

Distribution of population in 1865.

(*Atlas of Finnish history*, Helsinki 1959)

example, northern Tavastia to southern Ostrobothnia and from southern
Tavastia to Turku.[35] On the other hand, with a few striking exceptions,
the mortality-rate was higher along the coast than in the interior,[36] and the
amount of migration to Stockholm or St Petersburg was also greater from
coastal areas than from the interior.[37]

A linear extrapolation from 1749 to 1610 suggests that 19 per cent of the
population was Swedish-speaking in the latter year, but it is questionable
whether this extrapolation gives an accurate picture. It is possible that the
difference in the rate of natural population increase during 'normal' years
between coastal areas and the interior was less in the earlier than the later
period. On the other hand, the coast of southern Ostrobothnia suffered
more severely than any other part of Finland during the Great Northern
War. Moreover, emigration to Stockholm was of more importance during

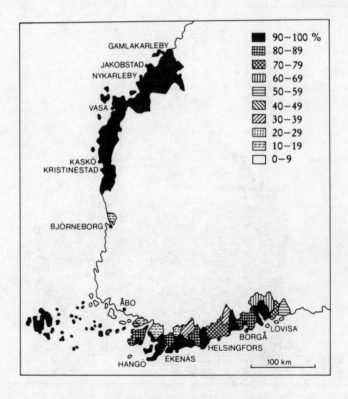

Swedish-speaking areas of Finland in 1880. Although Swedish-speakers made up only 14
per cent of the total number of inhabitants, they accounted for 38 per cent of the urban
population. (M. Klövekorn, *Die sprachliche Struktur Finnlands 1880–1950*, Helsinki 1960)

Sweden's age of greatness than in the eighteenth and especially the nineteenth centuries. Population growth in coastal areas as compared with the interior may therefore have been even weaker in 1610–1750 than in 1750–1865.[38]

However, the balance of strength between the two linguistic groups was influenced not only by the different rates of population growth in Swedish-speaking and Finnish-speaking areas but also by other factors as well. The geographic linguistic frontier sometimes shifted, and if those who moved into an alien linguistic environment were not assimilated, minorities emerged. Examples are provided by the coastal areas of Karelia, Finland Proper and Satakunta, which were Swedish-speaking in the Middle Ages, but which had been fennicised by the nineteenth century. Small changes to the advantage of the Swedish language can be noted in the case of western Nyland. There was also a virtually incessant stream of people from the Finnish-speaking interior to the Swedish-speaking parishes and towns of the coastal area, where the Finnish-speaking minorities were largely swedicised.[39]

Another process which influenced the population's linguistic composition was linguistic change as a social phenomenon. In the period we are considering, social mobility meant swedicisation if the movement was upwards and in its last stage usually fennicisation if the movement was downwards. Such downward mobility was quite widespread and its incidence should not be underestimated. Persons of standing constituted a small group: 2.7 per cent of the population in 1750 and 1.5 per cent in 1870.[40] The attitude they adopted in the language conflict aroused a good deal of attention, and it therefore has been, and still is, easy to exaggerate the importance of this group for the genetic composition of the people as a whole.

## NOTES

1. U. Salo, 'Pronssikausi ja rautakausi', in Y. Blomstedt, J. Tarkka (eds), *Suomen historia*, vol. 1, Helsinki 1984, pp. 127, 133–4; T. Seger, 'On the Structure and Emergence of Bronze Age Society in Coastal Finland: A Systems Approach', *Suomen Museo*, 88 (1981), pp. 31–44.

2. J. Koivulehto, 'Suomalaisten maahanmuutto indoeurooppalaisten lainasanojen valossa', *Journal de la Société Finno-ougrienne*, 78 (1983), p. 128.

3. K. Mark, *Zur Herkunft der finnisch-ugrischen Völker vom Standpunkt der Anthropologie*, Tallinn 1970.

4. C.F. Meinander, 'Om introduktionen av sädesodling i Finland', *Finskt Museum*, 90 (1983), pp. 5–20; J. Donner, 'Pollen av sädesslag och deras datering i pollendiagram från södra

Finland', *Finska Vetenskaps-societetens årsbok*, 3 (1983–4), pp. 9–13; T. Edgren, 'On the Economic Subsistence of Battle Axe Culture in Finland', *Iskos*, 4 (1984), pp. 9–15.

5. I. Vuorela, 'Suomalaiset — keitä he ovat ja mistä he ovat tulleet' (1982). This unpublished essay contains findings that were not available at the time of the Tvärminne conference.

6. V. Voionmaa, *Hämäläinen eräkausi*, Porvoo 1947, p. 22.

7. J. Vahtola, 'En gammal germansk invandring till västra Finland i byanamnens belysning', *Historisk Tidskrift för Finland*, 68 (1983), pp. 252–79.

8. T. Seger, 'The Plague of Justinian and other Scourges', *Fornvännen*, 77 (1982), pp. 184–96. The question is discussed in *Historiallinen Aikakauskirja*, 82 (1984), pp. 205–9 (J. Luoto), 83 (1985), pp. 97–102 (Seger) and 84 (1986), pp. 326–8 (Luoto).

9. O. Ahlbäck, 'Jomala', *Nordiska namnstudier, Festskrift till Harry Ståhl*, Uppsala 1983, pp. 251–65, assumes that the parish name Jomala is of Swedish origin. L. Hellberg, *Ortnamnen och den svenska bosättningen på Åland*, Skrifter utgivna av Svenska litteratursällskapet i Finland, 541, Helsingfors 1987, pp. 42–6, 218–19, maintains however that Jomala (Finnish *jumala* = god) 'is a typical Finnish name structure' and regards Ahlbäck's interpretation as 'very improbable'.

10. C.F. Meinander, 'Om svenskarnes inflyttning till Finland', *Historisk Tidskrift för Finland*, 68 (1983), pp. 229–51.

11. Unpublished material which I. Vuorela has kindly placed at the author's disposal.

12. K. Julku, *Kvenland — Kainuunmaa*, Studia Historica Septentrionalis, 11, Jyväskylä 1986, pp. 120–9.

13. P.-L. Lehtosalo-Hilander, *Luistari, 3, A Burial-ground reflecting the Finnish Viking Age Society*, Suomen muinaismuiston yhdistyksen aikakauskirja 82:3, Helsinki 1982, pp. 53–7.

14. Seger, 'The Plague of Justinian', pp. 184–96.

15. B. Gräslund, 'Befolkning, bosättning, miljö', *Fornvännen*, 69 (1974), pp. 1–13.

16. K. Pirinen, *Savon historia*, II:1, Pieksämäki 1982, pp. 50–64.

17. S. Sundqvist, 'Finlands folkmängd och bebyggelse i början av 1600–talet', *Meddelanden från Generalstabens krigshistoriska avdelning*, II, Stockholm 1931.

18. E. Jutikkala, 'Vad betecknar "näbb" i Borgå län?,' *Historisk Tidskrift för Finland*, 20 (1935), pp. 30–7.

19. H. Wallén, *Språkgränsen och minoriteterna i Finlands svenskbygder omkr. 1600–1866*, Turku 1932.

20. Jutikkala, 'The Way up', in S. Gissel *et al.* (eds), *Desertion and Land Colonization in the Nordic Countries, c. 1300–1600: Comparative Report from the Scandinavian Research Project on Deserted Farms and Villages*, Stockholm 1981, pp. 122, 140–2. Even more emphasis is placed on the role of the plague in L. Walløe, 'Pest og folketall 1350–1750', *Historisk Tidsskrift* (Oslo), 61 (1982), pp. 3–45.

21. A. Mäkelä, *Hattulan kihlakunnan ja Porvoon läänin autioituminen myöhäiskeskiajalla ja uuden ajan alussa*, Historiallisia Tutkimuksia 109, Helsinki 1979. E. Orrman, *Bebyggelsen i Pargas, S:t Mårtens och Vemo socknar i Egentliga Finland under senmedeltiden och på 1500–talet*, Historiallisia Tutkimuksia 131, Helsinki 1986.

22. Jutikkala, 'Asutus ja väestö'; in E. Jutikkala *et al.* (eds), *Suomen taloushistoria*, 1, Helsinki 1980, pp. 160–3.

23. It is true that parliament had decided that peasants who held land were only exempt from land tax if they had relinquished their farm to their descendants, but it must be assumed that the son placed himself on the taxation list when his father became too old to work. G. Lext, *Mantalsskrivningen i Sverige före 1860*, Meddelanden från ekonomisk-historiska institutionen vid Göteborgs universitet, 13, Göteborg 1968, pp. 249–51, independently reaches the same conclusion as I do in the essay mentioned in note 24. Old people who held no land may be regarded as excluded under the terms of a regulation which exempted 'the frail and the infirm' from taxation.

24. Jutikkala, 'Can the Population of Finland in the 17th Century be Calculated?', *Scandinavian Economic History Review*, 5 (1957), pp. 155–72. Lext, *op. cit.*, pp. 28, 43, 45–7.
25. P. Virrankoski, *Pohjois-Pohjanmaa ja Lappi 1600-luvulla*, Oulu 1973, pp. 98–105.
26. Jukikkala, 'Asutus ja väestö', pp. 150–2.
27. S.-E. Åström, *Hur stor var Finlands folkmängd under stormaktstiden?*, Institute of Economic and Social History, Helskinki University, 1978.
28. The province of Kexholm is included in this figure.
29. J. Lindegren, 'Krigsmakt och arbetskraft', unpublished essay 1987, pp. 86–97, 104.
30. R. Ranta, *Vanhan Suomen talouselämä 1721–1743*, Historiallisia Tutkimuksia 130, Helsinki 1986, pp. 79–83.
31. The areas ceded to Russia in 1721 and 1743 and incorporated into the grand duchy of Finland in 1812 are included at the beginning and at the end of the period. The total area involved is therefore unchanged apart from the parishes in northern Ostrobothnia and Lapland administratively treated as part of Sweden proper before 1809.
32. E. Jutikkala and M. Kauppinen, 'The Structure of Mortality during Catastrophic Years in a Pre-industrial Society', *Population Studies*, 25 (1971), pp. 283–6; O. Turpeinen, 'Les causes des fluctuations annuelles du taux de mortalité finlandais entre 1750 et 1806', *Annales de démographie historique*, 1980, pp. 287–96.
33. Y. Kaukiainen, 'Harvest Fluctuation and Mortality in Agrarian Finland (1810–1870)', in T. Bengtsson *et al.* (eds), *Pre-industrial Population Change: The Mortality Decline and Short-term Population Movements*, Stockholm 1984, pp. 235–54. A.M. Soininen, *Vanha maataloutemme. Maatalous ja maatalousväestö Suomessa perinnäisen maatalouden loppukaudella 1720-luvulta 1870-luvulle*, Historiallisia Tutkimuksia, 96, Helsinki 1974, pp. 382–94.
34. Wallén, *op. cit.* p. 147. Wallén states that 70–73,000 people lived in the Swedish-speaking areas during the second decade of the seventeenth century, and he believes that the number of Finnish-speakers living in these areas was about the same as the number of Swedish-speaking persons of rank residing in Finnish-speaking areas.
35. Y.S. Koskimies, 'Hallinto ja oikeuslaitos', in *Hämeen historia*, 3:1, Hämeenlinna 1966, pp. 309–11.
36. O. Turpeinen, 'Regional Differentials in Finnish Mortality Rates 1806–65', *Scandinavian Economic History Review*, 21 (1973), pp. 145–63.
37. M. Engman, *S:t Petersburg och Finland. Migration och influens 1703–1917*, Bidrag till kännedom av Finlands natur och folk 130, Helsingfors 1983, including the maps on pp. 196–200.
38. S. Carlsson, 'Stockholm som finnarnas huvudstad' in S. Huovinen(ed.), *Mitt sa' finnen om Stockholm: glimtar ur finnarnas historia i Stockholm*, Stockholm 1984, pp. 13–28; M. Engman, 'Finland — ett utflyttningsland' in M. Engman and H. Stenius (eds), *Svenskt i Finland, 2, Demografiska och socialhistoriska studier*, Skrifter utgivna av Svenska litteratursällskapet i Finland 519, Helsingfors 1984, pp. 122–6.
39. Wallén, *op. cit.*, passim.
40. K. Wirilander, *Herrskapsfolk. Ståndspersoner i Finland*, Nordiska museets handlingar 98, Stockholm 1982, pp. 124–43; Y. Blomstedt, 'Aleneva säätykierto', *Genos*, 45 (1974), pp. 12–26.

# THE FOREST AND THE FINNS

## Aarne Reunala

When the first inhabitants arrived in Finland thousands of years ago the country was almost entirely covered with dark coniferous forests. The only clearances had been made by storms and forest fires. Broad-leafed trees and bushy vegetation also flourished along the banks of the lakes and rivers. The game in the forest and the waters teeming with fish may have tempted the first settlers there. Game was not hunted simply for use by the hunter, but was needed also for trade. Beavers, elk, wild reindeer, bears, wolves, lynxes and foxes were hunted for the economy of the Roman world. The tax-collector, too, took his share in fur pelts.

Agricultural skills came to Finland with the first inhabitants. The trees in the fertile forests were felled and burnt, and on the soil enriched by the ashes crops were grown for a few summers. In the alluvial plains and river valleys of south-west Finland and also on the western shore of Lake Ladoga, agriculture became permanent in the course of the first 1,000 years. After burnbeating, the land was cleared to form fields whose fertility was maintained with the help of cattle manure.

*Hunting and fishing* were part of the annual work of the agricultural population from the very beginning of settlement. Hunting expeditions undertaken from the area of permanent settlement in south-west Finland could extend over a distance of up to 200 km. (125 miles) and take weeks. From the latter half of the sixteenth-century, hunting expeditions began to lose their importance because the forest wilderness was declared crown property and opened up to new settlement. Numerous affrays occurred as the former owners of the wild forest tracts and the new settlers, mostly from Savo, disputed each others' rights. Hunting had no radical influence on the Finnish forest landscape apart from conflagrations started by the hunters' camp fires, which, like the natural forest fires, freshened the monotony of the otherwise gloomy coniferous forests. Sometimes the forest was burned deliberately, for example during elk hunts. The elk would gather under the smoke to free themselves from their parasites and could then be shot.

Of all the ancient sources of livelihood in Finland, *burnbeating* had the greatest influence on the forests. The form of burnbeating practised from prehistoric times was the burning of broad-leafed and mixed forests on rich lands. This lost its importance as it was superseded by field cultivation in

The wilderness, by Pekka Halonen (1899). A

south-west Finland in the seventeenth century and in Tavastia and Upper Satakunta in the eighteenth. On the other hand, in Eastern Finland burnbeating in the coniferous forests remained a central means of livelihood up to the end of the nineteenth century.

Burnbeating in the dense coniferous forest demanded many years' labour. First the trees were dried out by peeling off their bark at the height of a man's reach. The stripped trees were left standing for about ten years so that broad-leafed brushwood had time to grow under the dry conifers; only then did the burnbeating take place. The cultivator had several tracts of stripped trees of different ages waiting at any one time, because burnbeating in coniferous forests produced only one or sometimes two rye harvests. After reaping, the burnbeaten land was left waste, serving at good pasture for a few years, and then becoming reforested in the course of time. The same land could be burnbeaten again after a period of twenty to forty years.

The development of the technique of burnbeating made possible the spread of settlement and the growth of population. Burnbeating was thus not a primitive form of squandering the forest but in its day was the most effective means of winning the coniferous forests for habitation. Timber had still no great value, while grain was easy to store, transport and convert into money. Burnbeating agriculture even made Savo into the granary of Finland, from which grain was sold to other provinces and sometimes even abroad. Burnbeating lands suitable for new settlement began to diminish from the latter half of the eighteenth century, when burnbeating became to some extent abusive. Luckily for the Finnish forests, the profitability of burnbeating began to diminish in the nineteenth century as Finland began to acquire duty-free grain from Russia and wood prices began to rise with the increasing use of timber by industry. At the end of the nineteenth century the new area used for burnbeating was only about 50,000 hectares (124,000 acres), and by the twentieth century burnbeating remained a curiosity which might still be employed as the first phase of field clearance.

Burnbeating brought new light and verdancy to the Finnish landscape. The dark spruce forests receded even further from inhabited areas and in their place came the brighter birchwoods and mixed forests. Around the villages, where burnbeating was carried out most often, birch had no time to grow but the ground was given over to the quick-growing alder. When burnbeating was coming to an end in the latter half of the nineteenth century, the whole of Southern Finland, with the exception of the coast, and the southern parts of Northern Finland had been almost entirely burn-

Burnbeating in Eastern Finland, photographed by I.K.Inha in 1896. *B*

beaten. Traces of the burnbeating era were already disappearing in western Finland but in vast areas of eastern Finland the original coniferous forest could no longer be seen.

*Tar* was exported from Finland to some extent already in the Middle Ages. The voyages of discovery and the growth of shipbuilding in the seventeenth century increased the demand for it and the centre of tar production moved to Sweden and above all to Finland. For two centuries tar became Finland's most important item of export. It was at first produced primarily in Savo, Karelia and North Tavastia. When Viipuri, Lappeenranta and Hamina were lost to Russia at the beginning of the eighteenth century, tar-burning ceased in Eastern Finland and the centre of Finnish tar production shifted to Ostrobothnia and Kainuu.

A tar pit under construction in 1930. Tar was Finland's principal export during the seventeenth and eighteenth centuries. *B*

Tar-burning began with peeling the bark in the same way as in burnbeating. The difference was that burnbeating was prepared in mixed forests and mature spruce forests, while young pine made the best tar. In spring the pines were stripped first at the base. In the following year, and perhaps even a third year, the stripping was continued higher up. Thus tormented, the pines began copiously to secrete resin, but nevertheless remained alive because a strip of bark was left on the north side up to the last bark stripping. After five or six years the dried trees saturated with resin were felled and hauled close to the tar pit where they were cut up for burning the following spring. At least four days were taken to burn the chips of wood in the tar pit. The tar was run into officially inspected barrels of 125 litres ($27\frac{1}{2}$ gallons) capacity; these were then transported by land or water to the export harbours. The trade in tar was so great that handling and warehousing centres were founded at Oulu and Kajaani; these were later called the tar courts. The name illustrates the great value of tar as the agent of prosperity.

A huge quantity of timber was used in tar-burning. It has been estimated that during the peak years at the end of the eighteenth-century, wood in Ostrobothnia was being used in a quantity amounting to about three-quarters of what can be felled in the managed forests of the present day. The marks left behind were correspondingly extensive. The young pine forests disappeared from their natural barren soils, replaced by tough but slow-growing spruce forests. These traces of tar-burning can still be seen even now in the forests of Ostrobothnia and Kainuu.[1]

Tar-burning was an industrial use of timber of its time. There were other similar uses. Many ironworks were founded in the south-western part of Finland during the seventeenth and eighteenth centuries. These needed quantities of charcoal and so *charcoal burning* became an important means of livelihood for the peasants and crofters of the region. In Ostrobothnia and Finland Proper (the south-western province) wood was used also for *lime-burning*; the *manufacture of potash* from the ashes of birch and aspen was concentrated in Ostrobothnia. Potash was needed by glass-factories and dyeing works. The marks left on the forests by charcoal- and lime-burning and the manufacture of potash nevertheless remained small and limited in extent compared with those left by burnbeating and tar-burning.

Cattle-raising was an important part of agriculture from prehistoric times. Winter was a lean time for cattle: animals were fed, for example, on straw, hay and mash made from dried leafy twigs and other plants. The situation was better in the summer when the cattle went out to *pasture in the forest*, although this was attended with its own dangers. The animals might wander too far or become lost and wild beasts were often a threat. To avoid disputes care also had to be taken that cattle remained in the common pasture area of their own village and did not stray, disturbing fields, meadows and burnbeating. Herdsmen were needed for this, taking the cattle into the forest in the morning and bringing them back to the village in time for evening milking.

Pasturage brought a new feature to the Finnish forest landscape. Light, park-like pastures were created where the trees took on peculiar and decorative shapes, often in fact decaying, from the effects of trampling and stripping by the animals. The juniper and the alder became more common as a result of pasturage. *Gathering branches for winter fodder* also gave a garden-like quality to the forest landscape around the villages. Moreover pasturage gave rise to the dense network of forest paths which was of use for all other movement in the forest. Nowadays the forest-pasture landscape and the forest paths have almost entirely vanished, the reasons being the end of forest pasturage and the coming of modern forestry.

*The use of timber for domestic needs* has been so varied in Finland that one could speak of a Finnish Wood Age lasting for centuries. Buildings were constructed of timber and their roofs were covered with shingles. The use of logs for building maintained its dominant position in country districts up to the 1920s. Wood was the most important fuel for domestic and

The main room of a peasant farm in Savo, painted by R.W. Ekman in 1848. The importance of the forest for the domestic economy is evident everywhere in this picture. The year's supply of bread hangs from the beams. *A*

industrial use until the Second World War. Wooden fence-making used up large quantities of thin timber. Wood was used for a multiplicity of purposes in the home: the few pieces of furniture, tubs, dishes, bakers' shovels, ladles, scoops, bowls and baskets were all made of wood. In Finland Proper the making of special wooden boxes became a domestic industry, the products of which were sold in the towns and even abroad. Wooden torches were used as a source of light, and around 20,000 of these were burned in a year by an average peasant household.

Sleighs and carts were made of wood as were collar-bows and horse collars, and often it was necessary to look in the forest for naturally curved trees suitable for these purposes. 'The lad Lauri is busy in the forest looking for crooked trees,' wrote Aleksis Kivi, describing a man of his time who when in the forest was constantly seeking valuable timber shaped by nature. In addition to timber, much else was found in the forest to ease the necessities of life. *Birch bark* was a particularly serviceable material for many purposes. Boxes and baskets, shoes and the inner soles of leather footware, floats for nets, herdsmen's horns and sheaths for knives were all made of birch bark. It was also a trading commodity, sold at fairs and exported as far as Stockholm.

Hunger was a perpetual threat to Finns in former times. A bad harvest year meant a shortage of food and sometimes outright famine. The particularly severe famine years 1542–5, 1601–2, 1695–7 and 1867–8 are fixed indelibly in the memory of the Finns. Even in normal years the flour used for bread-making was often eked out with substitutes. Over half of all Finns had to use substitute food regularly at the beginning of the nineteenth century. The most common substitute was *bark bread flour* which was made of the layer of bast stripped from beneath the bark of the pine. This was baked or boiled and then dried and ground into bark bread flour. Bark bread flour contained 40 per cent of material of nutritional value to humans, but if bread was made of dough containing more than half of bark bread flour this caused urticaria.

Other substitutes were used as well, such as husks, pea-stalks, straw, water arum, sorrel, ferns, lichen and moss. However, bark bread, the most frequently used substitute, above all associated the forest with the long-lasting image of former famine years when with the help of bark bread the people nevertheless managed to stay alive. From the forest also came resin used as *chewing gum*. This was already known during the Stone Age and remained a living tradition in Ostrobothnia until the 1920s. Spruce gum was used for preference but pine gum would do. It is said that the Finnish settlers in the forests of central Sweden even chewed their lumps of gum in church to keep awake during the sermon. The men in Kainuu had the habit of bringing chewing gum to the children as a souvenir of their expeditions into the wilderness.

To some extent wood was produced for sale from at least the sixteenth century. Firewood was exported to Tallinn and Stockholm, and the export of beams, hewn with an axe, began at the same time. The first water-powered sawmills were built in Finland in the sixteenth century but the export of sawn timber abroad began only in the eighteenth century when fine Dutch saw-blades came into use. Exports remained, however, comparatively small; at the beginning of the nineteenth century one-third of timber exports comprised sawn timber and two-thirds firewood.

The invention of steam power and the liberalisation of economic policy in the mid-nineteenth century drove the saw-milling industry into frantic expansion. Restrictions on sawing were removed, and production and exports rose rapidly. While exports in the 1850s comprised 50,000 standards, they had risen by the end of the century to nearly 500,000 standards and in 1913 to 900,000 standards. The Finnish saw-milling industry has remained at that level ever since.

The rise of the modern Finnish forest industry began with saw-milling. The first wood-pulp mills and paper factories were founded at the same time as the first steam-driven saw-mills in the 1860s. Wood-pulp was used in the manufacture of newsprint. Chemical processes of breaking down the wood fibres into cellulose were developed in the 1870s and 1880s. The sulphite process became predominant up to the 1950s because of the greater whiteness of the pulp and less waste. The plywood industry began in the 1910s, the wallboard industry in the 1930s and the chipboard industry in the 1950s.

The nineteenth-century philosopher and statesman J.V. Snellman did not believe that the development of Finland could be built on the wealth of its forests. He was convinced, as were German economists and cultural experts, that life supported by the forest signified primitiveness, poverty and lack of civilisation, and that only a prosperous agriculture offered the way to prosperity and enlightenment. Luckily for the Finns, Snellman was wrong. Finland's forest resources attracted foreign entrepreneurs from many countries, such as Britain, Norway, Sweden and Holland, and following their examples Finnish entrepreneurs began to build factories. This activity was profitable and the use of timber by industry increased quickly. As the industry grew, timber prices also rose rapidly, altogether ninefold between 1860 and 1880.

The income received from the sale of timber, which seemed absolutely incredible at the time, brought about all-round progress. The farmers were now able to modernise and improve their agriculture: arable land was thoroughly improved, buildings were renewed, equipment and machinery obtained. The rise in the value of timber made burnbeating unprofitable and it was now only practised by the poorest crofters and the landless.

Timber-felling offered work to a population which had greatly increased during the nineteenth century. Both farmers and those without land joined eagerly in timber-felling work. The typical tradition of forest work in Finland was born, in which the farming population has looked after part of the felling of timber while the rest has been done by temporary, itinerant, landless forest workers. After the Second World War temporary forest labour became gradually more permanent and finally in the 1970s changed into a valued trade, on a par with other industrial trades.[2]

The importance of the forest industry was at its peak at the end of the 1940s when 90 per cent of Finland's income from exports was derived from timber and processed wood products. During the dark post-war years the forests provided the possibility of paying war reparations and raising the standard of living. With the help of the forest the losses of the war were repaired in a surprisingly short time: the displaced population of Karelia was resettled, reparations were paid, industry was diversified, and the standard of living rose. The early 1950s were the great period for forestry and the timber industry in Finland. This confirmed the old saying that the forest was the most important support and safeguard of Finland's development.

Since the 1950s the relative importance of forestry and the timber industry has diminished as the national economy has diversified. The timber industry's share of export revenues had fallen to 37 per cent by 1984, but this diminution does not reflect the whole truth. The timber industry is based more than other industries on the use of domestic raw materials so that as a net producer of export income its share remains over 50 per cent. In spite of the diminution of its relative importance, the production of the timber industry has grown continually. In 1960 it used 32 million cubic metres of domestic raw wood, at the beginning of the 1980s the average was 40 million cubic metres, and according to the Forest 2000 Programme the domestic supply will rise to 62 million cubic metres by the year 2000. The timber industry is still a growing industrial sector, central to the national economy.[3]

*Private ownership of forests* in the immediate vicinity of farms and villages is of ancient origin. Severe years of war accompanied by increased taxation led in the seventeenth century to a large number of private hereditary farms coming into the possession of the state because of arrears of taxes. The farmers became crown crofters and tenants. With the improvement of the economic situation in the eighteenth century, tenant-farmers were given the right to buy back their farms as hereditary holdings. In 1870 four out of five farms had moved back into peasant ownership.

The extensive forests beyond the villages remained common land for centuries. Only the spread of settlement and the growth of the population made necessary the permanent arrangement of land ownership. The great programme of land enclosure was begun in 1757, and in about 100 years the main features of land-ownership in Finland were established: private owners often held the best forest lands near the settled, cultivated areas and the state retained the distant, barren regions, principally in eastern and northern Finland.

New pressures on forest ownership began at the end of the nineteenth century. The landless rural population had grown so large that even the growth of the forest industry had been unable to absorb it all and there was a growing awareness that the tenant-farmers, who were in a weak situation, should be given their own farms. On the other hand the rise in the value of timber had increased the interest of timber firms in owning forests. Both these questions provoked decades of discussion and argument.

The situation of the landless population was settled in 1918 when the so-called Crofter Law was passed. This led in all to the creation of about 150,000 new independent small farms by the end of the 1930s. The decision was remarkable and in keeping with the Finnish tradition of private land-ownership. The same principle, the formation of new independent farms, was followed after the Second World War when the refugee population from Karelia was resettled. A total of about 3 million hectares (7.4 million acres) of land was used for post-war settlement, almost 10 per cent of the area of Finland. The result of these settlement measures has been the fragmentation of forest ownership: in 1901 there were about 110,000 farms, while in the late 1980s there are 310,000 with over 2 hectares (5 acres) of forest, that is over three times as many. Settlement measures also meant the diminution of the state's share of forest ownership from 35 per cent in the 1920s to 24 per cent in the 1980s.

Land purchases by timber companies became a burning question at the end of the nineteenth century. The companies, which had become rich, bought entire farms with all their land and buildings and rapidly increased the amount of forest they owned. By 1910 companies already owned about 1.7 million hectares (4.2 million acres) of forest, a total which has hardly changed since. Their purchases aroused sharp public controversy because many feared that they would impoverish life in the rural areas. Companies were accused of speculation and of letting arable farming land decline. Individual negative examples were indeed to be found and although the companies endeavoured to show that the accusations were generally without foundation, a decree was promulgated in 1915 limiting land acquisition by companies.

Not all companies, however, were satisfied with the decision and they founded associated companies which, circumventing the decree, bought nearly 500,000 hectares (1.2 million acres) of land in a couple of years. This aroused great irritation, in consequence of which companies were required in 1925 to surrender farms they had acquired contrary to the decree. The mistrust still prevalent in Finland of land-ownership by companies has its origins in those times. This appeared, for example, in the 1970s when, as part of the reform of the laws governing land acquisition, restrictions on the purchase of farms were made more stringent than hitherto.

It is by these twists and turns that the proportions of forest ownership have developed over the years. At the beginning of the 1980s private individuals owned 63 per cent of forests, the state 24 per cent, companies 9 per cent and local authorities, parishes and other organisations 4 per cent. The importance of privately-owned forests is emphasised by their location on the best land: the privately-owned share of the growth of standing timber is in all 76 per cent.

The social structure of Finland has altered profoundly in the decades under considertion. The country was predominantly a primary producer, but has become industrialised and urbanised. This change· has influenced the ownership of the forests. Migration from the countryside and the system of inheritance have led to circumstances where the forests owned by farmers have been transferred to an increasing extent to forest-holders rather than farmers. In the 1950s scarcely 10 per cent of private forests belonged to the owners of forest holdings. Since then their share has risen to 41 per cent in 1983, and if development continues at approximately the same pace, owners of forest holdings will possess about 65 per cent of private forests by the year 2000. This change will place Finnish forestry in an entirely new situation.[4]

The traditional use of the forests — burnbeating, tar-burning and lumber-felling — involved living from hand to mouth without regard for what happened to the forest after it had been used. Only the development of the timber-consuming industry created an awareness that the forests ought to be used sufficiently sparingly for the timber to last into the future. The first such ideas were put forward by the owners of the ironworks to ensure the requirements of their blast furnaces for timber as fuel, but only the strong development of the timber industry in the latter part of the nineteenth century prompted the idea of *forest management* approximately as it is now understood.

In the 1850s the National Board of Forestry was founded, and advanced forestry instruction was started at the Evo forestry college.[5] Estimates made at that time of the extent and state of the forests were disturbing: forests in abundance remained only in northern Finland and the rugged districts of the watersheds; elsewhere there was a lack of timber. A German forestry expert invited to Finland was equally worried: if burnbeating, tarburning and reckless felling continued unchanged, the forests of Finland would be reduced to only second-rate wasted woodland.

A new forest law, which demonstrated rare foresight, was brought into effect in 1886. The principle of sustaining yield was set forth there in a way which has been transferred in almost identical terms to all subsequent forest laws: 'Forest land shall not be laid waste.' This means that forests have to be felled intelligently and their regeneration cared for. The enactment in the current law on private forests, dating from 1967, has been modernised in the form 'The forest may not be devastated.'

In practice the supervision of felling and the care of the forests made progress gradually, dependent on resources. The personnel of the National Board of Forestry was increased, and voluntary associations were founded to promote private forestry; in 1928 these became forestry boards, funded by the state but based on self-government by the forest-owners. Forest management associations were founded, and their activity became more intensive in the 1930s and above all in the 1950s when as a result of the law on forestry management associations, they were set up in all rural communities. At present scarcely any country has a more effective organisation of support and advice for forest-owners than Finland. In 1985 it employed over 2,500 trained forestry professionals.

A more active concept, too, became associated with forest management already at a fairly early stage: it was not enough that forests should be felled intelligently but attempts should also be made to improve them in the same way as fields were improved in agriculture. The forest improvement law was passed in 1929 under which the state began to support the drainage of wetlands and the afforestation of open spaces and wasted woodlands. Subsequently state aid has extended to the construction of forest roads, forest fertilisation, the tending of young stands, and finally the pruning of standing timber.

Forest management long remained based on natural methods. This situation began to change in the 1950s. The timber industry had grown at such a pace that already by the end of the decade excessive felling was taking place. The solution was seen in more efficient timber production, and several forestry efficiency programmes were drawn up in the 1960s of which the best known became the Mera (Forestry Funding) programmes produced with the backing of the Bank of Finland.[6] Clear cutting became more general and the soil began to be treated more intensively: in the 1950s clearings were burned over but in the 1960s burning gave way to site preparation: the dressing and ploughing of the soil. Young stands were tended more purposefully than before, first with bill-hooks, then also chemically and with clearing saws. Use of fertilisers became common at the end of the 1960s. Harvesting became mechanised: the power-saw displaced the frame-saw and the axe, and agricultural and logging tractors displaced the horse. Forest improvement work increased: the drainage of wetlands reached its peak at the end of the 1960s, and the network of forest roads needed by mechanised forestry has become more dense from year to year.

All told, the 1960s marked a leap in the move from natural forestry to cultivation forestry. The change was so swift that the Finns had still not really become accustomed to it a couple of decades later, in spite of the fact

that the intensification of silviculture was interrupted in the mid-1970s by
the rise in costs caused by the oil crisis and the swing from overcutting to
cutting savings. Thoughts of intensifying the forestry industry have
gained a new emphasis in the 1980s. In the view of the Economic Council,
the growth of prosperity for the Finns has made it essential to have
recourse once more to the forests. The Economic Council thus sponsored
the Forest 2000 Programme in which an attempt has been made to raise
forestry to a new and higher level than before. This programme, drawn up
in 1985, also contained a new element in that for the first time a careful
attempt was made to reconcile timber production with the protection of
the environment and the use of the forests for recreational purposes.[7]

The forests and trees have not only provided material sustenance but at the
same time many beliefs have been linked with their use.[8] One series of
beliefs has developed from ancient ideas according to which the firmament
is kept in place with the support of a mighty *world tree*. To support the
world system the Finno-Ugrians built their dwellings as miniatures of the
universe: the roof of the hut curved like the sky above its dwellers and in
the centre was placed a strong pole to represent the world tree, with a
purely ritual function. It is thought that the final form of development of
the centre pole was the pillar supporting the corner of the stove in a
Karelian house.

Numerous customs have arisen throughout the world from the myth of
the world tree. The tree has a central and benevolent part in them. In a religious ceremony the spirit of the bear killed by the hunter was sent to the
bears' heaven along the pine where its skull was hung up. Special memorial
trees or other sacred trees, which were common in eastern Finland as late as
the nineteenth century, protected the household and brought good luck.
Damage to them would be followed by misfortune. In the middle of the
burnbeaten clearing, the farmer might leave a tree to protect the land's
fertility. And wooden objects, foliage and branches were used in numerous
spells for curing diseases, protecting people and domestic animals, bringing good luck in hunting and fishing, and arousing affection.

The tradition of the world tree has remained alive to the present day. In
Sweden and the Åland Islands a decorated pole is raised on Midsummer
Day. The fire, smoke and ashes of the Midsummer and Easter bonfires have
provided protection from spirits and from disease, and in the ceremony of
dancing round the fire, the rotation of the universe around its axis, the
world tree, is repeated. The Christmas tree dates from the seventeenth

Bear-skull fir tree in north-eastern Finland, photographed by Samuli Paulaharju, 1915. *B*

century, creating primarily for urban dwellers a new bond with nature and the natural, age-old world system. By bringing an evergreen tree indoors at the darkest time of the year people take a ritual part in the course of the seasons and confirm the coming of the new spring and summer. The mid-summer birch has the same meaning of confirming the course of the year. The use of the sauna whisk and, at Easter, the flicking of people with willow branches are the heirs of old healing spells. The well-known act of 'touching wood' may also have its origin in belief in the world tree. The close association of tree and man is depicted also in the planting of trees to honour significant events and perhaps even in speaking of the genealogical tree.

In addition to the tree, *the forest has been seen as benevolent and protective*. People have fled to the forest to shelter from their enemies, and the trees of the forest have given comfort to the deceived individual, lamenting his loneliness. The forest comforting the lonely is a basic theme of Finnish national lyric poetry. There has always been in the mind of the Finns a certain echo of freedom in the forest.

But the forest has not only been a safe and protective place. *It has also aroused fear*. Spirits and gods were capricious, therefore there was cause to be wary of them and, to be on the safe side, to appease them. Mysterious diseases could be caught in the forest, and accidents, wild animals or simply getting lost threatened men and cattle alike. Numerous spells were cast to ward off the evil that threatened in the forest. Wolf bailiffs hung coloured pieces of cloth and bits of wool on bushes and tied the branches of bushes into knots to keep the wolves away. When cattle were let out in spring into the forest pasture for the first time, protection was given to the animals against the dangers of the forest by tarring their udders or by making them walk through a wooden hoop.

Besides its identification with the ancient myths that blend safety and fear, the forest has also meant bread to the Finns. Thus the *landscapes of burnbeating and cultivation*, cleared from the forest, became symbols of prosperity already at an early stage. The open cultivated landscape breathed gently, and nothing in the eyes of the burnbeating farmer seemed more beautiful than the burnbeaten clearing, burned black, smoking and soon to bring forth grain. The bright broad-leafed and mixed forests which grew in the overgrown burnbeated clearings brought variation to the dark coniferous forest and aroused memories of the livelihood secured by burnbeating cultivation.

Appreciation of the beauty of the original primeval forests was learned only later, when industrialisation and urbanisation made the forest more distant. Artists who had studied abroad were the pioneers here, one of the first being Werner Holmberg, who as early as the 1850s saw 'incomparable treasure in the forests which have been touched only by the Creator's hand'. Many other artists followed Holmberg, such as Hjalmar Munsterhjelm, Berndt Lindholm, Viktor Westerholm, Akseli Gallen-Kallela, Eero Järnefelt and Pekka Halonen, as a result of whose work the primeval forest became the symbol of Finnishness and patriotism. Pictures of the forest and of trees were printed on banknotes and stamped on coins. Share certificates were decorated with pictures of the forest, musical compositions depicted its mood, and societies and municipal buildings were given names associated with it. In provincial songs a patriotic mood was raised by images of the dark, primeval coniferous forests and the soft broad-leafed forest. Finnish architecture developed an original 'forest style' in which international trends were blended with the Finnish forest landscape. Finnish literature has been to a great extent literature about the forest,

Forest motifs were widely used in the *Jugend* style of architecture at the turn of the nineteenth century. Detail from the building of the Pohjola insurance company (1899), designed by Gesellius, Lindgren and Saarinen. *C*

The Independence Spruce, planted in Helsinki in 1930, and in the foreground the monument proclaiming its dedication to the Finnish parliament 'in memory of the sixth of December 1917, when parliament smashed the fetters of slavery from its people, lighting the torch of its liberty'. (Contemporary photograph) *B*

describing the tensions between life in the wilderness, daily life in the countryside, and urban life. And hardly had the Finns moved to the towns in the 1950s than they were hurrying back to spend their holidays in the midst of the countryside and the forests.

The old values of the forest are still living in the mind of the modern, even the urban, Finn. Finns are hunters and pioneers, they seek protection in the forest, where they experience an ancient pantheistic union with nature, and the dark conifers and light broad-leafed forests arouse in them feelings of patriotism. Even the principle of sustained use has in the course of time become part of Finnish values.

The present day has even given rise to completely new values concerning the forests. *Their recreational use* has become an activity for the masses, uniting the desires to enjoy the many traditional values of the forests, to have a change and to break free from the pressures of daily life. *The movement for the protection of nature* which spread worldwide at the end of the 1960s has drawn attention, as far as the Finnish forests are concerned, above all to the ecological consequences of silvicultural methods and to the need for conservation areas.

The image of the forest among people living in the unprecedented plenty of industrialised Finland is manifold and even conflicting. The forests ought to offer the possibilities for the continual improvement of the standard of living, and at the same time to provide a link with the special cultural heritage of the Finns, with the life of previous generations and with age-old myths. They ought also to provide recreation, and they must be kept healthy and diverse in their plant and animal life. The fulfilment of all these different needs, of course, presents many problems.

Modern forestry is so recent that it has still not become adapted to the traditional values of the forests. There are conflicts between nature protection and forestry which are difficult to resolve. On the other hand urban recreation frequently accords well with the environment of commercial forests. An attempt is made in forestry to reconcile these numerous values by drawing more attention than hitherto to the many uses of the forests. Directives and recommendations have been issued for paying attention to the landscape, recreation and conservation in conjunction with forestry.

A number of general factors add to the possibilities of using the forests in an impartial way that would satisfy most users. Examples from Finland and abroad show that as years go by the conflict between silviculture and the traditional values of the forest diminishes and that well-managed forests can become environments which are seen as beautiful and refreshing. Moreover, all forest-users are facing a new threat in common: air pollution. All forces can unite to prevent it, and the resulting common effort will make for greater mutual understanding in other matters concerning the forest as well.

## NOTES

1.  Methods and effects of tar-burning are described in detail in P. Alho, 'Utilization of Forests in North Ostrobothnia and its Effects on their Condition' (English summary, *Acta Forestalia Fennica*, 89 (1968).

2.  Forest workers' growing social status is seen in the fact that forest labour studies began in the 1950s with the dissertation of L. Heikinheimo, 'Method of Surveying Forest Labour' (English summary, *Acta Forestalia Fennica*, 61, 1954). A whole series of studies followed, of which the most comprehensive was L. Heikinheimo, M. Heikinheimo, M. Lehtinen and A. Reunala, 'Level of Living of Forest Workers in Finland', *Comm. Inst. For. Fenn.*, 81.1 (1974).

3.  J. Raumolin, 'The Impact of Forest Sector on Economic Development in Finland and Eastern Canada', *Fennia*, 163.2, 1985, gives a historical-comparative perspective on the importance of forests in Finland's economic development.

4.  A. Reunala, 'Structural Change of Private Forest Ownership in Finland', *Comm. Inst. For. Fenn.*, 82.2 (1975).

5.  E. Laitakari, 'A Century of Finnish State Forestry', *Silva Fennica*, 112, 1963, describes the history of state-owned forests but gives a good overview of forest use in general.

6.  The principles of the first Mera-programme are presented in S. Ervasti *et al.*, 'The Development of Finland's Forests 1964–2000', *Silva Fennica*, 117 (1965).

7.  'The Forest 2000 Programme', *Silva Fennica*, 20.1, (1986).

8.  The following text on the forests' role in Finnish culture and traditions is principally based on A. Reunala and P. Virtanen (eds), 'The Forest as a Finnish Cultural Entity', *Silva Fennica*, 21.4, 1987 (English summaries). The publication contains articles from many different fields of study, mainly humanities and social sciences.

# KARELIA: BATTLEFIELD,
# BRIDGE, MYTH

## Hannes Sihvo

The historic Finnish province of Karelia no longer exists (see map), having been ceded to the Soviet Union in 1940, although in present-day Finland the administrative province of North Karelia is creating its own identity and there are some south Karelian towns in parts of the administrative province of Kymi. These areas today have a strong inclination for maintaining cultural traditions relating to the Karelian identity by fostering them and keeping them alive. Karelia and Karelian features always seem to find a new start to life, as has traditionally been the case over the centuries.

As part of an ideological tradition of Finnish patriotism inherited from the nineteenth century, Karelia and the Karelians evoke idealistic and ideological sentiments, Karelia is 'the land of Destiny', 'the Karelia of joy and sorrow', 'the land of folk poetry', 'the lands of the Kalevala epic', 'the Karelia of past, faded golden memories'.

In an historical perspective the drastic changes which afflicted Karelia and its population as the result of the Second World War are part of the same process which has been going on for centuries in the tidewater between east and west. This process may be approached from different angles, but what is essential is that Karelia should be regarded specifically as a changing phenomenon and not as a centuries-old fossilised outdoor museum, as tends to be the case nowadays among the Finnish population at large and those interested in Karelian folk and popular culture.

The shape of Karelia has changed greatly over the centuries. Its contraction or expansion has been an offshoot of the designs of east and west in relation to their spheres of power, and cultural, religious, economic and political boundaries. It has known long periods of peace but has also very often been an area of conflict and aggression. The best rewards may be achieved by regarding Karelia as both the battleground and the bridge for the two spheres of power, but even the most objective inquirer will find it impossible to avoid the duality of influence that is closely connected with Karelia, i.e. eastern and western; indeed, acceptance of these two varying interests must form the starting-point for inquiry.

Although controversy about the physical possession of Karelia is a thing of the past and a settled matter, there is still sufficient material for research, for art and for the more general debate about the Karelian identity to allow

Karelian folk singers, photographed at a song festival in Helsinki in 1900. *B*

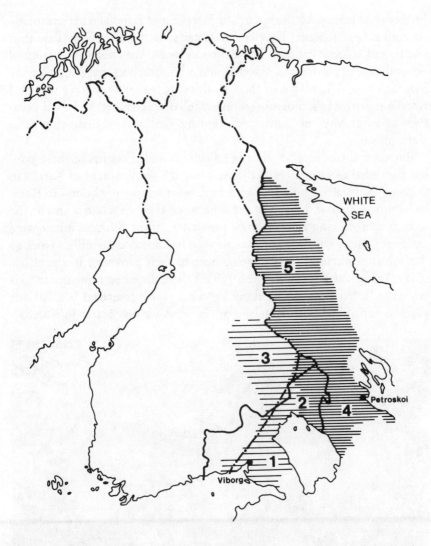

Map showing the historic Finnish province of Karelia, which consists of the Karelian Isthmus (1), Frontier or Ladoga Karelia (2) and North Karelia (3). The unbroken line running to the west of Viborg marks the 1743 frontier. The Karelian Isthmus and Frontier Karelia formed the *guberniya* of Viborg in the eighteenth century, but was united with the grand duchy in 1812 and constituted the province of Viborg until the Second World War. The part of the province (west of the broken line) which remained to Finland after the war was made into the province of Kymi, while North Karelia became a separate province in 1960. The area to the east of the 1812 frontier (East Karelia) was divided between the administrative districts of Olonets (4) and Archangel (5). Both districts also embraced large regions that were purely Russian. The narrowly shaded area denotes Orthodox population.

further deliberation of the essence of Karelia and Karelian characteristics. As cultural phenomena, Karelian characteristics and components are thus not bound to political and national boundaries; but students of cultural phenomena, in particular folklorists and ethnographers, have been largely indifferent to or ignorant of these realities. It is they who have regarded Karelia as a great folk museum crammed full of folk-singers and the decorative ethnography of nineteenth-century national romanticism and Karelianism.

But then again, it is largely the reflections and thoughts of those who left the ceded areas in 1944 that have created a public image of Karelia in Finland. Naturally, those thoughts have been temporally bound to Karelia's immediate past, to its best times between the two world wars. At the time of their leaving Karelia, these promoters of the Karelian image were no longer young, or they were people who had devoted their life's work to the vigorous phase of rapid development in their province. In the classic study *Accommodating the Refugees* (1952) there appeared some quotations which reflected Karelian thinking — 'Our youth remained behind; our dreams, too, filled with Karelia', or 'Everything was better in Karelia'.

Karelian Romanticism in full bloom. The photographer I.K. Inha (bearded) and friend returning from Archangel Karelia to Finland, enjoying a picnic in the company of some village women by the lake at Kuittijärvi. *B*

The loss of the area, the fading of memories and daydreams of the native locality, have changed to a Karelian nostalgia — a kind of tribal therapy for 'the last Karelians'. It has its psychological significance but has also given rise to a tasteless and trivial souvenir industry.

The greatest danger in recent Karelian cultural activity has been the attempt to give a one-sided impression of Karelian characteristics, in the building of either the Bomba log mansion in the Karelian border style as a tourist attraction, or of a new Valamo in memory of the monastery on the Ladoga islands, or in the creation of a miniature model of the town of Viipuri as it was on the eve of the war. A student of Karelian culture might nowadays feel exasperated with the prevailing fervour for building Karelian mementos, perhaps a complete 'Karelian country', a Karelian Disneyland, but on the other hand it is some comfort to know that even in the tourist and travel industries the eastern and western components of Karelia come to the fore. There is now a lively tourist trade to Viipuri, to Terijoki in the Karelian Isthmus and also, to a certain degree, to Petrozavodsk on Lake Onega. Perhaps Lake Ladoga and the lakeside towns of Sortavala and Käkisalmi and the old Valamo monastery will soon be opened to tourists. Then it would be possible to see a good deal of Karelia with one's own eyes.

As a land of memories Karelia is a double-sided phenomenon. On the one side it is already a myth, part of the national archetype, in which historically realistic events have been simplified or wrapped up in the guise of legends. The picture of Karelia has begun to parallel that romantic illusion about the past of the Finnish people created by Lönnrot's *Kalevala*. However, on the other side there still exists an enormous amount of private, personal, family, kindred and community 'memory albums' which will carry forward the traditions far into the future. A large part of the golden memories is taken up by the extraordinarily substantial and flourishing Karelian literature. Although there is an abundance of literature with a refugee theme, there might at least be a comparative 'world record' in the output of the Karelians, who have recorded their reminiscences of their native locality, kinsfolk and community.

Popular literature associated with Karelia is thus thriving, and it includes the occasional work of real literary merit, but conversely there has not been much scholarly research into Karelian history and culture. Research on Karelia does not have a large following. For example in the 1970s and 1980s there has been more interest in the East Karelian question and the development of the idealisation of the Karelian people than in basic research into Karelian history. The most important studies of the latter

have clearly been Heikki Kirkinen's work on Karelia in the Middle Ages
and modern times, Veijo Saloheimo's history of Northern Karelia and
Erkki Kuujo's history of Border Karelia. An extensive project on the history of Southern Karelia has just been started. The settling of refugees in
Finland and their adjustment was the subject of social studies in the 1950s,
and younger researchers have made studies of similar topics. A popular
scholarly general interpretation of Karelia and its varying circumstances
appeared in the 1980s as a five-part series.

Around 700 AD the Karelians lived in some kind of 'Ancient Karelian'
tribal area south and southeast of Lake Ladoga dealing chiefly in the fur
trade. The view now prevalent among philologists is that they belonged to
a proto-group which also included the Ingrians, Estonians, Votians and
Vepsians. From south of Lake Ladoga they moved in different waves of
settlement to the west and north. They moved westwards at least as far as
the vicinity of present-day Mikkeli where they constituted the foundation
of the Savo tribe. The Olonets, Vepsians and Ludic (a tribe of former Vepsians living on the eastern border of Olonets) moved to the area between
Lakes Onega and Ladoga. Those living on the western shores of the White
Sea were later considered as the 'purer' Karelians. By the beginning of the
eleventh century there was vigorous North Russian migration into the
eastern borders of the Karelian lands, with a good deal of peaceful assimilation taking place. It was in the western rather than the eastern border of
the Karelian lands that conflict tended to occur.

The Karelians' earliest contacts with the east and west were peaceful.
The Varangians, the travellers on the road to the east in Viking times,
traded with the Karelians in Aldeigjuborg, the 'Staraya Ladoga' of the
sagas, along the River Volkhov. The Vikings' 'Karjálabotn' (or
'Kirjálabotn', a term for the eastern part of the Gulf of Finland in Icelandic
legends) at the lower end of the River Vuoksi and the 'Korela' of the
Russian chronicles are proof that the inhabitants of these areas derived their
names from that place.

Lake Ladoga has been the 'primary sea' for the tribe which was given the
name 'Karelian' in the Novgorod chronicle in 1143. By then the Karelians
constituted a relatively independent group or nationality, allies of Novgorod and companions-in-arms of the Novgorod people in the violent raid
on Sigtuna in 1187. The time of greatness in Karelian history was in the
twelfth and thirteenth centuries. In the thirteenth century Novgorod
strengthened its position by founding a fortification in Karelia, later to be

Karelian village, with Orthodox church in background. The large, closely-grouped buildings, often housing up to sixty members of an extended family, were typical of the region. (J. Krohn, *Suomen suku*, Helsinki 1887)

enlarged as Käkisalmi castle. The work of conversion in the east proceeded in an unspectacular fashion, in spite of the mass baptism of the Karelians by Prince Yaroslav in 1227. In 1293 the Swedish commander Tyrgils Knutsson began the building of a castle at Viipuri as a frontier-post of Western Catholicism.

A period of border wars between Novgorod and Sweden followed, after which the fundamental peace treaty in Karelian history, that of Nöteborg, was signed in 1323. Here the secular forces of the two churches, namely Rome and Byzantium, concluded 'an eternal peace', kissing the cross and swearing in the name of God to respect the agreement. However, the treaty was soon violated, and the Karelians suffered the consequences.

The peace treaty split the Karelian Isthmus in two, with the border designated as running from the river Siestarjoki by way of the river Vuoksi to the region where Savonlinna now stands, and from there, according to some historians, to the Gulf of Bothnia, and according to others, to an ill-defined area between the Gulf of Bothnia and the Arctic. The border to the north was not specified in detail. This gave grounds for disputes, for moving the border a little at a time and even for falsifying the border deeds, and the exact location of the border has been a source of difficulty for researchers since. More important, the border continued to have an effect over the centuries on the structure of folk culture, and provided the justification for the division of Finland into east and west.

The border thus split the old Karelian area in two. The Karelia centred around Viipuri developed in the Swedish/western sphere of culture, while the area under the rule of Novgorod was subjected to eastern influences. The differences manifested themselves in religion and administration but most notably in matters of taxation and in the mode and established form of society. In the culture of the people the border divided the Karelians by language, religion and customs. In Novgorod Karelia, the Orthodox religion inculcated more peaceable habits, and tolerated the pagan customs and beliefs of the people. Whereas in western Finland the peasant Lalli slew the missionary bishop Henry, the eastern church, with its secluded monks and monasteries set in the backwoods, encountered less hostility from a pagan people.

Settlers and merchants traversed the border created under the Nöteborg peace treaty, but it was also crossed thick and fast during tribal wars. The Häme tribe was Novgorod's adversary, although it was in the balance for some considerable time whether they were willing to subject themselves to Swedish rule.

At the beginning of the modern period, King Gustav Vasa (1523–60) actively encouraged the colonisation of the forested interior; this policy meant that the frontier war imperceptibly moved eastwards. The decades of warfare in the second half of the sixteenth century brought destruction and desolation to Karelia. Finally, the peace of Teusina in 1595 moved the border further to the east. In 1617, King Gustav II Adolf forced Russia to sign a treaty at Stolbova after an exhausting struggle for power. As a consequence, both Lake Ladoga and the Gulf of Finland became inland seas within the Swedish empire, with Finland, the former eastern hinterland, becoming the outpost of the West. The newly-acquired parts of Karelia were united with the Swedish realm, but they were dealt with as conquered lands coupled with Ingria, and were not incorporated administratively into the rest of Finland.

In its conquered territory of Karelia, Sweden set up a system of farming out the land revenues. The peasants who came under the control of the lessees were often wretchedly exploited. An unscrupulous bureaucracy, the heavy burden of taxes and, worst of all, the assault on the Orthodox faith of the inhabitants by forced conversion to Lutheranism caused a mass exodus to the Russian hinterland. This was mostly to Tver, where the

Karelians created a settlement in which the Karelian language and culture have been preserved to the present day.

The Karelian Isthmus was further devastated in the wars of the early seventeenth century; with the return of peace, settlers from western Finland, Ostrobothnia and particularly Savo began to move in. The Savo migrants, who together with the other settlers in the Äyräpää district in the 1600s and 1700s became known as the Savakko people, gave the Isthmus a new, distinctly Western character. Up to the nineteenth century a great number of those living in the Isthmus were descendants of the Savakko. This intensive settlement has also meant that the area's dialect belongs to the south-eastern sub-group of the eastern Finnish dialect. The region of the true Karelian language begins on the north-eastern and eastern sides of Lake Ladoga.

The treaty of Stolbova in some respects united Karelia, but it also ultimately separated a section of the Karelians to become a distinct eastern group under the Russian realm in the administrative districts of Olonets and Archangel. The Karelian-speaking population living in the Olonets and Lake Onega areas were in lively contact with the neighbouring Russian settlement in and around Petrozavodsk. To the west of the White Sea, but mainly in the area towards the Finnish border, the Archangel Karelians continued to live by their own archaic culture in the peace of the backwoods. This settlement originated both from the Ladoga Karelians of the Middle Ages and from the migrants from more westerly Finland in modern times.

In the first decade of the nineteenth century, nationalistic ideologies regretted the fact that the Archangel Karelians had been separated from the rest in perpetuity and therefore had no possibility of participating in the promotion of Finnish culture. This was indeed the case, and later attempts to unite East Karelia with Finland collapsed because there was not the time for the East Karelians to develop even a literary culture, still less an educated class which would have adopted the cause of promoting the nationality concept. Attempts at cultivating and annexing East Karelia remained a matter for a small but significant group of Finnish activists.

It might also be asked whether the 'Karelian culture' of the Archangel Karelians would have been preserved had they been subjected to the miseries, as well as the benefits, which affected the rest of Karelia. The Archangel Karelians were left in peace, isolated from civilisation and wars; they were left alone as if living on a reservation, waiting for their Finnish national romantic discoverers in the nineteenth century.

Following the fall of Viipuri castle in 1710, Karelia became a Russian possession with a strategic value for launching a conquest of Finland. After the Great Northern War and the period of Russian occupation in Finland (1714–21) the border was moved under the terms of the treaty of Nystad in 1721 to resemble to a great extent the Soviet-Finnish border of today. Karelia, not including the area approximating to present-day Northern Karelia, was now under the sceptre of Russia. Peter the Great's border has proved to be more permanent than that dictated by Sweden when it was a great power. The Tsar, with an eye on the West, strengthened his position by establishing a new capital city at the mouth of the River Neva, which flows from Lake Ladoga into the Gulf of Finland. The new metropolis of St Petersburg turned the geopolitical position of Karelia on its head. The border between Russia and Sweden was to become increasingly significant.

At the conclusion of peace of Åbo in 1743, after a brief Russo-Swedish war (1742–3), the border was moved to the river Kymi. The provinces of Viborg and Kexholm became the Russian *guberniya* of Viborg. At the turn of the eighteenth century this was renamed the *finlyandskaya guberniya*, commonly called 'Old Finland'. In its administration the laws of the Swedish kingdom were retained but Russia regarded it as being coupled with the Baltic lands for administrative purposes. The *gubernii* of Archangel Karelia and of Olonets were not incorporated into Old Finland.

The most difficult social problem that has ever existed in Karelia arose — rather, it grew worse — at the end of the eighteenth century. At that time a large part of the Isthmus and of Ladoga Karelia came under the control of special favourites of the sovereign who were given gifts of land ('donations'), or estates, upon which the peasants were reduced almost to the status of serfs, or had to pay rent in the form of day labour.

At the conclusion of the Russo-Swedish war in 1809 the whole of Finland was transferred to the Russian empire, and in 1811–12 Old Finland was transferred to the Finnish grand duchy, or — as the Russians maintained — the grand duchy was united with Old Finland. In Finnish eyes the eastern border, which remained substantially unaltered between 1812 and 1940, was regarded as stable and historically sanctioned: it was 'legitimate' and for that reason the only rightful one, whereas other phases were merely 'transitional'.

The union with Russia obliged the Finns to look to the east for the expediting of their affairs. In principle, the relations of the Karelians with St Petersburg ought to have been easy, but they were not always so, at least not at first. The difficulties had been many, and the uniting of Old Finland with the grand duchy did not improve the lot of the peasants in the so-called donation lands. On the contrary, their miserable situation was made even worse in 1826 when the peasants were deprived in every respect of the proprietary rights to their farmsteads. When the tenant farmers refused to perform the burdensome day labour or sign conveyance agreements, the Cossacks were ordered in. Many farmers were tried and given sentences of exile in Siberia. In 1867 the liability to perform day labour was finally abandoned when the states started to purchase the granted lands, after which the peasants were allowed to buy (their own) farmsteads back. This dragged on for many decades.

The persecution of the Orthodox religion and the flight from the land following the treaty of Stolbova had been a severe blow to Karelia. Another period of repression was brought about by the feudal donation land grants. However, at the end of the century the peasant was able to get on to his feet both spiritually and economically. In the Isthmus and in Ladoga Karelia there was a noticeable revival of economic activity and cultural life. There were several cultural centres, the most important being Viipuri and Sortavala. Viipuri developed noticeably as a commercial city, and with its literary societies and schools also became a base of support for Finnish-language nationalism. When the railway link between Viipuri and St Petersburg was opened in 1870, the Isthmus was reinvigorated and an unprecedented economic boom took place.

The Isthmus was strongly oriented towards St Petersburg. In addition to the railway, the road network carried food and other produce from Finland to the capital. The peasant traders of the Isthmus were well known throughout Finland, as were their more distant colleagues, the pedlars who traded from the provinces of Archangel and Olonets. A number of the peasants trading with St Petersburg, together with some small farmers in the Isthmus who had just redeemed their plots, turned away from agriculture, and made easy extra cash by selling or renting their land to the flood of holiday-makers from St Petersburg, into the ambit of which the Isthmus was progressively drawn before the First World War, becoming in a sense a 'Russian Isthmus'. The economic and cultural significance of this phenomenon has yet to be thoroughly investigated.

In the building of a Finnish national identity in the nineteenth century, Karelia played a central role. The Finnish nation did not have its own history in the political sense, but with the publication of Elias Lönnrot's *Kalevala* in 1835 it gained an imagined past. Lönnrot compiled his epic from old Karelian folk poetry which he had collected from the Russian part of Karelia — Archangel Karelia. He created 'the dream of a land of happiness, which had been preserved for a poetry-less era in its original innocence'.

Karelia thereafter enjoyed a prodigious reputation, and towards the end of the century became the shrine for holy pilgrimages from across the border. At the same time as famous writers (Juhani Aho, Eino Leino), artists (Akseli Gallen-Kallela, Eero Järnefelt, Pekka Halonen, Emil Wikström), composers (Jean Sibelius) and ethnologists were creating a national culture drawing its inspiration from Karelia, the ideological view that the Archangel Karelians would have to link up with the Finnish cultural community also gained ground.

When Finland severed its connections with Russia in 1917, some activists aspired to bring the Karelians across the eastern frontier into the newly-independent state. This eastern Karelia was seen as a Finnish irredenta. During 1918 and the following years, the normally peaceful and remote corner, which had been disturbed only by the border raids of the sixteenth and seventeenth centuries, found itself a theatre of war filled with the soldiers of many armies together with some seekers after financial gain. The people of Archangel Karelia were bewildered, and to a certain extent it was in that state that they were transferred straight from an illiterate hunting and fishing culture to the sphere of enlightenment of a new Soviet state. After the wars and conflicts, the East Karelia question became an international issue. The cherished dream of the educated class and the political activists in Finland that Karelia would become Finnish dated back to the nineteenth century. It gained strength around 1918, and perhaps more so between the World Wars when the Academic Karelian Society was founded by university students inspired by the nineteenth-century vision of the unity of the Finnic peoples. They swore oaths for a Greater Finland 'out of a hatred for Russia and love for their Karelia', of which East Karelia was a natural and inseparable part.

On the Karelian coat-of-arms the curved scimitar of the east and the true sword of the west tussle for the Karelian crown. This dispute has been fought in literature and in general discussion, at times vigorously, throughout the twentieth century. Typical of the Western view is that presented by T.G. Aminoff: the Finnish title of his general work on Karelia is *Karelia — A Frontier-Post of the West*. (More neutral is the original Swedish title *Between the Sword and the Scimitar*.) According to Aminoff, the Karelians have generally defended the West from an Eastern or Russian offensive. The opposite viewpoint is apparent in the book published in Petrozovodsk by the Russian D.B. Bubrikh in 1947 under the title *The Birth of the Karelian Tribe — the Story of an Ally and Friend of the Russian People in the North*, according to which Karelia, as a Russian outpost, has borne the brunt of Sweden's repeated attacks.

Both sides have indulged in propaganda. It was at its most passionate in the nineteenth century and the first decades of the twentieth. If Finland spoke of making Karelia Finnish and Lutheran, so Russia for its part defended the Orthodox faith and promoted Russian culture in Karelian schools. This battle took place mainly in border Karelia where the Orthodox faith was used as the main weapon in the russification process. The founding of the Finnish Orthodox diocese in 1892 helped to boost the identity of Karelian Orthodoxy in Finland; on the other hand, an entire monastic order was founded for the purpose of russianising Karelian Othodoxy.

The threat of Russian cultural dominance in the Isthmus provoked counter-measures in Finland. In 1908, patriotic inhabitants of Viipuri erected a statue of Tyrgils Knutsson. The Russian historian General M. Borodkin, in a book published in 1909, called the uniting of the province of Viipuri with Finland in 1812 'the most distressing chapter'. In 1910, at the bicentenary celebrations of the Russian capture of Viipuri castle, the response of the Russians to 1908 was to unveil a statue of Peter the Great, who for them was the 'restorer of ancient Russian lands'. In 1911 there was a Russian plan to transfer the easternmost districts of the Isthmus from Finnish to Russian administration as a buffer zone for St Petersburg.

It has been argued that those districts could well have been given up at that time, thereby avoiding the threat of later conflict over the security of St Petersburg-Leningrad. This argument, however, tends to ignore the importance of the economic and cultural resurgence in the Karelian Isthmus. Furthermore, a kind of death sentence was pronounced on the Isthmus when the Treaty of Dorpat in 1920 cut off the vital connections with St Petersburg. At that stage Karelia really did become a 'frontier post', the mainstay of which were the Finnish Civil Guard and the army. On the other hand, we must take into account the tense situation as the world braced itself for war. On the eve of the Second World War all the pressure and tension of this preparation fell on the Isthmus where the atmosphere was that of the calm before the storm. As the recollections of many witnesses have testified, the gay, exotic and even cosmopolitan mood of the Isthmus, Terijoki and Viipuri had an almost macabre quality.

Significantly the historian Arvi Korhonen concluded his work *The Origin of Finland's Eastern Border*, published in 1938 by the War History Department of the Defence Ministry, by discussing the 1617 treaty of Stolbova and the fact that 100 years later the eastern border had again changed, 'but fate, which in this case is not the same as chance, has decreed that the border [that of the Stolbova Peace] with all its advantages and

Carrying the flag: a school in the East Karelian town of Petrozavodsk during the Finnish occupation in 1941. The new Finnish name of the town and school is above the door; the Russian name remains affixed to the wall. *B*

The Finnish army in retreat, summer 1944. *D*

disadvantages is now the eastern border of Finland and at the same time the border between eastern and western culture, now more evident than ever before.' The historian Jalmari Jaakkola also paid attention to the mental. effort or, more appropriately, the mental assault which had to be made on East Karelia. Jaakkola even transferred the origin of the old folk poetry from Karelia to western Finland. The full force of the Academic Karelian Society's propaganda on East Karelia followed in Jaakkola's footsteps.

There is also good reason to remember the propaganda from the East. O.V. Kuusinen's 'Finnish Democratic Government' set up in Terijoki at the outbreak of the Winter War declared on 3 December 1939: 'The time has come to fulfil the centuries-old hopes of the Finnish nation of reuniting with the Karelian nation, thereby unifying the kindred Finnish people to become a homogeneous Finnish race.' The prophets of both East and West were, however, to be proved wrong.

In the Second World War Karelia was crushed on every front. In the Winter War the whole Finnish nation defended itself on the frontier which had been fought over for centuries. The Isthmus and Ladoga Karelia changed to the icy Tuonela (land of death) of the *Kalevala*. The departure of the first evacuees and the treaty of Moscow in March 1940 with the loss of Karelia was endured as an ordeal of destiny, but equally Dame Fortune was appealed to. In the spirit of 'Back to Karelia', the Finnish army even crossed the Stolbova border in 1941. This conquest of East Karelia became an epilogue in the long history of Karelianism. Little Finland felt that it was on a crusade bearing Western civilisation to Karelia and destroying Bolshevism.

The pattern of history stretching from Nöteborg to the treaty of Paris (1947) wound to an end: the relations between East and West started afresh in a manner as tragic as they had begun. The Kalevala tale of the destruction of a military expedition to Pohjola was repeated. The story which appealed most to the Finnish nation was one of the most important Finnish twentieth-century epics, Väinö Linna's *The Unknown Soldier*, translated into German as *Kreuze in Karelien*.

One hundred per cent of that section of the population which returned to their home districts during Finland's reoccupation of Karelia in the Continuation War (1941–4) had to leave again, in itself an historically unparalleled movement of population as a consequence of war. There was to be no problem in the formulation of articles in the peace treaty of 1947 relating to any remaining population: only the graves of their forefathers and the corpses of the fallen remained. These too have had monuments erected to their memory on the Finnish side. The Karelians brought everything with them, even their dreams. All in all, some 400,000 moved across the frontier into Finland. At the time of writing, about 150,000 of these refugees survive.

The Soviet Union put new inhabitants in the empty dwellings and russianised place-names. The transfusion was accomplished by bringing in a new population from the distant interior of Russia. Viipuri became 'the brother of Leningrad' and 'the outpost of peace' at the extremity of the Baltic. Viipuri however kept its name in the Swedish form Viborg, unlike for example the East Prussian town of Königsberg which the Russians renamed Kaliningrad. In the 1950s a Soviet history text called Viipuri 'an old Russian town', and it is so described to tourists from both East and West. The statue of Peter the Great, whose head had become detached when the Finns pulled it down, was restored to its original condition. Symbolism is an important weapon when Russian culture is being grafted on to conquered territories.

Over the decades since 1940, the Karelians have become assimilated into the Finnish community. The process has taken more than four decades, and it could be suggested that, to some extent, the whole of southern and central Finland has been affected by Karelian culture. That is to say that the Karelians were as far as possible settled in areas resembling their former home districts. The map of these groups of evacuees almost completely covers southern Finland with the exception of the Swedish-speaking coastal areas. Finland has thus been 'karelianised' with Karelian woven wall-hangings and Karelian rice pasties. The exuberant but soft Karelian dialect and even the traditional wailing for the dead have become part of the Finnish scene.

The last resettlement of the Karelians was of its kind a unique feat, although from the architectural and cultural viewpoint it disrupted the milieu of the southern and western Finnish countryside. The extensive emergency resettlement programme makes one wonder whether perhaps the highly-praised Karelian building tradition faded a long time ago.

The hospitable Karelians, themselves always calling on acquaintances, have never been familiar with separatism. Perhaps the distinctive traits in their traditions are over-emphasised when they meet, in their local district celebrations, and in the Karelian press and literature. However, other Finns easily excuse it. It is a small price to pay for what Karelia has given to the rest of Finland.

# OSTROBOTHNIA IN FINNISH HISTORY

## Heikki Ylikangas

In many countries there is a province whose history differs to a greater or lesser extent from the general national trend. In Sweden this is true of Dalecarlia and in Norway of Tröndelag. A special place has been ordained for Bavaria in German history and for the Don basin in Russian history. In Finnish history an exceptional image has been characteristic of Ostrobothnia.

Ostrobothnia is in itself a broad territorial concept. Historic Ostrobothnia extends from Satakunta north of the town of Pori far into the remote north of Finland. To the west it is bounded by the Gulf of Bothnia, and to the east the proper boundary is the watershed, the Suomenselkä ridge, though the present administrative borders actually permit its extension across the watershed. However, only a part of the historic province of Ostrobothnia is meant when one speaks of Ostrobothnia's special position. This part is South Ostrobothnia which lies along the coast roughly between Kristiinankaupunki and Pietarsaari and extends eastwards for some 100 miles (150 km.). The population living along the coast is Swedish-speaking while Finnish-speakers live to the east. The Finnish-speaking population is divided into two dialect areas. The Ostrobothnian dialect, a Western Finnish dialect, is spoken to the west, while to the east — in what is called the South Ostrobothnia lake district — the dialect resembles that of Savo and is Eastern Finnish.

What in the development of South Ostrobothnia has in fact been so special in its character? Chronologically, the divergent character of South Ostrobothnia first becomes apparent at the end of the sixteenth century. Finland had at that point reached a phase of development which England had experienced almost 300 years, France about 200, and Germany not quite 100 years earlier. The peasants rose in revolt to defend themselves against the combination of a centralising state and a new nobility. Disturbances and even armed risings also occurred in other parts of Finland, but South Ostrobothnians formed the hard core of the army of club-wielding Finnish peasants. In South Ostrobothnia almost every adult male entered the ranks, whereas elsewhere recruitment was based on the principle of one man from each household. Because of this the decisive battle of the 'club war' was fought in South Ostrobothnia, the principal base of the insurgents. Cavalry, gathered mainly from the nobles' estates in the south,

The south Ostrobothnian landscape is characterised by flat, almost treeless plains, dotted with hay-barns. Detail from a painting by Vilho Lampi, *Saunan Katto* (1933). *A*

crushed the last resistance of the peasants at Ilmajoki in South Ostrobothnia on 24 February 1597.

Despite this defeat, the special character of South Ostrobothnia was maintained, and indeed during the seventeenth and eighteenth centuries its profile became sharper and its silhouette darkened. Witch-hunting was rife during the seventeenth century, affecting equally the north and south of the province. About half of the 500 known witchcraft trials in Finland took place in Ostrobothnia. Opposition to enfeoffment (the royal assignment of lands or revenues in return for specific services) was also at its most powerful in South Ostrobothnia. The form in which taxes were paid was a matter for particular dispute; the fief-holders wanted tax to be paid in kind — in the form of tar — while the peasants wanted to pay in money. During the Great Northern War (1700–21), South Ostrobothnian peasants joined the Swedish army fighting in Finland in greater numbers than peasants from elsewhere to defend their province from the advancing Russians. These militiamen were drawn up in the rear of the army, and when the Russians succeeded in surprising the Swedish rear with their cavalry at the decisive battle of Napue in Isokyrö parish in 1714, the losses of the militia reached horrifying proportions. In some parishes (e.g.

Vähäkyrö) not a single able-bodied adult male is known to have survived. Similar popular resistance was repeated in the Russo-Swedish war of 1808–9 when Russia conquered Finland from Sweden. Then, too, the South Ostrobothnian peasants took part in military operations on an exceptionally intensive scale.

During the eighteenth century two new special features unfolded in the development of South Ostrobothnia. On the one hand the religious revivalist movements, known earlier as Pietism, won a foothold beginning in the coastal districts. On the other hand, towards the end of the century, various disturbances to public order increased. Both phenomena grew in strength and continued into the nineteenth century. In the following decades Ostrobothnia became the hotbed of revivalist movements in Finland. At the same time violent crime in the region swelled to huge proportions. About 2,000 South Ostrobothnians perished in criminal acts of violence between 1790 and 1890. Although the province represented only just over one-tenth of the country's population, at least one-third of all homicides were committed there; the ratio per 100,000 inhabitants per annum being almost ten. For short periods and in certain limited areas (Ylihärmä, Alahärmä and Kauhava) the ratio even rose to between fifty and sixty. Traditionally this period is known as the age of the knife-carrying thugs or villains (*puukkojunkkarit*).

National as well as religious revival met in South Ostrobothnia the strongest response of any Finnish province. The first authorities of the national movement (Zachris Topelius, J.V. Snellman, J.L. Runeberg and Yrjö Koskinen) all had roots there. The province became the strongest base of radical fennomanism in the 1870s and 1880s; thus activity aimed at strengthening the social and cultural position of the Finnish-speaking element in the population won strong support in Ostrobothnia. The youth association movement exemplifies this. Started by the people in the 1880s, this movement was intended to train citizens, by means of self-education and information, for participation in political and cultural life. Special club-houses for young people were set up in the parishes where newspapers were provided and evening and special educational activities arranged. The movement subsequently spread to other rural areas.

A new powerful mass movement, with totally different objectives, made its appearance at the same time as the youth society movement was beginning. From about 1885 onwards there was a surge of emigration from Ostrobothnia to America, involving about 2,000 South Ostrobothnians a year. By 1930 about 120,000 of the inhabitants of the province had migrated across the Atlantic. (The population of Ostrobothnia grew

A group of distinctively-dressed Pietists, photographed by Samuli Paulaharju at Laihia in 1929. *B*

from about 100,000 in 1800 to about 300,000 in 1900.) Although almost a third of the emigrants returned, South Ostrobothnia (and even part of Central Ostrobothnia) incontrovertibly showed higher migration figures than other parts of Finland.

South Ostrobothnia played a significant part in the attainment of Finnish independence. In the first place the greatest number of *Jägers* in proportion to population came from Ostrobothnia. In 1915–16 the German empire agreed to give military training to Finnish volunteers, and the resulting 2,000-strong *Jäger* unit, trained in Germany, decided the course of the Finnish civil war of 1918. Because the numbers of men involved in the civil war on the White and Red sides were approximately the same, and because there was no significant disparity in their weaponry, the final outcome was decided by the relative proportion of trained men. As far as training was concerned, the Whites enjoyed superiority over the Reds because the *Jägers* fought almost exclusively on the White side and the Reds derived less benefit from Russian soldiers in Finland than the Whites did from the *Jägers*, Finnish ex-Russian Imperial army officers and Swedish volunteers. The role of South Ostrobothnia in the events of 1917–18 was further emphasised in that it constituted the Whites' principal base. The Senate fled there from Helsinki, and South Ostrobothnian volunteers held the Reds in check until the conscript army raised in the north could be assembled and organised.

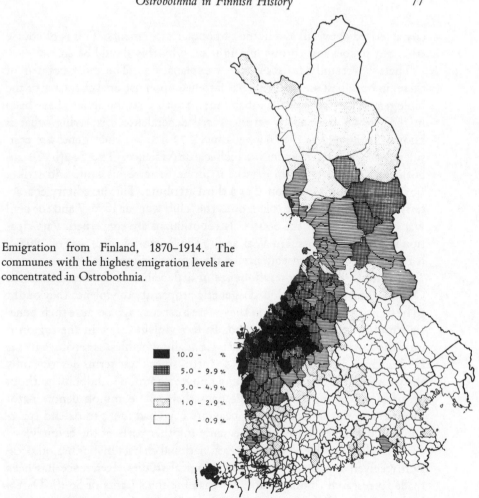

Emigration from Finland, 1870–1914. The communes with the highest emigration levels are concentrated in Ostrobothnia.

| | |
|---|---|
| ■ | 10.0 –    % |
| ▦ | 5.0 – 9.9 % |
| ▤ | 3.0 – 4.9 % |
| ▨ | 1.0 – 2.9 % |
| □ | – 0.9 % |

The last display of the distinctive character of South Ostrobothnia was in 1929–32 when right-wing radicalism became active. This radical movement aimed first at the prohibition of the Communist Party. After attaining this objective the movement turned against representative democracy. The crisis reached its peak in 1932 in the so-called revolt at Mäntsälä. The disturbances were swiftly halted after the government had appealed successfully for the support of the army. Throughout these years of crisis South Ostrobothnia stood out as the most active hotbed of the right wing. The period has even become known as the time of the Lapua movement, taking its name from Lapua in South Ostrobothnia.

These, briefly chronicled, are the special features of South Ostrobothnia in a historical context. What do they reveal? The region has been characterised above all as a home of popular movements. This is of course true, but it does not throw any light on why this should be so.

There is certainly no shortage of explanations. The most popular of these, in both past and present, has fastened upon national character or the biological inheritance of the inhabitants. South Ostrobothnians have been marked down as ruled by strong social dependence, displaying what is known negatively as the 'herd instinct'. Moreover, their genes are considered to contain elements which cause violence. The South Ostrobothnian, especially when drunk, is prone to seize his knife and strike. Love of freedom is mentioned as a third attribute. This hereditary characteristic has been used to explain both the 'club war' of 1596–7 and the civil war of 1918 as far as the South Ostrobothnians are concerned. Participation in the Great Northern War and in the Russo-Swedish war of 1808–9 is reckoned to be a consequence of the same characteristic.

Such myth-like interpretations are of little value. If the heredity of the Ostrobothnians really included a genetic propensity to violence they ought to be fighting as much today as they were a century ago because their genetic structure cannot have changed. In fact violent crime in the region is now the lowest in the entire country. Equally worthless is recourse to the herd instinct, love of freedom and so forth, since these terms describe only the nature of the phenomena from a known common standpoint without properly explaining anything. Perhaps their sole common denominator may be that the Ostrobothnian peasants have had more to defend (prosperity and independence) than peasants in other parts of the country.

An explanation based on biological national characteristics has on occasion received support from anthropological studies. Reference has been made to research findings showing that the inhabitants of South Ostrobothnia are the darkest people in Finland. It may also be pointed out that South Ostrobothnia would once have been inhabited by the mysterious ancient Kainuu people. A prosperous Iron Age culture flourished in the region, although finds relating to it cease from the first half of the ninth century. It is evident that these people were called the Kainuu because even as late as the 'club war' members of other Finnish proples called the Ostrobothnians Kainuu peasants. The Kainuu people are located in the same areas in Alfred the Great's 'History of the World' at the end of the ninth century. Possibly the heredity of the Ostrobothnians includes traces of the ancient Kainuu even if the ancestors of the majority of the present-day inhabitants have undoubtedly come from Satakunta and Tavastia. Despite this information, explanations based on genetic structure remain weak. Here-dity of a permanent character can in general be explained only by permanent characteristics and features. The strength of the explanation becomes badly strained when variations occur. And as far as Ostrobothnia is concerned, variations are the rule rather than the exception.

Other approaches exist which shed light much more effectively on the special characteristics of South Ostrobothnia. Let us first examine witch-hunting, which in general terms flourished in areas where a primitive trading economy had taken off but had not yet led to the accumulation of wealth and hence to increased security. This characteristic, regularly applicable elsewhere in Europe, is also valid in Finland. There, too, witch-hunting occurred principally where a primitive trading economy existed. Initially furs were exported from Ostrobothnia, then provisions (derived from animals), and finally tar. An early capitalist economy thus existed which during the sixteenth century was already producing a multitude of peasant traders in the coastal regions and along the rivers.

Trade never comes alone. It produces individualism, responsibility and equality. Partners in trade require sufficient personal freedom and have to own the product they are selling. A man engaged in commercial enterprise has to accept personal risk, assume individual responsibility and begin to plan his own future. It may be observed that on the one hand trade encouraged witchcraft in that it enticed tar-burners to buy the services of professional witches; success was to be purchased from the spirit world even in tar-burning. On the other hand doubts arose about the witches' tricks when one man experienced personal misfortune and failed while things went well for others. Men engaged in primitive trade were exposed to just such possibilities. Before trading, the blows of fate — crop failures, epidemics, wars — struck society collectively. Brewing, tar-burning and trading expeditions, on the other hand, succeeded or failed on the part of individuals.

Ostrobothnia became the chief centre of the revivalist movement for exactly the same reason — the spread of primitive trading. The characteristic of revivalism was the expression of a person's individual responsibility in relation to God. Moreover, the revivalist movements aimed at a new and better life and thus imparted regular concern for the morrow and anxiety about the future. The collective redemptive rituals of the church were felt to be inadequate. The adoption of that sort of attitude was possible only when people had already experienced similar occurrences in their daily lives. Primitive trade had brought individual responsibility and an individual future, or more precisely the possibility of influencing one's own future. Economic gains could be utilised in a way which influenced the future.

Pietist children, photographed by Samuli Paulaharju. *B*

During the eighteenth century the significance to Ostrobothnia of tar-burning markedly increased. The growing fleets of sailing ships that made colonial conquests and waged colonial wars demanded endless supplies of tar. The shift westwards of Sweden's eastern frontier by the peace of Åbo in 1743 to the Kymi river cut communications between the forests of eastern Finland and the coast of the Gulf of Finland. In Ostrobothnia the course of the navigable rivers and the long coastline made transportation cheap. These conditions made possible the establishment of Ostrobothnia as the most important source of tar first for the whole of Sweden and then for the whole of Europe. The tar towns on the coast invested their money in large-scale shipbuilding while the peasants in the interior built imposing houses and engaged in land clearance and different forms of forestry. Although the depletion of the pine forests moved the centre of tar-burning ever further from the south and the coast towards the east and north, the age of tar nevertheless left something permanent behind — an active early capitalist economy. Compensation was sought and found for the decline in tar. The region moved from a natural economy to a money economy.

This situation caused the rector of Kokkola, Anders Chydenius, who died in 1803, to become a critic of mercantilism and a champion of the free market economy. He advanced the same ideas as Adam Smith but a decade earlier. The social background to which Chydenius responded in his writings was the struggle of the coastal towns of the Gulf of Bothnia (such as Kokkola), made rich through tar, to be able to trade free from regulation by Stockholm. He drew up a theoretical framework for the arguments which the coastal towns put forward in this struggle.

During the period when tar-burning flourished, a set of values was born which strongly emphasised the principle 'Man forges his own fortune'. These values take as their starting-point the idea that enterprise and diligence guarantee success independent of one's social origins. No problems arise so long as this doctrine holds good in practice. A crisis only occurs when the doctrine and people's experience of daily life come into deepening conflict with each other. This happened in the latter half of the eighteenth century. The expanding economy fostered a growth in population which soon exceeded growth figures in other parts of the country. Before long a growing proportion sons were left without farms of their own. At first the younger sons were allocated crofts, then they became more generally cottagers or scrapholders, and finally they had to earn their living by working as day-wage-earners for their more prosperous fellow-peasants. It was above all the young men who sank in the whirlpool of downward social drift.

The culture of the knife-carrying thug recruited its most numerous and eager supporters from precisely this last category. The typical violent criminal was a farmer's son who had been left without his own farm. He therefore felt unsuccessful and became disposed to self-reproach and feelings of inferiority. To escape these pressures he turned to alcohol, and protested against them by behaving with indifference towards the values and norms of society. A stubborn fighter was thus born, a type of man who has 'no pity for himself and does not spare others'.

Despite the fact that the landless proportion of the rural population grew even in South Ostrobothnia, the province nevertheless preserved its character of a strongly successful peasantry. Handsome old two-storey farmhouses still bear witness, remotely but tangibly, to those times. This situation explains why radical fennomanism attained such a firm foothold in the region. The economic and social activity of the Ostrobothnians in particular was fettered by a society based on rank and privilege. Mercantilism restricted trade to the towns while the Swedish-speaking upper class fended off attempts by outsiders to rise in the social scale. Finnish-language nationalism promised the removal of the obstacles in both these directions.

Two of the most famous *puukkojunkkarit* in police custody, and still exuding defiance, in spite of their monstrous shackles. *B*

It promised approval and success in society. In short, it justified the aims of the prosperous peasants.

The pressure that built up was able to burst out in one additional direction. In some respects emigration to America steered the development of South Ostrobothnia into new channels, but above all it broke through the impasse into which the development of society had drifted. America opened up once more opportunities for success to those elements in the population for whom they had been reduced. Ostrobothnians were both mentally and materially prepared to emigrate as soon as the opportunity arose. The values of the early capitalist world sanctioned the pursuit of money, while inherited wealth helped to finance the journey. Both these preconditions were lacking among the poor people in southern, and above all in eastern, Finland. For them the idea of migration was terrifying quite apart from the fact that they could not have imagined how to find the cost of the passage. Only in Ostrobothnia, influenced by early capitalism, was it possible to stake everything on one card: to sell property, take a loan, put the wife and children into a rented house and send the head of the family off to America to earn the money to pay for the family's tickets.

In the course of time a new type of society emerged following the great wave of emigration. The Great West had absorbed a considerable proportion of Ostrobothnia's poverty and wretchedness. Although not everyone living in poor circumstances had been able to leave, even the situation of the poor who remained was improved because wages rose as the available labour force diminished and even land prices fell or at least remained at tolerable levels. In this way South Ostrobothnia succeeded in unloading in America the very social problem that constituted a time-bomb in southern Finland. This bomb exploded in the civil war of 1918 with well-known destructive consequences. Radical socialism never penetrated into South Ostrobothnia because migration to America had turned that previously leftist province to the right. A society matured there in which wealth was distributed comparatively equally and which was even relatively egalitarian. That type of society does not support insurrections; on the contrary it suppresses them. Thus at the turn of the century South Ostrobothnia found its political home on the right. It tried to defend what it possessed, which was why it became the base of White Finland. In simple terms, social equality explains the rise of the Whites, while the lack of it explains the rise of the Reds. The Reds attempted to gain by force of arms the realisation of that equality (carried to a relatively extreme degree) which South Ostrobothnia had already attained.

During the period of the Lapua movement, South Ostrobothnia was only continuing along the same road upon which it had set out at the turn of the century. The province tried to prevent the creation of a society based on the working class and on a service economy. At the same time, opposition to the Lapua movement was also at its strongest in South Ostrobothnia. The farmers' party, the Agrarian League, placed Artturi Leinonen, editor-in-chief of its principal newspaper *Ilkka*, at the head of the front organised to defend legality. According to Leinonen's analysis, the parliamentary system was more advantageous to the independent small farmer than a corporative state supported by large landowners, big industry and higher civil servants. The game was decided when the Agrarian League joined the socialists, the Swedish People's Party and the Liberal Party in support of the parliamentary system. In crude terms the country was saved from right-wing dictatorship by the prevalence of smallholdings in Finnish agriculture and by the independence of the farmers.

Leading figures of the Lapua movement posing for the camera near the Alexander II statue in Helsinki during the farmers' demonstration at the height of the agitation for the suppression of communism (summer 1930). *E*

The Lapua movement was banned in 1932, and with its defeat the unique character of South Ostrobothnia in Finnish politics and social development was finally weakened. The country's political and economic centre of gravity shifted permanently to southern Finland. Weak in forests and in major industry, South Ostrobothnia remained a declining backwater. With its agriculture and small industries, the province maintained and continues to maintain the values created in the time of Anders Chydenius. Its political map bears the imprint of the right and seems in every respect to be one step to the right compared with Finland as a whole. In other words a social democrat there is more right-wing than one in Helsinki or Tampere. In this respect South Ostrobothnia resembles a memory of past times.

# FINLAND FROM PROVINCE TO STATE

## Osmo Jussila

J.V. Stalin and the White Russian generals were agreed on at least one thing: they were prepared to acknowledge Poland (though not the Baltic lands) as an independent state. In the matter of Finland, however, they differed. Stalin clearly recognised Finland as a state separate from Russia, while the White generals were only prepared to concede autonomy. At the Tehran conference in 1943, Stalin justified the incorporation of the Baltic lands into the Soviet Union by virtue of the fact that they had not enjoyed autonomous status during the final period of tsarist rule. Finland, according to Stalin, had been a distinct state entity at that time; clearly it was not now his intention to make the country into a Soviet republic, but rather a people's democracy. More than two decades earlier, in 1919, the White Russian minister in London, K.D. Nabokov, had acknowledged that Finland had its own 'national identity', its own constitutional laws, culture and social structure, all of which Estonia lacked. The White Russian General N. Yudenich put it more succinctly: 'There is no such thing as Estonia. There is only a piece of Russian land — a Russian province.'

Although Estonia, as well as Latvia and Lithuania, became independent states in the aftermath of the First World War, Finland had acquired an identifiable profile as an embryonic state even before the outbreak of war. The idea that Finland constituted a separate state, linked to Russia either in a *Realunion* or by association, had been propounded and had acquired common currency in Finland at the beginning of the 1860s. The Baltic lands at this time were commonly regarded, not only in the empire as a whole but also in the region itself, as provinces in which the nobility and towns enjoyed special privileges. Certain student circles in Dorpat did indeed envisage a status for Estonia similar to that already enjoyed by Finland, but even their perspectives stretched no further than the vague idea of a provincial state. It was not until after 1905 that autonomy similar to that of Finland became an overall objective in Estonian circles.

Ever since the relationship between Finland and Russia began to deteriorate in the late 1890s, when the historian J.R. Danielson urged his pupil U.L. Lehtonen to study Alexander I's Polish policy, there has been a tendency to seek parallels between Finland and Poland. This is justifiable in 1832–63, but not 1815–32, since Congress Poland enjoyed a far more

The wreaths which surround the statue of Alexander II in the main square of Helsinki were laid in protest at the 'February manifesto' issued by Nicholas II in 1899. Although plans to bring Finland under closer and more immediate central control had been considered by Imperial authorities for a number of years, the emperor's manifesto was the first major public statement of Imperial aims, and as such caused much anguish and distress among hitherto loyal subjects in the grand duchy. The laying of wreaths at the memorial to a ruler commonly regarded as a benevolent promoter of the welfare of Finland is a poignant reminder of that loyalty. *E*

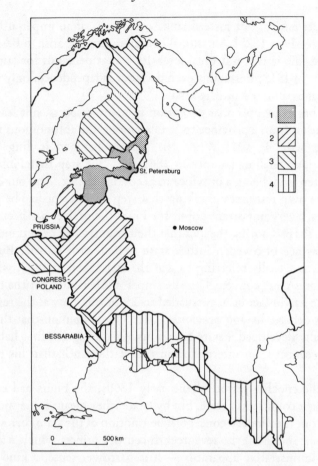

The expansion of Imperial Russia, 1710–1815. The acquisition of Baltic lands in 1721 and 1743 (1) was followed by territorial gains in the three partitions of Poland between 1772 and 1795 (2). Russia also acquired territory during the Napoleonic wars (3) and from the decaying Ottoman empire (4).

distinctive status and a higher degree of autonomy than Finland did at that time. Finland during this early phase can be likened more to less-known parts of the empire such as Bessarabia, conquered by Russia from Turkey in 1812. Comparison can also be made with the Baltic lands: thus, plans which would have given Lithuania a status similar to that obtained by Finland in 1809–12 were drawn up under the direction of Count M. Oginski in the 1810s.

Why and how did Finland succeed in following a different path to that of the Baltic lands? Why did Bessarabia, which in principle at least had just as much going for it as the grand duchy of Finland, fail to develop into a separate state entity, but instead sink to the level of an imperial Russian province as early as 1828? A national consciousness did arise in Bessarabia, but like Estonia it was not until after 1905 that demands for autonomy were raised. In 1918, Bessarabia even declared independence, only for part of it to be incorporated into Romania.

Finland has been a peculiar exception in many respects, not least in its transformation from a province to a state among the autonomous frontier lands of imperial Russia. When the philosopher and leading Finnish nationalist J.V. Snellman wrote in 1861 that 'the step that Finland has taken is a step from being a province to becoming a state. And our country relied on its own resources in taking that step',[1] he seemed to be putting his finger on a very important point: the Finns themselves had been largely responsible for promoting the idea that their country had been transformed from a province of Sweden into a state united with Russia. But what Snellman was actually referring to was the step taken in 1809, when the Finnish estates were convened by the emperor Alexander I at the town of Porvoo. He had in fact been persuaded to adopt this view as the result of a fierce press debate, having previously been of the opinion that the Finns had gradually developed a state-consciousness during the first half of the nineteenth century, an interpretation nearer the truth than his position after 1861.

Before the epochal period of the early 1860s, the Finns had certainly regarded their country as a state, but by 'state' they meant something quite different from the modern concept. Their notion of the state corresponded to the 'finance state' of the seventeenth-century prince, which was essentially an administrative apparatus — in a narrower sense, a kind of tax-gathering machine. J.A. Ehrenström, for example, used the expression 'the supreme court and government or state council' in 1812, where 'state' meant the same as the fiscal department of the recently-created Finnish council of government. This notion of the state did not mean that 'province' and 'state' were mutually exclusive terms: Finland could be at once and the same time a province and a state.[2]

This 'finance state' was not created at the meeting of the emperor and the estates in Porvoo cathedral on 29 March 1809: it came into being in the autumn of 1809 with the establishment of the council of government in Turku. This somewhat limited idea of the state underwent a decisive change around 1840, thanks to a Swedish professor, Israel Hwasser, who with some justification can be called 'the father of the Finnish state'. It was Hwasser who adapted the natural law theory of the origins of the state to the act of swearing fealty which took place in Porvoo cathedral. This act

Alexander I opening the Diet of Borgå, 29 March 1809. Painting by E. Thelning. *B*

thus became for Hwasser the founding moment of the Finnish state; a 'state treaty' had been concluded in Porvoo in accordance with the principles of natural law.[3] This was a radically new interpretation, for solemn pledges of loyalty, such as took place in Porvoo on 29 March 1809, had never been nor were an occasion for the founding of a state, but were part of a tradition stretching back to the Middle Ages, when the prince and representatives of the 'land' met. Agreements were concluded at such meetings, but they usually had to do with status — that is, both the prince and the representatives of the land bound themselves to uphold the existing framework of laws and justice. Solemn and binding oaths of loyalty (*Huldigungsakten*) of this traditional type were made in Europe up to the revolutionary year of 1848. The last known case is from 1835, when the estates of Lower Austria 'acclaimed' the emperor Ferdinand as their ruler.[4]

The pseudonymous Olli Kekäläinen strengthened Hwasser's argument in a pamphlet which drew on the opinion of a number of legal experts to demonstrate that a '*pactum gratuitum*' or '*donatio*' (a true, irreversible treaty) had been concluded at Porvoo, and that this treaty was binding on all subsequent rulers of the empire.[5] Professor J.J. Nordström further developed this concept of the state in his lectures into a theory of a *Realunion* between Russia and Finland. Hwasser's views were not taken up in Finland before the 1860s. Fredrik Cygnaeus, J.V. Snellman and in particular the historian Robert Castrén discovered and rehabilitated Hwasser, whose adaptation of natural law principles to the act of swearing fealty became the generally accepted view in Finland. From the 1860s onwards, Finland was no longer regarded as a province or a 'finance state', but a state in the meaning which Snellman had expounded in his work *Om statslära* (On the theory of the state).[6]

The most effective and skilful exponent to a foreign readership of this new concept of the state was the senator and professor of jurisprudence, Leo Mechelin. His most important contribution in this respect was the *Précis du droit public de la Grand-Duché de Finlande*, published in 1886. Because notions of Finnish sovereignty as well as the *Realunion* theory had encountered difficulties not only in Russia but also among European jurists, Mechelin made a subtle distinction between the notion of sovereignty according to constitutional law and that according to public law. Finland was sovereign in the former but not in the latter sense. The union of Finland and Russia was therefore not one of equals, but a *'unio realis inaequali jure'*.

Mechelin knew that whether Finland was a state or not was not in itself particularly important for the maintenance of Finland's special status, but he was well aware that it was important for Finland's future that the country should be ranked as a state in international opinion. Rafael Erich, in a 1939 article commemorating the centenary of Mechelin's birth, made the telling point that subsequent experience had shown 'that an unconditional recognition of [Finland] as constituting a state was valuable not only from the point of view of ambition, but also in practical political terms. Finland had no need first to constitute itself as a state. . . .'[7]

Let us now turn to the Baltic provinces, to study more closely the differences and similarities *vis-à-vis* the Finnish case. Although Estonia and Livonia had been incorporated into Russia a century earlier than Finland, the two events had rather more in common than the mere fact that the conquered territories had all been under the Swedish crown. In both instances, the meeting between the estates and the new ruler, and the forging of ties between them, followed a tradition dating back to the Middle Ages. In accordance with this time-honoured practice, a *Herrschaftsvertrag*, or an agreement to uphold existing laws and customs, was made: the subjects

Leo Mechelin (1839–1914), seen from two different angles. The drawing, *left*, by Oscar Furuhjelm has him resting on the 1734 law code. The caricature, *right*, by an unknown Russian cartoonist, drawn in 1907 when Mechelin was still leading the Finnish government, or Senate, seems to suggest that the doughty defender of the Finnish constitution was also willing to act in a Russian manner when it was politically expedient to do so.

swore fealty and the prince confirmed existing rights and privileges.[8]

In the case of the Baltic provinces however, these agreements were rather more advantageous, for the indigenous nobility had been able to force greater concessions out of their feudal overlords during the late Middle Ages. The 'capitulations' signed by the estates of Livonia and Estonia and Peter the Great in 1710–11 were also given international confirmation by their inclusion in the peace treaty between Sweden and Russia, signed at Nystad in 1721. The treaty of Fredrikshamn in 1809, whereby Sweden formally ceded her former Finnish provinces to Russia, made no mention of any corresponding agreement between the Finnish estates and their new ruler. In comparison with Finland, therefore, the autonomy and privileges of the Baltic nobility and towns rested on firmer ground from the outset. In another important respect, however, Finland enjoyed a more favoured position than the Baltic provinces, for the country was given its own administrative autonomy right from the start.

The status of the two regions was often perceived in St Petersburg as being similar: both were called privileged provinces. This parallel is most obvious in the law codification begun in the 1830s.[9] The Governor-General of Finland, F.W. Berg — a man of Livonian origin — was still able to equate the Finnish and Livonian Diets at the end of the 1850s. Finnish hopes for the convening of a Diet were strengthened by Berg's assertion that this would indeed be granted if the Finns displayed the same kind of moderation as the Livonians, who had been rewarded with the calling of the *Landtag*.[10]

Although special regional bodies, such as the Collegium for Livonian, Estonian and Finnish Affairs (the last-named referring to the province of Viborg, detached from Finland in 1721), were set up to bind the Baltic lands to the central administration, these bodies were placed under the control of the Russian Senate, as were all other colleges. When ministries replaced the collegial system in 1802, it was obvious that their area of competence would also extend to the Baltic lands: after 1809 however, they could only interfere in Finnish affairs through the mediation of the 'minister for Finland', i.e. the state-secretary for Finland ('minister state-secretary' after 1834). The Finns were nevertheless obliged to carry on a long bureaucratic campaign before this arrangement began to work in practice. An important step in this process was taken in 1816 when the council of government was renamed the Senate, which gave it a comparable status to the Senate in St Petersburg. However, it was by no means certain initially that Finland was to be left outside the area of competence of the ministers. That this did occur — and this disparity in the administrative system was later to be of great importance — was, in the last resort, a matter of chance.[11]

It was therefore a drawback for the Baltic lands that the region was joined to Russia at a time when the collegial system of government, under the direction of the Senate, was being introduced, since this system was more centralised than the ministerial system of the nineteenth century. Within the collegial system, self-governing regions had no special minister who could directly refer their matters to the emperor. The Baltic lands also had a dualistic legal system from the outset. On the one hand, there was the internal legislation passed by the corporate nobility in the local Diets, and on the other, there was the Imperial administrative legislation implemented through the office of the governor-general. In comparison with the Baltic lands, this Imperial sector was extremely narrow in Finland.

In addition to these differences in the administrative system, there were important distinctions between the nobility of Finland and of the Baltic lands. In comparison with the Baltic nobility, the Finnish aristocracy were few and weak, constituting only one of the four estates of the Diet. In the Baltic provinces, the Diets were completely dominated by the nobility, with the exception of two representatives from Riga, who only had one vote. During the late Middle Ages, the Livonian *Landtag* had consisted of several estates (though not the peasantry), but during the seventeenth century the Estonian and Livonian Diets had become virtually confined to the nobility. The reverse side of this noble 'absolutism' was that it ultimately hindered the development of state-consciousness: the nobility became inward-looking, content merely to defend their own privileges. Even though the Baltic German nobility constituted a powerful pressure group in St Petersburg, to the extent that the entire Russian empire was characterised as being under the 'knoutish-German'* yoke, this also meant that these nobles adopted an imperial outlook and identified themselves with Russia rather than their native land.[12]

Finland really had nothing to compare with the numbers and influence of the Baltic Germans in St Petersburg, other than the minister state-secretary and his assistant, and a few officials in the imperial chancery such as Theodor Bruun, who was shunned in Finland because of his 'Russianness'. The numerous Finnish officers serving in the imperial army cannot be compared in terms of influence with the Baltic Germans, for few

---

* A 'knout' was a Cossack whip. One interpretation of this expression was that, since the Baltic Germans had occupied all the important offices of state, the Russian nobles were left with nothing else to do but whip their subjects.

of them served in the élite units or on the staff in St Petersburg. The great majority were stationed in remote garrisons and had little or no opportunity to influence Russian policy towards Finland.

The Baltic German nobility cut themselves off from other social groups, even from the German burghers. With the exception of the group of bureaucrats in St Petersburg, they also remained aloof from any close collaboration with the ruler. Unlike the Finns, they failed to maintain a close watch over their administrative autonomy. The separate status of the Baltic lands, in short, was founded upon the autonomy of a privileged estate: that of Finland upon an administrative autonomy.

In Finland, the work of keeping an eye upon privileges and the country's distinctive administrative autonomy was undertaken not by the nobility alone but by all four estates. Far from simply pursuing their own interests as a privileged estate, the aristocracy actively promoted the development of Finnish autonomy. In the Baltic lands, the gap between the nobility and other groups was insurmountable, and in such circumstances no general notion of the 'national idea' emerged, not to mention a concept of the state. The Baltic nobility clung obstinately to their privileged status, even during the revolution of 1905, when the Finnish nobility freely abandoned theirs in the national interest. Not without good cause was the term 'ill-liberal' applied to the Baltic nobility.[13]

The isolation of the Baltic-German nobility from other groups was clearly demonstrated during the famous debate of the 1860s, when the professor of Russian history at the University of Dorpat, Carl Schirren, defended the special position of the Baltic provinces against the criticisms of the Russian journalist, Yuri Samarin. Ranged alongside Schirren were the president of the Livonian High Court, Woldemar von Bock, and Julius Eckart. Already in 1841, Otto Mueller had maintained that the acts of 1710 had the character of a treaty in his book, *Die livländische Landesprivilegien und deren Confirmationen*. Schirren and his allies pursued the same line of argument, claiming that the privileges accorded in 1710 could not therefore be changed unilaterally: any changes would need the consent of both sides to the agreement. Schirren specifically presented the acts of 1710 as agreements between vassal and provincial ruler. In the event of the provincial ruler not fulfilling his promises, the vassals were also entitled to regard themselves as freed from their obligations under the agreement.

Schirren dressed up the old notion of *Landsrecht* in contemporary nationalist garb in his famous work *Livländische Antwort an Herrn Juri Samarin* (Leipzig 1869), but he spoke and wrote simply of 'the German nation', not of a Livonian, Latvian or Estonian nation, or of a Baltic nation. The Latvian and Estonian peasants should be emancipated, Schirren conceded, but only as peasants, not as Latvians or Estonians. The culture of the country was 'German-Lutheran', not Latvian or Estonian. Like many of his contemporaries, Schirren used the term '*Landesstaat*', which he contrasted with the ruling (Russian) state: but Livonia was simply a *Landesstaat*, and only the state of the German nobility at that — and therein lay its weakness.[14] This juxtaposition of the ruling and the ruled state is reminiscent of the ideas put forward by Olli Kekäläinen, and it was at this level that notions of the state remained in the Baltic lands.

Among the Baltic intelligentsia and the so-called *Literaten*, however, there were ideas in circulation around the middle of the nineteenth century which could well have been developed into a doctrine of a Baltic state, or states. These intellectuals closely followed developments in Finland, such as the setting up of a committee to prepare a programme of legislative reforms in 1861 and the calling of the Diet by the emperor Alexander II two years later. A detailed 'constitution [*Verfassung*] for a united Livonia or for the duchy of Livonia, Kurland, Estonia and Ösel' was drafted by students at the University of Dorpat. This document referred to the then little-known constitutional plan of 1819, and proposed that the constitution forfeited in the rebellion of 1830–1 should be restored to Poland, and that Finland's constitutional rights should be extended. But, although this draft constitution for a united duchy proposed that the office of state-secretary be established to link the administration of the empire and the duchy — as in the Finnish case — the term 'provincial state' (*Provinzial-Staat, Gesamt-Provinzial-Staat*) was used to describe the duchy. Even for these constitution-drafters, the union of the three provinces was not sufficient to elevate their duchy to the rank of a state which would no longer bear the stamp of 'province'. The end-result was an amazing mishmash of the old and the new: a province in a personal union with the empire, in which there were also to be 'provincial ministers'. Justice, internal affairs and finance were to be handled by special 'provincial ministers', other matters would fall under the competence of imperial ministers. The Russian emperor would have been 'provincial master' (*Landesherr*) in the Baltic lands.[15]

Woldemar von Bock's thinking ran along similar lines. When Yuri Samarin warned the Russians that the Baltic lands might become 'a second Finland', von Bock retorted: Why should the Baltic provinces not have their own state-secretary with his own office, like the Finns? Why should the emperor not bear the title 'grand duke of the united Baltic duchies', as he had earlier adopted the title 'grand duke of Finland'?[16] It seems as if von Bock was unaware that the emperors since the days of Peter the Great had in fact borne the title 'grand duke of Estonia, Livonia, Kurland and Semgallen' which they continued to do till 1917.

Von Bock also proposed the creation of a common Diet for the three Baltic provinces, which could present itself as a single corporation with regard to Russia, in the same way as the Finnish Diet. This plan failed to get off the ground, mainly because of the particularist interests of the three provinces and the unwillingness of the nobility to broaden the representative base of the Diets. The Estonian nobility showed themselves to be even more reactionary than the nobility of Livonia and Kurland. The German burghers in the towns were also unwilling to cede a place in the Diets to representatives of the indigenous population, although their own estate was represented only by the two burghers of Riga in the Livonian *Landtag*. It has been calculated that fourteen proposals for an administrative reform along the lines proposed by von Bock were made between 1864 and 1880 in the Livonia Diet alone, but they were all rejected. An important reason for this negative attitude was that neither the Estonian nor the Livonian Diet demanded unanimity in the same way as the Polish *Sejm*, where all had to give their approval in matters of privilege. The Diets in the Baltic lands sought to avoid putting decisions to the vote, but it was difficult to achieve unanimity, since there was always someone who disagreed.

The essential differences between Finland and the Baltic lands — which meant that Finland became a state and the Baltic provinces remained provinces — had their origins in the time before union with Russia, but they were also shaped by the specific circumstances of the time at which incorporation occurred. The position of the nobility and their relationship to other social groups were inherited factors, while the Russian system of administration at the time of union was an institutional, environmental factor.

After its incorporation into the Russian empire in 1812, Bessarabia was also given a governor with the right of direct access to the emperor, in the same manner as the Finnish state-secretary.[17] Bessarabia was given a 'political existence', and the emperor confirmed its religion, laws and rights. Taxes collected in Bessarabia, as in Finland, were used to cover local expenditure, and the emperor promised to rule the region in accordance with local laws. As early as 1812, a provisional constitution — which became permanent in 1818 — was confirmed. This decreed that the administration of Bessarabia was to be in the hands of a council of government consisting of two departments, one dealing with fiscal and internal matters, the other a department of justice — exactly as in Finland. The 1818 'constitution' stipulated that the highest administrative body should be a supreme council; although the majority of its members were appointed, six were elected by the nobility for a term of three years.

The formal prerequisites and the institutional framework for an advance from autonomy towards separate statehood were thus at least as favourable in Bessarabia as in Finland. In certain respects, it enjoyed an even more advantageous position. The Bessarabians were given their own special constitution, a document of some 58 pages — something which the Finns never succeeded in obtaining during the entire period of the union with Russia. On the other hand, the Russian central administration was able from the start to use this detailed system of government to claim a major role in running the affairs in Bessarabia. The submissions of the supreme council, for example, were dealt with by the Russian state council before being passed on to the emperor, and the supreme council itself dealt with business in Russian and Moldavian, and according to Russian and Moldavian law. Matters of general order, taxation, criminal offences and investigations were dealt with in Russian and Moldavian, but in accordance with imperial Russian law, whereas Moldavian law and the Moldavian language were used to expedite business relating to civil law, land ownership and judicial procedure. Although the governor had the right of direct access to the emperor, Bessarabia was never given its own state-secretary. Count Capo d'Istrias (Ioannis Antonios Kapodistrias), one of Alexander I's closest advisers, Russian foreign minister and expert on Balkan questions (1816–22), did however act as a kind of supreme watchdog on Bessarabian matters in St Petersburg, performing a similar kind of role to that of the Finnish aristocrat, Count G.M. Armfelt.

Bessarabia's system of self-government was abolished — more precisely, its status was significantly reduced — in 1828, even though the region continued to belong thereafter to the so-called specially administered provinces ( *gubernii*). Bessarabia was thus downgraded from the rank of state to province or *guberniya* of the empire, and a major reason for this was the failure of the system of self-government, despite much hard work and many changes in the corps of administrators. It did not work because the Bessarabian nobility were not in the least interested in making it work. The Russians sent to get the system working were surprised to discover that only the chairman and secretary turned up to meetings, and then irregularly. The system of government had been created from above, in a mechanical fashion, as a part of Alexander I's borderlands policy (the same however could be said of Finland's autonomy).

But although some Finns complained bitterly that their countrymen lacked a national spirit and were indifferent to the destiny of the fatherland, and although the exiled patriot A.I. Arwidsson looked in vain for a 'statesmanlike spirit', Finland nevertheless possessed a far greater measure of national and statesmanlike spirit than did Bessarabia. Unlike Bessarabia, Finland had social corporations and a 'corporative spirit', and above all a far more developed legal system. The Finns were careful to ensure that imperial ministers and officials did not interfere in Finnish affairs other than through the prescribed channels. A watchful eye was also kept on the regulations which delineated the areas of competence of the governor-general and the procurator, and a successful campaign was waged to limit the powers and authority of the governor-general. Although no new Diet was to be convened until 1863, and no written constitution was ever granted, the very fact that these issues were kept in the public eye greatly increased awareness of self-government. The successful rejection of the Russian plan to codify the laws in the 1840s is clear evidence of a highly-developed national consciousness, even a state consciousness.

But, in spite of all this activity and self-awareness, Finland's separate administration was sometimes at risk before the reign of Alexander II. Count R.H. Rehbinder, minister state-secretary in the 1820s, was by no means sure that Nicholas I would renew his predecessor's assurances. It is conceivable that only the Decembrist rebellion ensured that he did. The committee for Finnish affairs established by Alexander I in conjunction with the state-secretariat for Finland was wound up at this time, and Russian attempts to codify the laws were largely frustrated by Governor-General Menshikov, who was persuaded to take the view that such a step would seriously encroach upon his own preserve.

A comparison of Finland and Bessarabia thus shows that it was primarily the stronger political traditions, not only of the nobility but also of the other three estates, in addition to a national and state consciousness, which made the difference in Finland's favour. As the example of Bessarabia demonstrates, a 'political existence' was not to be created simply by imperial edict; it also needed a solid foundation of deep-rooted traditions.

These advantages meant that self-government in Finland was from the outset more independent of the central imperial government than the Bessarabian administration. Bessarabia was also russified to a far greater extent: there was a steady inflow of migrants from Russia, and they formed a powerful pro-Russian party. One in four offices in Bessarabia was

*The Attack*, painted by Edvard Isto in 1899, showing the Finnish maiden, desperately clutching the lawbook which the double-headed Russian eagle is trying to tear from her grasp. Thousands of lithographed copies were sold. *B*

held by a Russian, and Russians also bought up large estates. In Finland on the other hand, the local nobility was significantly stronger than the handful of returning emigrants. Although the first governor-general was appointed from the ranks of these men, their influence on Finnish affairs remained slight.

Nations, especially those which are small and relatively young, seem to have need of a glorious moment of parturition which can be celebrated as a national day. The occasion of a declaration of independence is often chosen for this purpose, however mundane that occasion may have been. In some cases, actual independence may not even have followed the declaration, as in the case of Ireland, where the republic was proclaimed by Patrick Pearse in front of the Dublin post office during the Easter rebellion of 1916. Before 1940, the Estonians celebrated the declaration of independence made at the beginning of 1918, even though the country was overrun by the Germans almost immediately after this had taken place.

The sixth of December 1917 is nowadays celebrated as independence day in Finland. The assurance given by Alexander I, which was prominently displayed on the walls of Finland's churches for more than a century may enable the event which took place in the cathedral at Porvoo on 29 March 1809 to be considered as the moment of Finland's birth as a nation and as a state. What happened on 6 December 1917 was that Finland ceased to be merely an internally independent state, and became an externally independent, sovereign state. The event passed virtually unremarked at the time, and has not given rise to much mythologising since. There seems to be one only painting of the event, Eero Nelimarkka's *The Sixth of December 1917* (1940). It is not to be found in Heimola, the building where the declaration of independence was made, which has been demolished; nor is it to be found in the Senate building, the headquarters of the Finnish government, which does however have a canvas by R.W. Ekman of the Diet of Borgå.* The fact is that Finland was already a state in December 1917. Even though there were different views on the country's juridical status within the Russian empire, all agreed that it was a state, a view which had also been effectively disseminated abroad.

If we reject the idea that the Finnish nation and state were born in Porvoo cathedral, then it is difficult to find a more suitable occasion for national celebration. It is even harder to come up with ideas for commemorative statues, although the development of a Finnish doctrine of the state traced above might suggest some. This doctrine was a unique phenomenon in the Russian borderlands and a rare event in Europe. Something similar can however be seen in the case of Hungary, where the 'country' (*ország*) was changed into a 'state', and the Hungarian language, like Finnish, needed a new word (*állam*) to describe this concept. The Hungarians too dressed up an old '*Herrschaftsvertrag*' (dating from 1723) in modern garb as a state treaty; as in the Finnish case, this was largely the work of the law faculty of the university in the capital. Finland had its Leo Mechelin, Hungary its Ernö Nagy.[18]

When the 175th anniversary of the Finnish state council was being celebrated in 1984, there were plans to erect some kind of memorial to the Finnish state in Porvoo. Strictly speaking, there is no need of a new statue; trimming the tree which now conceals the bust of Leo Mechelin on the wall of the House of the Estates in Helsinki should be suffi-

---

* The painting now hangs in the Nelimarkka museum in Alajärvi, Ostrobothnia.

cient — although perhaps it might also be a good idea to put up in Turku a complementary bust of Israel Hwasser.

## NOTES

1. Snellman was writing in response to articles in the Swedish press: his article appeared in *Litteraturblad för allmän medborgerlig bildning*, Helsingfors 1861, pp. 332–3.
2. G. Oestreich, *Ständetum und Staatsbildung in Deutschland.*, 6 (1967), pp. 63–6.
3. Hwasser presented his new interpretation in two polemical tracts: *Om allians-tractaten emellan Sverige och Ryssland år 1812*, Stockholm 1838, and *Om Borgå landtdag och Finlands ställning 1812*, Uppsala 1839.
4. O. Brunner, *Land und Herrschaft. Grundfragen der territorialen Verfassungsgeschichte Österreichs im Mittelalter*, Vienna 1959, esp. pp. 423–36.
5. There is some doubt about the identity of 'Olli Kekäläinen'. The man behind the pseudonym is generally held to be A.I. Arwidsson, but there is also reason to believe that Professor J.J. Nordström may have helped write the pamphlet *Finlands nuvarande statsförfattning*, which appeared in Stockholm in 1841.
6. On the development of the 'idea of the state' in Finland, see O. Jussila, *Maakunnasta valtioksi*, Helsinki 1987.
7. R. Erich, 'Leo Mechelin som rättslärd och rättspolitiker', *Tidskrift utgiven af Juridiska Föreningen i Finland*, 1939, pp. 27ff.
8. The capitulations and confirmation of privileges were published by C. Schirren, *Die Capitulationen det livländischen Ritter — und Landschaft und der Stadt Riga von 4 Juli nebst deren Confirmationen*, Dorpat 1865: E. Winkelmann, *Die Capitulationen der estländischen Ritterschaft unter der Stadt Reval vom Jahre 1710 nebst deren Confirmationen*, Reval 1865.
9. See O. Jussila, 'Finnland in der Gesetzkodifikation zur Zeit Nikolajs I', *Jahrbücher für Geschichte Osteuropas*, 20 (1972).
10. In his memoirs, Snellman recalled that Berg frequently returned to this theme. J. Snellman, *Samlade arbeten*, 9, Helsingfors 1896.
11. For a comparison of the system of presenting the affairs of Finland and the Baltic provinces, see O. Jussila, 'The Presentation of Baltic and Finnish Affairs within the Tsarist Government in the 18th and 19th Centuries', *Journal of Baltic Studies*, 4 (1985), pp. 373–82.
12. See G. Pistohlkors, *Ritterschaftliche Reformpolitik zwischen Russifizierung und Revolution*, Göttingen 1978, and M. Haltzel, 'The Baltic Germans', in E. Thaden (*ed.*), *Russification in the Baltic Provinces and Finland*, Princeton 1981, p. 151.
13. Pistohlkors, p. 257.
14. See Haltzel, pp. 124–33; R. Wittram, 'Carl Schirrens "Livländische Antwort 1869" ', *Ostdeutsche Wissenschaft*, 1 (1954), pp. 292–3; and E. Thaden, *Russia's Western Borderlands, 1710–1870*, Princeton 1984, pp. 181–2, 194–6.
15. R. Wittram, *Liberalismus baltischer Literaten. Der Entstehung der baltischen politischen Presse*, Riga 1931.
16. G. von Rauch, 'Der russische Reichsgedanke im Spiegel des politischen Bewusstseins der baltischen Provinzen', *Ostdeutsche Wissenschaft*, 1 (1954), p. 200.
17. G. Jewsbury, *The Russian Annexation of Bessarabia, 1774–1828: A Study of Imperial Expansion*, New York 1976.
18. L. Peter, 'The Dualist Character of the 1867 Hungarian settlement' in G. Ranki (*ed.*), *Hungarian history — world history* (Indiana University Studies on Hungary, 1), Budapest 1984.

# FINLAND AS A SUCCESSOR-STATE

## Max Engman

The new, more or less independent Finland which emerged on the international stage between 1917 and 1920 was the object of lively interest among observers in neighbouring countries and diplomats stationed in the Nordic region. Many of them saw the dissolution of the Russian state as a transient phase and regarded plans which presupposed a permanently weakened Russia as a potentially dangerous opportunism. It was therefore an open question whether an independent Finland was viable or even, from its neighbours' point of view, desirable.

Colonel von Giese, the German military attaché in Stockholm, argued at the beginning of 1918 that Germany could gain a dominant role in Scandinavia with the help of a Finland that had become independent of Russia. He believed that Finland, as a kind of 'Nordic Bulgaria', would replace the militarily insignificant Sweden after the world war. This assessment was disputed by the German minister in Stockholm, Baron Helmuth Lucius von Stoedten, who took a very sceptical view of Finland. He tried to reinforce his arguments by citing various Swedish and other authorities, including the 'pleasant' Frans Seyn, a former Russian governor-general of Finland, who — according to Lucius — had often complained that the Finns were a difficult people to govern and only wished to obtain advantages from their association with Russia without giving anything in return. Lucius also thought that Germany ought to take into account the Swedish view of the Finns as 'awkward, distrustful and often unreliable people'.[1] As for the question of Finland's future, Lucius declared that he shared the view expressed by the Swedish minister in Petrograd, General Brändström, namely that a fully independent Finland, stretching as far as the immediate vicinity of Petrograd, could not last long, and that the economically decisive influence of Petrograd, which had as many inhabitants as the whole of Finland, could not in the long run be warded off by political measures.[2]

Similar thoughts were expressed in the conversation the German minister in Kristiania had a year later with his Swedish counterpart, Baron Fredrik Ramel. The latter believed that the three Scandinavian kingdoms had drawn closer to each other during the war, but that Finland occupied a special position because of its German orientation and cultural backwardness. As a result, there could be no question of cooperating with Finland

The end of the old regime: Russian sailors on board the Imperial yacht *Standard*, shortly before their evacuation of Helsinki in April 1918. *B*

except in certain special questions. In Ramel's view, Finland would become a very awkward neighbour for Sweden, 'something similar to what Serbia had been for Austria–Hungary'. However, Lucius pointed out that every Swedish politician was convinced that Russia was an even more awkward neighbour and that, because it was necessary to choose between two evils, the Swedes were prepared to give a certain amount of support to Finland against Russia.[3]

In Norway too, the emergence of a new independent Finland was not regarded with unalloyed satisfaction. Finland was seen as a potentially aggressive state which might threaten Norwegian interests in the north. Norway wished to forestall Finnish demands for territory along the Arctic coast and for a time even considered making territorial demands of its own in northern Finland. Considerable attention was aroused in 1920 when Norway approached Soviet Russia, a state with which it did not have diplomatic relations, and informed Moscow that Norway would not demand a revision of frontiers if the two states remained neighbours but would do so if Russia ceded territory along the Arctic to a third power.[4]

There was also widespread scepticism about the new Finnish state among various Russian groupings. Finland saw itself as being at war with the Soviet government; the White generals refused to recognise Finnish independence. Many Russian politicians resident in the West believed that Finnish desires could be satisfied within the framework of a restored Russia and that Finnish independence without strategic guarantees for Russia was unthinkable.

Even after the situation had begun to stabilise, the representatives of the great powers regarded this newcomer with a certain amused condescension. In May 1920 the new British minister in Helsinki, George Kidston, reported his first impressions to the Foreign Office as follows:

The first thing which has struck me is the intense nervousness of all those in authority with whom I have hitherto come into contact, from the president himself to the prime minister and the minister for foreign affairs. They are all intensely anxious to do the right thing and to find out what is the right thing to do, while at the same time desiring to avoid giving the impression that they are new to the business.[5]

Such more or less sceptical statements and expressions of doubt about Finland's viability as a state — manifestations of that superior gossip of which diplomatic reporting consists — could be counterbalanced by citing statements, by both Finns and others, that are full of confidence about Finland's future prospects. However, the gloomy prognostications, even if offset by more hopeful attitudes, are important as a manifestation of the situation in Europe during the last phase of the world war and the first post-war years. It was difficult for established members of the European state system and for diplomats of the old school to become accustomed to the idea of a 'balkanised' Europe or to see the new states as anything other than a means of weakening the powers which had lost the war. There was also a certain condescension towards these new or 'artificial' units, these *'Rand- und Schandstaaten'* ('peripheral and shameful states').

The Europe that was destroyed by the First World War had been dominated by the great powers, and in the central and eastern parts of the continent by three empires. Small states were to be found only on the periphery of the continent. The empires ruled by the Habsburgs and the Romanovs were dynastic units which had developed over centuries. They regarded themselves as upholding a traditional order in which the language, culture and ethnic affiliations of the subject were subordinate in relation to the empire's unifying principle. The foremost form of patriotism was to be *'Kaisertreu'* (loyal to the emperor). The largest national groups in these empires, the groups which readily saw themselves as sustaining the state, were politically and culturally dominant, but the Russians were in a minority within the Russian empire as were the Germans and Magyars in their respective parts of the Dual Monarchy.

Radically different ways of looking at the legitimacy of political authority emerged in the nineteenth century because of nationalism and democracy. As the practices of total war gained an increasing hold on the belligerents during the First World War, both sides attempted to exploit the nationality problems of their enemies. As a result, the principle of national self-determination came to play an ever more significant role and was turned into practical politics during the last phase of the war by the United States under Woodrow Wilson and Soviet Russia under Lenin. The consequences were most far-reaching for Austria-Hungary and Russia.

The Habsburg empire was the hardest hit by the triumph of national self-determination. The Dual Monarchy was dissolved when its territory was divided between seven states: the new order was established by essentially peaceful means through the Versailles peace settlement. The Romanov empire was thrown into turmoil by two revolutions in 1917, and a number of peripheral areas then seceded from the state. After a series of wars and revolutions, the new order was regulated by the conclusion of separate peace treaties between Soviet Russia and the new states in 1920 and 1921.

In many respects, Finland is a rather typical example of the new states which were created as a result of the collapse of the old empires. It belongs to the category of successor-states which emerged in the broad zone of territory between Russia and Germany, from Finland in the north through the Baltic states, Poland, Czechoslovakia and Hungary to Yugoslavia in the south. As in the case of some other successor-states, Finns speak of a First Republic, which is regarded as coming to an end in 1944; Austrians, whose country in its new form can also be called a successor-state, treat 1938 as the dividing-point, and Czechs see 1948 as the year in which their First Republic ended.

The creation of the new states was a difficult process in relation not only to frontiers, territorial conflicts, constitutions and diplomatic orientation but also to questions directly connected with the dissolution of the old empires like the division of their administrative apparatus, property and traditions. It was a question of considerable economic and, not least, emotional assets — a struggle for loyalties and symbols. Even if the new states readily saw their own emergence as self-evident, old bonds whose effects could be felt on many levels needed to be dissolved. Bohemia had been ruled by the Habsburgs since 1526 and Hungary since the Turkish wars at the end of the seventeenth century. The Baltic provinces and the province of Viipuri had belonged to Russia for 200 years, and the rest of Finland for more than 100 years. These shared centuries had created — despite special administrative arrangements, autonomy and federalist tendencies in varying measure — a considerable degree of integration in such areas as legislation, the economy, communications, culture and urban systems.

In short, the new states all faced the problem of creating national integration, even if their prospects of survival varied. To adopt the perspective of examining Finland as one of the successor-states may contribute to identifying what is specific in Finland's development after independence.

The Finnish declaration of independence on 6 December 1917 was followed in January 1918 by the disarming of some of the Russian troops who were still in the country and by revolution and civil war. These upheavals subsequently gave way to a period of neither war nor peace in relations with Soviet Russia, but Finland's international position was eventually stabilised by the Peace of Dorpat in 1920. Finland declared her independence as a republic and was ruled until the middle of 1919 by a series of regents. The first of them, P.E. Svinhufvud, followed a German orientation which had resulted in the election of Kaiser Wilhelm II's brother-in-law, Prince Friedrich Karl of Hesse, to be king of Finland. The second regent, General Carl Gustaf Mannerheim, tried to orient Finland towards the Western powers, and finally confirmed a republican constitution which stabilised the country's domestic politics and which, with relatively few amendments, is still in force today.

Although Finland managed in the course of just over two years to have an emperor, an interim government, a regent, a king and a president as head of state, the constitutional changes involved were in practice small and all these forms of government rested on the principles of enlightened despotism as enunciated in the fundamental laws of Gustav III of Sweden. The degree of continuity was even more striking at lower levels of government. The economics department of the Senate was renamed the council of state (*valtioneuvosto*); the Senate's role in the administration of justice was transferred to the supreme administrative court, while its justice department became the supreme court. No great changes occurred in practice.

In 1918 the various bodies which had been responsible for relations with

A demonstration by troops and sailors passing the university library in Helsinki during the early days of the revolution, April 1917. *B*

Russia — the state secretariat and passport office in St Petersburg and the governor-general's office in Helsinki — were abolished. The Finnish state also assumed control of the telegraph service, which had previously been administered by the Russians. Two new branches of the administration did need to be created: the armed forces, which emerged in the spring of 1918 in the form of the White army that had fought and won the civil war; and the foreign service, which grew out of Finland's attempts to gain recognition for its independence. The exceptional circumstances which prevailed during the first years of independence demanded a number of emergency measures, but in all essentials Finland moved from being an autonomous grand duchy to a sovereign republic with an unaltered administrative and legal system.

The situation was quite different for those successor-states which, like the three Baltic states, were obliged to build up a central administration from scratch. In the cases of Czechoslovakia and Yugoslavia, the strongest region within the new state, Bohemia and Serbia respectively, came to be administratively dominant, a development which further increased the difficulties of these two states in maintaining a regional balance and gaining legitimacy among their national minorities. Austria faced the opposite problem in that it possessed an inflated administrative apparatus and had to accommodate a great many former civil servants from the other successor-states. This placed a heavy economic burden on the country, and the necessary reduction in the size of the bureaucracy, the so-called *Beamtenabbau*, which the League of Nations made a condition for granting Austria a loan, led to a further increase in discontent with the new republic among its inhabitants.

Several of the successor-states were an agglomeration of regions from different earlier states with different administrative and legal traditions. In the new Poland, Prussian law applied in West Prussia, Austrian in Galicia, quasi-French law in Congress Poland, Russian in the rest of Poland that had previously been under Russian rule, and Hungarian in certain small areas in the Carpathians. In Czechoslovakia, Austrian law applied in Bohemia and Hungarian in Slovakia. Yugoslavia initially had seven legal codes, although the differences were in fact relatively small. However, wholly different legal systems confronted each other in the case Poland, and the taxation systems also varied considerably: primarily indirect in the former Russian areas, direct in the German and a combination of the two in the Austrian. The different legal systems in force in certain small areas were quickly abolished, but it still proved necessary to appoint a codification commission in Poland and establish a special ministry for the harmonisation of legislation in Czechoslovakia. The great schemes of codification which were set in motion had not usually been completed before the coming of the Second World War, and this meant that the old Austrian law was even extended to new regions, since some of the successor-states made it apply to the whole country. For example, Austrian land and bankruptcy law was extended to the whole of Yugoslavia, including Serbia and Montenegro where it had never applied before.[6]

This mixture of different administrative traditions was foreign to Finland, where the legal and administrative systems remained unchanged. The only exception was the army, which combined Russian and Prussian traditions: the high command of the new army was largely made up of former officers in the imperial Russian armed forces, while the young officers had received their military training in the *Jäger* battalion of the German army. This mixture led to many conflicts between the different catagories of officers.

The dissolution of the old empires involved much more than the new frontiers which were the most visible manifestation of the changes in sovereignty that had occurred. The successor-states also made demands in relation to the common property of the empires to which they had belonged; they sought a division of the old imperial assets among the parties concerned. In addition, the many different kinds of relationship across what had now become national frontiers had to be regulated.

In Finland, dozens of committees were appointed which had to deal directly with questions created by the dissolution of the union with Russia. Of particular importance was the joint Russo-Finnish committee stipulated in the peace treaty, which — assisted by various sub-committees — worked for several years and prepared about thirty special treaties between 1921 and 1924. These treaties regulated matters which could previously have been settled by administrative decisions, but which now had to be codified through difficult negotiations in bilateral inter-state treaties. The relevant treaties included agreements on such matters as frontier incidents, railways, fishing rights, the return of Soviet and Finnish citizens to their homelands, transportation in the Petsamo area, timber-floating, transportation on the Neva, sealing on Lake Ladoga and the exchange of official archives. Many of these agreements were prepared and put into effect by special or joint committees. In addition, special committees and other bodies were needed inside Finland to deal with new questions created by the dissolution of the union with Russia. Several committees were responsible for the administration of the fortress of Svea-borg and for real estate, schools and other property belonging to the Russian state; one committee discussed the position of the Orthodox Church in Finland; and another how the patrolling of the frontier should be organised. The negotiations between Finland and Russia were generally protracted, even over quite technical questions, partly because of the bad relations between the two countries but also perhaps partly because the Russians were simultaneously engaged in similar negotiations with other states along their borders.

Such questions necessitated wide-ranging administrative measures and difficult negotiations, but Finland enjoyed the advantage that its administrative system was already quite separate from Russia's. In com-parison with the Baltic states, for example, the questions that had to be resolved were relatively few and uncomplicated. In Austria, matters were more difficult. In November 1918 the new Austrian republic took over the old imperial ministries, albeit with the explicit proviso that the rights of the other successor-states would be taken into consideration. Special commissions, containing representatives of the successor-states, were appointed to administer and in time wind up the ministries. These commissions worked under the supervision of the envoys of the new states, but the armistice commissions of the victorious powers also became involved. The Italian armistice commission in particular made very free use of Austrian state property. Once the peace treaty of St Germain came into force, the division of the old imperial assets became an internal Austrian affair, but this simply meant that the difficult negotiations to come had to be dealt with at the diplomatic level.[7]

Most of the problems created by the division of property that had belonged to states which no longer existed were solved by the territorial principle. Each new state took possession of the assets — government buildings, fortifications, railways and so on — which were located within its frontiers. During the peace negotiations at Dorpat, Finland and Soviet Russia attempted to calculate the value of Russian state property in Finland in relation to the value of Finnish state property in Russia, which incidentally included the Valkeasaari-Petrograd railway line; the Finland Station; and the offices of the state secretariat and the Bank of Finland in Petrograd. However, on each occasion the two sides produced very different results because they could not agree on either underlying principles or the value of individual assets. The Finns argued that Russian state property in Finland now belonged to Finland as spoils of war, while the Russians disputed that a state of war had ever existed under international law. The ultimate outcome was an agreement to allow the demands of the two sides to cancel each other out on the basis of the status quo. However, the Russians refused to do more in relation to the demands for compensation of private Finnish individuals and firms than to promise that they would be treated in accordance with Soviet law and in the same way as the affairs of other foreigners. Finland's position in this respect as 'most favoured nation' was of little significance in practice, and the question of compensation remained topical until well into the 1930s.

The territorial principle was also adopted in the case of the former Dual Monarchy, but many questions could not be solved in this way. The navy was divided between the victorious powers and those successor-states with a coastline. In central Europe, seven states had to divide between them the Austro-Hungarian railway network, which included several important private railways. At the time of the armistice, several of the successor-states had seized large quantities of rolling stock, and this development — combined with the shortage of coal and the introduction of visa requirements and new tariffs — soon threatened to bring the whole railway network to a halt. In order to ensure the transportation of food, the great powers forced the seven states concerned to appoint a joint committee to administer their rolling stock. The division of assets in the proper sense began after the conclusion of peace, but it was not till 1933 that the international *Fahrparkaufteilungskommission*, which had a British chairman, was able to regard its work as largely complete, and even then some questions were not resolved until shortly before the *Anschluss*.[8]

In the case of Finland, questions connected with the railway network were resolved at Dorpat and through the detailed transportation agreements concluded in 1921 and 1925, but the problem recurred at a different level. The railway network in Finland had the same gauge as that in Russia, but in the summer of 1918 the possibility of changing to the narrower West European gauge was discussed in various quarters in Finland, including the communications committee. The main argument advanced in favour of this proposal was the opportunity of direct communication with Western Europe, but other factors were also mentioned. The specialist railway journal *Järnvägsmannabladet* conceded that such a change would involve considerable costs, but added that 'the very feeling of orientation towards the countries of high culture would make them worthwhile'.[9] However, the desire for a clean break with Russia in this field too had to give way to the expectations entertained in many quarters of deriving advantage from the Russian market and the opportunities presented by the transit trade between Russia and the outside world. Towns like Turku and Riga hoped to become major centres for the large-scale export of Russia's immeasurable natural resources, which was expected to begin once the situation stabilised.

One problem which generally proved very difficult to resolve was the fate of what might be described as imperial cultural assets. Particular controversy was caused by certain *objets d'art* and by the former imperial archives, which had a current administrative, historical and, not least, symbolic importance. The territorial principle was followed in this case too, with the successor-states assuming control of the archives within their territories, but conflict raged over the central historical and administrative archives in the former imperial capitals. Appeals like that made by the director of the Austrian state archives that the archives in Vienna should be allowed to remain untouched as a memorial to bygone days, like the Pyramids of Egypt, fell on deaf ears. Each successor-state demanded whole archives, parts of archives or individual documents on the grounds that they had originated in or been removed from its territory, or that they concerned its territory, or simply because they were regarded as important for the new state. In some cases, such demands had devastating effects on the archives as organic entities. Austria, which was in a relatively weak

negotiating position, entered into a series of agreements with the
successor-states concerning its archives during the 1920s and 1930s, but
the continuing unresolved dispute between Austria and Yugoslavia over
the application of the treaty they concluded in 1923 bears witness to the
difficulties inherent in this issue.[10]

Generally, Finland attempted to demand from Russia — though without success — documents concerning Finland in the Russian archives; the
main Finnish demand related to the archive of the Finnish state secretariat
in Petrograd, while the Soviet government for its part was interested in the
Russian military and police archives in Finland. At one stage the Russians
also demanded the Slavonic library of Helsinki University, which had
obtained free copies of Russian publications between 1828 and 1917. After
heated discussions, the archive question was left to some extent open at
Dorpat, since the Soviet government reserved to itself documents in the
state secretariat's archive which 'solely or primarily' concerned Russia.
This form of words was hard to interpret, and even after four years of difficult negotiations and the taking of an inventory of the archive's contents,
the agreement concluded in 1924 still listed about 2,500 documents about
which the two sides could not agree. This would appear to be the only list
of an archive's contents to be published as a state paper. Most of the documents concerned, which filled several railway trucks, were exchanged in
the mid-1920s, but the ownership of the last disputed documents was not
resolved until five years later.[11]

When the old activist Konni Zilliacus returned to Finland in September
1918 after many years of exile, he said to a journalist that it was a liberating
feeling 'to discover that the Russian presence which had previously been so
noticeable had been totally swept away'.[12] What Zilliacus meant by this
remark is not immediately apparent — Finland had its own administration, the number of Russian civilians was smaller than in any other part of
the Russian empire, and in peace-time the military garrisons were small.
Since the turn of the century the Russian government had pursued a policy
of centralisation which was regarded in Finland as russification. After May
1918 that policy was replaced by energetic measures designed to promote
what might be called Finland's de-russification.

The post of Russian translator in local government offices and other
state institutions was abolished in the summer of 1918. A series of regulations was also issued which did away with the earlier stipulations concerning the use of Russian in state institutions. When the telegraph service
passed into Finnish hands, those of its employees who were not Finnish

citizens were dismissed. In accordance with the view that Russian property in Finland had become Finnish as spoils of war, the Senate issued a long series of regulations sequestrating Russian barracks and other buildings, ships, stocks of food, debts owed to the Russian crown, hospitals, schools and soon.

The Orthodox church in Finland, which had been a separate diocese under the patriarch in Moscow since 1896, was administratively a Russian institution, even though three-quarters of its *ca.* 63,000 members were Finnish-speaking. The Orthodox church was compromised in the eyes of many by its role in the policy of russification in Karelia. For national and security reasons, the Finnish government therefore introduced a number of measures designed to 'fennicise' the Orthdox church by establishing a separate communion and demanding that its priests and monks be Finnish citizens, the use of Finnish as its language of internal administration, the adoption of the Gregorian calendar, and that it should free itself from Moscow's authority with a view to becoming an autocephalous church. These issues led to conflicts which continued for several years. The dispute over the calendar, and in particular over the time when Easter should be celebrated, led to the voluntary departure or expulsion from the country of some of the monks in the monasteries of Valamo and Konevitsa. The Russian archbishop Serafim refused to accept some of the reforms; he was first suspended from office and then not appointed to the newly-established archbishop's post on the grounds that he did not meet the requirements of the language law. The attempt to create a completely independent church failed, but the Finnish Orthodox church was removed from the authority of the Moscow patriarchate and placed under the ecumenical patriarchate in Constantinople in 1923, a development which Moscow did not accept until 1957. Similar efforts to free the Orthodox church from the authority of Moscow occurred in several of the other successor-states. The Orthodox church in Poland became completely independent in 1924, but its Estonian counterpart had to be content with autonomy under the authority of the Constantinople patriarchate.[13]

The garrison areas in Finland with their Orthodox churches had been strongly Russian in character, and these churches were now seen as unnecessary. The Alexander Nevsky church on Sveaborg lost its onion cupolas and became a Lutheran church, as did the church at Lappeenranta, while that at Hämeenlinna was turned into a library. Several others were demolished or rebuilt to house soldiers or perform some other useful function. The so-called Resvoysky chapel which had been built in Helsinki to celebrate the centenary of the Peace of 1809, that is to say Finland's

A detachment of the Vaasa battalion, the first Finnish troops to enter the eighteenth-century fortress of Sveaborg for over a century. The cupolas on the Orthodox church were soon to be removed. *B*

incorporation into the Russian empire, was tarred by anonymous nationalists on Palm Sunday in 1919, and the congregation agreed to its demolition the following year.

Other visible symbols of the former Russian presence were also subjected to de-russification. As early as the spring of 1917 revolutionary Russian soldiers and sailors had removed the double eagle from monuments, and in the summer of 1918 the Finns turned their attention to other such symbols. Russian stamps and coins were made invalid, and directives were issued stating that all official seals bearing a Russian text had to be replaced as soon as possible. By 31 May, all Russian road-signs had been removed in Helsinki at the expense of the city council. The Russian Alexander theatre, which had been specially favoured by the governor-general, was closed and the building given to the Finnish Opera. A number of Russian archives and libraries were destroyed deliberately or through carelessness.

The University in Helsinki was at the centre of some of the attempts at de-russification. In September 1918 the newspaper *Svenska Tidningen* demanded, in a leader with the headline 'Away with the Russian professorships!', the abolition of the long-established chair in Russian language and literature and of the two chairs in Russian law and the one in Russian history and politics established at the beginning of the century to promote 'devotion to the throne and sympathy for Russia'. These three posts were either abolished or transferred to a different area of study. In September 1918 the University made a distinct break with the past century which had been so important for its development by proposing, after a vote among its members, that its name be changed from 'the Imperial Alexander University in Finland' to 'Helsinki University'. The sort of continuity the majority wished to emphasise is shown by its unwillingness to retain the former emperor's name while adding, for example, 'founded in Turku in 1640' after the full title. However, one group of students, which included Urho Kekkonen, wanted to go further, and in 1924 covered Alexander I's monogram on the University's façade with tar. The students also initiated a long campaign to have a bust of the emperor removed from the University's main hall, a campaign which finally succeeded in 1932.[14]

De-russification — or similar measures against Austrian or Magyar traditions and symbols — were on the agenda in other successor states. The University in Prague had been partitioned on a linguistic basis in 1882, and both the Czech and the German universities had been allowed to retain the name of 'the Charles-Ferdinand University'. In 1920 this name was abolished and the Czech University was rechristened the Charles University in order to eliminate the name of a Habsburg and to emphasise continuity with the ruler who had founded the University in 1348, Emperor Charles IV of Luxemburg.[15]

In 1930 the memorial at Sarajevo for Archduke Franz Ferdinand and his wife was destroyed and replaced by a plaque commemorating their assassin Gavrilo Princip. This action prompted a public protest in London from one of the instigators of the Yugoslav state, Professor R.W. Seton-Watson.[16] Three years later a plaque commemorating the man who shot Governor-General Bobrikov in 1904, Eugen Schauman, was unveiled at the top of the main staircase in the Senate building in Helsinki. An observer like Seton-Watson might have wondered whether the text on the plaque, '*Se pro patria dedit*', did not apply to the victim as much as to his assassin.

Some aspects of de-russification consisted of administrative measures occasioned by changed circumstances, and others represented an attempt to expunge the past. There were, however, those who felt that the elimination of features of the Russian period was not enough. The groups that rallied round the Academic Karelian Society were particularly vehement in demanding that the Finnish people, especially young people, ought to be educated to take an actively negative attitude towards the country's eastern neighbour, a hatred which combined older traditions of russophobia with antipathy towards Bolshevism and efforts to create the basis for an expansionist policy or at least heightened defence preparedness. It is hard to know how deeply such attitudes affected public opinion, but they were at any rate strongly present in the books on relevant topics published in this period. One indication that agitation of this kind was not wholly without effect is that the number of Russian literary classics translated into Finnish declined during the 1930s and that there was a considerable fall in the number of copies sold. The Siestarjoki river which marked the new frontier had become a barrier which permitted few contacts, even with the past.[17]

One of the characters in a novel by the Austrian writer Joseph Roth complains that he had previously lived in a house but that after the war he was forced to live in a cupboard. The sort of national limitation to which Roth referred also affected Finland, which turned inwards intellectually during the inter-war period. National culture was strengthened, but the younger generation also experienced a need, in Olavi Paavolainen's words, 'to open the window towards Europe'.

The dissolution of the old empires had far-reaching economic consequences. In the case of Central Europe, an integrated economy was destroyed. Most of the commodities produced in the Dual Monarchy had been exchanged between mutually complementary areas like industrialised Bohemia and agrarian Hungary. About four-fifths of the commodities produced by the different regions of the Dual Monarchy were marketed within the Habsburg empire itself. When the empire collapsed, its natural resources and industries were distributed unevenly among the successor-states (Czechoslovakia obtained 70 per cent of the industry in the former Austrian half of the Dual Monarchy), and lopsided economies were created which were extremely dependent on exports. In addition to the general economic problems of the post-war years, these new states experienced difficult problems of adjustment, which they sought to solve by making themselves as economically independent as possible by measures like high tariffs and import prohibitions. In practice, the negative effects of such measures were felt most strongly by neighbouring states. The high tariff walls made it cheaper to buy, for example, British machinery and American grain. The outcome was that trade between the countries of

Central Europe fell to an insignificant 10–15 per cent, a development further underlined by the virtual exclusion of the Soviet Union from international trade. General autarkic tendencies — the attempt to create a self-sufficient economy — created a situation in which Austria and Czechoslovakia sought to build up the agrarian sector and Hungary the industrial.[18]

The new Poland faced the opposite problem: 80–85 per cent of her trade and been with the powers which partitioned Poland at the end of the eighteenth century. The textile and engineering industries of the former Congress Poland were dependent on the Russian market, while the agrarian areas of German Poland supplied food to the great German cities. The closure of the Russian market and the high tariffs introduced by the successor-states made it difficult for Poland to build up a national economy, a problem exacerbated by the fact that existing communications had been developed to meet the needs of the old empires. Fifty Austrian or German railway lines in Poland led to the former Russian frontier, but only ten of them continued on the other side.[19]

Many of the successor-states also tried to build up their consumer industries, while other countries gave priority to heavy industry. Per capita steel production rose substantially in Britain and Sweden during the inter-war period, but it remained more or less static even in relatively industrialised successor-states like Czechoslovakia and Poland. The relatively slow pace of growth was not particularly noticeable during the good years in the 1920s, but the shock created by the depression was all the greater and had direct political consequences.

In the case of Finland, the dissolution of the union with Russia did not create such severe problems of adjustment. Before the war Finland's share of the imports and exports of the whole Russian empire had been about 3–5 per cent, and Russia's share of Finnish trade had been around 30 per cent. The Russian market was of particular importance to the paper industry, 80 per cent of whose exports went to Russia. The world war led to a considerable increase in Russia's share of Finnish trade. The interruption of trade with the West enhanced Finland's dependence on Russian grain (Finland's level of self-sufficiency was only 40–50 per cent) and led to a stagnation in its timber exports. Sectors like the engineering, leather, shoemaking and textile industries, which were able to produce goods for the Russian armed forces, experienced rapid and substantial expansion.[20]

In the years after the revolutions the Finns continued to regard Russia as an important market, but Russia never accounted for more than 1–4.5 per cent of Finland's total foreign trade between 1922 and 1937 because of political conditions and Russia's economic decline. This would have led to very difficult problems of adjustment if Finland had not enjoyed the advantage of having been relatively unscathed by the world war. As a result, stocks of commodities in short supply on Western markets could be sold, and the paper and timber industries in particular had gained a good foothold by the time the post-war depression set in. This was of special importance to Finland because the industries which had expanded through supplying the Russian armed forces were unable to compete on Western markets and declined to the position of industries serving the home market only. However, in the case of the engineering industry, for example, Finland's problems of adjustment were less severe than those of Estonia, which had been an important centre for the shipbuilding and armaments industries before 1917. The capital, expertise and raw materials had all been Russian or foreign, and production had been entirely geared towards the Russian market and the navy's building programme. When these two factors disappeared from the scene after the war, the Estonian engineering industry completely collapsed, while the crisis of economic adjustment in Finland between 1917 and 1919 only involved a brief decline before the prewar level was reached again.[21]

Finland experienced severe shortages in 1918, but grain imports from the West then began to reach the country. Throughout the whole of the inter-war period Finland tried to increase its level of self-sufficiency in food, and imports from Russia therefore remained at a very low level.

The dissolution of the union with Russia thus only led to a short crisis of economic adjustment for Finland, which the Finns were able to solve because of favourable circumstances without the economic convulsions that afflicted Central Europe. However, in regional terms, the dissolution of the union and above all the closure of the frontier did lead to difficulties for the south-eastern parts of the country and a dramatic change for the Karelian Isthmus. The population of the Isthmus lost the many opportunities for earning money in and around St Petersburg, and fishermen lost some of their traditional fishing grounds. The stream of Imatra tourists and summer holiday-makers from St Petersburg also ceased.

The number of villas on the Isthmus had reached a level which was not attained in Finland until the 1960s in the area surrounding Helsinki, and the number of summer holiday-makers visiting there before the war was over 50,000 each summer. The closure of the frontier led to a considerable loss of income, but also created problems in the sense that there were several thousand unoccupied villas after the revolution, and nothing was known about the fate of their owners. In order to solve this problem, a law

was introduced in 1922 which was unique in Finnish terms: it gave the
state the right to administer and ultimately to confiscate real estate owned
by foreigners which was left unattended. Close to 5,000 properties and
buildings had been confiscated under this law by 1936, and through sale at
auction not a few of the villas were dismantled and re-erected in other parts
of the country.[22]

The dissolution of empires led to radical changes for their capital cities, and
two of them — Petrograd and Istanbul — even lost their position as capitals. As Stalin pointed out during the negotiations which preceded the
Winter War, Leningrad had become a city which lay within artillery range
of the frontier on the Karelian Isthmus. The troops of a foreign power had
never been stationed so close to the city since its foundation. The boundaries of the new Austria were very similar to those of the Habsburg
possessions in 1365, while Vienna ceased to be situated at the centre of the
Austrian state and became once again, as it had been during the Turkish
wars, a capital lying on the very frontiers of the country.

Petrograd and Vienna were also cut off from large parts of their traditional hinterland, a development which contributed to the shortages both
cities suffered after the war. Vienna was too large a capital for the republic
of Austria: a third of the country's population lived in '*Wasserkopf-Wien*'
(Vienna with water on the brain), and major conflicts occurred between
the cosmopolitan capital, governed by social democrats and containing
large Jewish and Czech minorities on the one side, and the conservative
alpine districts dominated by the farming community on the other.

While regent of Finland, Svinhufvud emphasised in April 1918, and on
later occasions also in conversation with German diplomats, that under no
circumstances could Petrograd be allowed to remain the capital of Russia.
His preferred solution was to turn the city into a sort of city-state and free
port in order to minimise the Russian threat of Finland. The German
minister in Helsinki, von Brück, took the view in the spring of 1918 that
Finnish plans should be governed by reality and that the unparalleled
successes of German arms had deprived the Finns of their sense of proportion and their grasp of what lay within the bounds of the possible. In the
summer of 1919, when a march on Petrograd played a large part in the
conspiratorial plans of the Finnish activists, von Brück found that these
'fanciful' and 'chauvinistic' schemes enjoyed the support not only of the
regent but also of large sections of the Finnish press. He deplored the effect
on 'uneducated people' of constant chauvinistic agitation, when the leader
of the Agrarian Party, Santeri Alkio, demanded in his newspaper that

Russia should be driven back from the shores of the Baltic and that the
political importance of Petrograd should be eliminated by turning the city
into a separate republic independent of Russia and a centre for trade
between East and West. *Svenska Tidningen*, using the slogan '*Écrasez
l'infame*', also wished to attack this 'gigantic spider' and 'pestilential boil'
in the conviction that 'the future of Europe depends on our swords.'[23]

Finnish opinion was generally most interested in acquiring Eastern
Karelia and Northern Ingria and was content in the case of Petrograd with
eliminating the city, as it were, as a geopolitical reality. The march on
Petrograd discussed in 1918 and 1919 was therefore seen as a means
less of acquiring the city than of securing other territorial objectives
with the support of the Germans, the Western powers or the White
Russians.

It is clear that von Brück's sober assessment of the bounds of the possible
was the correct one, but the adoption of a comparative perspective shows
that Finnish plans had their counterparts elsewhere. During the post-war
period Danzig and Fiume were turned into international free cities, and for
a time a similar solution was considered in the case of Istanbul. An important section of Greek opinion wanted Istanbul to form part of a future
Greater Greece embracing both shores of the Aegean Sea. The victorious
powers were at one stage willing to hand the city to Greece or to turn it
into an international city, but the Greeks preferred to stake the fate of their
plans on an invasion of Anatolia. Similarly, the Finns ultimately abandoned
the idea of a march on Petrograd after long hesitation, and instead
supported expeditions into Eastern Karelia. The small states concerned
were not able in either case to impose their territorial demands and at the
same time lost any chance of achieving a different solution to the problems
presented by the former imperial capitals.[24]

In the case of Finland, the 'Leningrad problem' remained. The topical
nature of the problem is demonstrated by the publication between 1918
and 1934 of six novels, all works of science-fiction, which described how
little Finland — because of its courage, the unity of its people, its
possession of miraculous weapons or the support of the oppressed minorities in Russia — conquers and, in most of the books, destroys the great
city on the Neva. During the Second World War the Germans again raised
the possibility of either destroying Leningrad or of turning it into an international city. These were tempting perspectives, but the Finns refrained on
this occasion too from staking everything on the conquest of the city.[25]

The altered position of the former imperial capitals is also demonstrated
by their loss of some of their multi-national character through the volun-

tary emigration or expulsion of important minority groups. The Greeks in Istanbul, who had numbered several hundred thousand before the war, were not included in the agreement between Greece and Turkey concerning the exchange of national minorities, but at least 150,000 were forced to leave the city between 1922 and 1924, and their number fell continuously thereafter. Migrants from Finland had formed an element in the population of St Petersburg since the foundation of the city, but most of the Finns left the city after the revolution or were evacuated under the terms of a special agreement concluded in 1922. The Czechs in Vienna, who numbered 200,000 before the war, were protected by a minority rights agreement between Austria and Czechoslovakia, but the size of this group was reduced by migration back to Czechoslovakia even before its members, like the Jews of Vienna, were affected by Hitler's measures against the city where he had formerly lived.[26]

The dissolution of empires created an enormous number of refugees: close to 2 million in the case of the Russian revolution and its consequences alone. Finland became the first place of refuge and a transit country for refugees from the Petersburg region and Eastern Karelia. The Senate decided in the spring of 1918, as part of its programme of de-russification, to expel all Russian subjects from the country. As a result, a large number of them were sent over the border into Russia, but as early as the autumn the tide had turned and was flowing the other way. The number of refugees in Finland reached about 15,000 in 1919, and in 1922 the figure was 33,500. In proportional terms, this was about the same as in the other states which bordered Soviet Russia. The refugees occasioned a number of political disputes, but they never became such a burden on the country as they did in some other successor-states. For example, Greece, with a population of about 5 million, had to cope with the crushing burden of accommodating well over 1 million Greeks from abroad because of agreements with Turkey and Bulgaria concerning the exchange of national minorities.[27]

One of the arguments used to justify the emergence of the successor-states was the principle of 'national self-determination'. In most cases, the people were not asked whether they wished to belong to these new states, and if so on what conditions. In some cases, it was perfectly clear that a national group did not wish to belong to the new state within whose borders it was now accommodated. The Germans in Bohemia and in south Tyrol and the Magyars in Transylvania are examples. Plebiscites were arranged in only a few cases, and treaties guaranteeing minority rights could not change the

## NATIONAL MINORITIES IN THE SUCCESSOR STATES
## DURING THE INTERWAR PERIOD

|  |  | *All minorities as a percentage of the total population* |
| --- | --- | --- |
| Yugoslavia | 1931 | –57 |
| Czechoslovakia | 1921 | –52 |
| Poland | 1921 | 31–35 |
| Romania | 1930 | 29–34 |
| Latvia | 1930 | 27–28 |
| Albania | 1930 | 22–24 |
| Lithuania | 1923 | 16–18 |
| Bulgaria | 1934 | 13–16 |
| Hungary | 1920 | 10–15 |
| Estonia | 1934 | 12–13 |
| Finland | 1930 | 10 |

*Note.* These figures are derived from R. Pearson, *National Minorities in Eastern Europe 1848–1945* (1983), p. 148. Pearson regards the nationality which sustained the state as the 'majority' and the other nationalities as minorities. Of the two figures given in the right-hand column, the first is derived from the census statistics (which generally underestimate the size of the minorities) and the second from other calculations. There are no separate census figures for Serbs and Croats and for Czechs and Slovaks. The figures in the table do not take bilingualism into account and are only meant to give an approximate picture.

fact that the ethnic map of Europe did not provide a basis for 'pure' national states.

Before 1914 about half the population of Eastern Europe was in the position of belonging to a national minority. This proportion fell to about a quarter as a result of the settlement after the First World War, but many of the successor-states still faced the same problems as the old empires and several of them were in effect small multi-national empires. All of them had quite substantial national minorities (see table), and in some of them the peoples which sustained the state were in fact minorities, even if they sought to disguise this fact in their dealings with the outside world and in their official statistics by using aggregated descriptions of nationality like Czechoslovaks and Serbo-Croats. In some respects, the difficulties the successor-states experienced in dealing with minority problems were perhaps greater than those of the old empires, because they were economically and politically unstable and because they lacked the non-national cohesive principles which the old empires had been able to expound. The creation of the successor-states had been legitimated by the polite fiction that they were nationally homogeneous. Sharp conflicts therefore sometimes occurred when the nationalism of the state clashed with the nationalism of the minorities, which often received external support in the 1930s. The new 'national states' came into conflict with the reality of their own multi-national character, and this provided fertile soil for the authoritarian and fascist regimes which came to power in nearly all the successor-states.

In the case of Finland, in so far as one can speak of a nationality problem, it was a small one in quantitative terms. However, a particularly important difference between Finland and the other successor-states was that the world war and independence led to no, or at least very few, changes in relations between the country's linguistic groups. In contrast, the creation of Czechoslovakia, for example, meant a complete revolution for the so-called Sudeten Germans, who had previously belonged to the dominant national group within the empire, but who now became a minority which constituted one-fifth of the population of the new state. Other factors — like widespread bilingualism and the traditionally high level of mobility over linguistic boundaries within all social groups — were also of great importance in the case of Finland. The divide between the majority and the minority was not a sharp one, and the social composition of the two linguistic groups was not decisively different in that all social groups contained speakers of both Finnish and Swedish. It is true that Swedish-speakers were over-represented in the higher and intermediate social

No ferries to the zoo; and the Swedish name of the island on which the zoo is situated has been tarred over by Finnish nationalists. Photographed by A. Rönnberg in 1927. *E*

categories, but this was outweighed by the fact that they were too few to become dominant.

Both linguistic groups identified unreservedly with the Finnish state. Their respective members took part on both sides in the country's social and political conflicts. The emergence of an independent Finnish state did not create political losers, like the Croats and the Slovaks, prepared in their bitterness at the dominance of another ethnic group to destroy the state. Nor were there in Finland social losers like German landowners in the Baltic states or Magyar landowners in Romania, who were hard-hit by agrarian reforms and regarded this as a manifestation of ethnic persecution.

An important factor was that Finland's language struggle did not become internationalised. Swedish interest in any aspect of this conflict other than the Ålands was very lukewarm, and the Ålanders were the only group to turn to a foreign power over an ethnic question. The opinions expressed in Sweden about the language conflict certainly aroused irritation in Finland, but Finland's Swedish-speakers made few appeals to Sweden. Whatever Finnish-language nationalists might think, there was a world of difference between the implications of organisations like the Verein für das Deutschum im Ausland, with Hitler in the background, for states with German minorities and the implications for Finland of Riksföreningen för svenskhetens bevarande i utlandet (the national union for the preservation of Swedish culture abroad) with the Swedish socialist leader P.A. Hansson in the background. The question of international guarantees of minority rights was only raised in the case of Finland in relation to the Ålands, and Finland provided far-reaching guarantees for the protection of the Swedish language there within the framework of the League of Nations, but without entering into a treaty concerning minority rights in other respects.[28]

Swedish non-socialist politics in Finland were activated soon after independence. Svenska Finlands folkting (the popular assembly of Swedish Finland) was founded, and the use of the term 'Finland–Swedish' (*finlandssvensk*), which had been introduced during the second decade of the twentieth century, was supported. Swedish-speakers argued that the kind of international guarantees protecting minority rights which were being discussed in Europe were adequate and unsuited to Finnish conditions. Such attitudes are illuminating because they show how the leaders of Finland–Swedish opinion did not generally regard the country's Swedish-speakers as a minority except in purely quantitative terms. They saw both linguistic groups as having equal rights and an equal role in sustaining the state.

During the years 1918–21 the country's Swedish-speakers pursued two different and partly contradictory goals in response both to domestic conditions and to developments in Europe as a whole. The first goal, which was realised in the country's constitution and language laws, was equality for the two linguistic groups. The second goal, which was encapsulated in the term 'the idea of self-government', was to achieve guaranteed minority rights, self-government and regional autonomy. Reforms within the administration of the Finnish church (the creation of a Swedish-speaking bishopric) and the education system (the establishment of a Swedish section within the schools administration and guarantees concerning the use of Swedish at Helsinki University) created a limited measure of cultural autonomy, but it was not possible to realise the far-reaching demands of the Swedish-speaking minority in other respects.

The language conflict in Finland aroused great attention among the public, but it should be emphasised that it largely concerned the use of Swedish at Helsinki University and that the foremost victims of the conflict were Swedish road-signs which were covered in tar. In contrast, ethnic and national conflicts in many other parts of Europe took a violent form and occasioned terrorism and armed clashes.

The first Finnish republic was a quite typical representative of the new states which emerged after the First World War. Finland had to face most of the problems caused by the disintegration of 'the world of yesterday', as Stefan Zweig in his memoirs called the Europe which was destroyed by the First World War and which was characterised by supra-national empires, peace, material progress and a stable monetary system.

The emergence of the new states after the war led to the realisation of many hopes, but also left many of their inhabitants disappointed. In some respects, the Europe of the successor-states had to pay for the dissolution of the old empires with new conflicts, which ultimately led to a new world war, and with authoritarianism, economic instability and narrow nationalism.

The dissolution of the union with Russia led in Finland to a bitter civil war in 1918, but in most other respects Finland suffered less than the other successor-states. An important factor in the background was that in 1917 Finland had long been a state and that the country emerged from the period of upheaval with largely unchanged frontiers and constitution. It would be a gross exaggeration to regard Finland as 'complete' within the Russian empire before 1917, but the period which a parochial nationalism chose to call 'the Russian parenthesis' did give Finland many of the preconditions for political sovereignty, and this was a point of contrast with most of the other successor-states.

The Austrian journalist Ernst Trost claimed that the peoples of Eastern Europe carried an 'inner double eagle'.[29] The degree to which this was also true in Finland is an open question, but the Finland which ultimately disproved the sceptical assessments expressed during the first years of independence was a country that had taken shape under the wings of the double eagle.

## NOTES

1. Lucius to Auswärtiges Amt (AA) 7.3 and 31.10.1918, Hauptarchiv des Auswärtiges Amts, Abteilung A, Finnland, Bd 1 and 19 (copies in Finnish National Archives).
2. Lucius to AA 1.5.1918, ibid. Bd 5.
3. Mutius to AA 14.6.1919 and Lucius to AA 27.6.1919, ibid. Bd 22.
4. K.E. Eriksen and E. Niemi, *Den finske fare. Sikkerhetsproblemer og minoritetspolitikk i nord 1860–1940*, Oslo 1981, pp. 139–41, 164–5, 173–5.
5. Kidston to Curzon 22.5.1920, Foreign Office, Confidential print, Baltic States and Finland II, 1920, Public Record Office, London (copy in Finnish National Archives).
6. H. Slapnicka, *Österreichs Recht ausserhalb Österreich. Der Untergang des österreichischen Rechtsraums*, Schriftenreihe des österreichischen Ost- und Südosteuropa-Instituts 4, Vienna 1973, *passim*.
7. U. Freise, 'Die Tätigkeit der allierten Kommissionen in Wien nach dem Ersten Weltkrieg', unpublished D. Phil. diss., University of Vienna 1963, pp. 4–31, 59, 110–12.
8. P. Mechtler, 'Internationale Verflechtung der österreichischen Eisenbahnen am Anfang der Ersten Republik. Die Trennung des altösterreichischen Eisenbahnwesens nach dem Zusammenbruch der Donaumonarchie', *Mitteilungen des österreichischen Staatsarchivs*, 17–18 (1964–5), pp. 399–426.
9. *Rautatieläislehti-Järnvägsmannabladet*, 5–6 (1918), p. 61.
10. L. Bittner, 'Die zwischenstaatlichen Verhandlungen über das Schicksal der österreichischen Archive nach dem Zusammenbruch Österreich-Ungarns', *Archiv für Politik und Geschichte*, 4 (1925), pp. 58–96, esp. p. 64. G. Rill *et al.*, '60 Jahre österreichisch-jugoslawisches Archiv-übereinkommen. Eine Zwischenbalanz', *Mitteilungen des österreichischen Staatsarchivs*, 35(1982), pp. 288–347.
11. M. Engman, 'Arkivförhandlingarna mellan Finland och Rådsryssland', manuscript, 1984, and 'Böcker i kristid. Biblioteken i relationerna mellan Finland och Rådsryssland 1917–1926', *Helsingfors universitets-biblioteks skrifter* 50 (1986), pp. 32–50.
12. *Hufvudstadsbladet*, 22 Sept. 1918.
13. U.J.V. Setälä, *Kansallisen ortodoksisen kirkkokunnan perustamiskysymys Suomen politiikassa 1917–1925*, Porvoo 1966, *passim*.
14. *Svenska Tidningen*, 2 Sept. 1918; M. Klinge, *Ylioppilaskunnan historia*, IV: 1918–1960, Porvoo 1968, pp. 97–103.
15. H. Slapnicka, 'Die Teilung der Prager Karl-Ferdinands-Universität in eine deutsche und eine tschechische Universität im Jahre 1882' in F.B. Kaiser and B. Stasiewski (*eds*), *Deutscher Einfluss auf Bildung und Wissenschaft im östlichen Europa*, Studien zum Deutschtum im Osten, 18, Köln 1984, pp. 137–57.
16. Arthur J. May, *The Passing of the Hapsburg Monarchy, 1914–1918*, I, Oxford 1966, pp. 42–3.

17. M. Klinge, 'Ryssänviha', in *Vihan veljistä valtiososialismiin*, Porvoo 1972, pp. 57–112; K. Immonen, *Ryssästä saa puhua . . . Neuvostoliitto suomalaisessa julkisuudessa ja kirjat julkisuuden muotona 1918–39*, Helsinki 1987, pp. 286–93.

18. I.T. Berend and G. Ranki, *Economic Development in East-Central Europe in the 19th and 20th Centuries*, New York 1974, pp. 172–200.

19. R.F. Leslie (*ed.*), *The History of Poland since 1863*, Cambridge 1980, pp. 139–40.

20. E. Pihkala, 'Suomen ja Venäjän taloudelliset suhteet I maailmansodan aikana', *Historiallinen Aikakauskirja*, 78 (1980), pp. 29–42.

21. J. Ahvenainen, 'Suomen ja Neuvostoliiton väliset kauppasuhteet 1920– ja 1930–luvulla', *Turun Historiallinen Arkisto*, 41 (1986), pp. 168–85; T. Herranen and T. Myllyntaus, 'Effects of the First World War on the Engineering Industries of Estonia and Finland', *Scandinavian Economic History Review*, 32 (1984), pp. 121–42.

22. V. Hämäläinen, *Karjalan Kannaksen venäläinen kesäasutuskysymys maamme itsenäisyyden kaudella*, Tampereen yliopisto, Historiatieteen laitoksen julkaisuja 6, Tampere 1983, *passim*.

23. V. Brück to AA, 17.4.1918, Hauptarchiv des Auswärtiges Amts, Abteilung A, Finnland 1, Bd 5, and 16.6.1919, *ibid.*, Finnland 2, Russisch-Finnische Beziehungen, Bd 3 (copies in Finnish National Archives); *Ilkka*, 7 June 1919; *Svenska Tidningen*, 26 June 1919.

24. Alexis Alexandris, *The Greek Minority of Istanbul and Greek-Turkish Relations 1918–1974*, Athens 1983, pp. 52–4; M. Jääskeläinen, *Die ostkarelische Frage*, Porvoo 1961, *passim*.

25. Immonen, *op. cit.*, pp. 240–2. Ohto Manninen, *Suur-Suomen ääriviivat*, Helsinki 1980, p. 249 and *passim*.

26. Alexandris, *op. cit.*, pp. 83–7, 103–4. K.M. Brousek, *Wien und seine Tschechen. Integration und Assimilation einer Minderheit im 20. Jahrhundert* Schriftenreihe des österreichischen Ost- und Südosteuropa-Instituts 7, Vienna 1980, *passim*.

27. Toivo Nygård, *Itä-Karjalan pakolaiset 1917–1922*, Studia Historica Jyväskyläensia 19, Jyväskylä 1980, pp. 71–2; M.R. Marrus, *The Unwanted: European Refugees in the Twentieth Century*, New York, 1985, pp. 100–9.

28. G. v. Bonsdorff, *Självstyrelsetanken i finlandssvensk politik åren 1917–23*, Bidrag till kännedom av Finlands natur och folk 94:1, Helsingfors 1950, *passim*.

29. E. Trost, *Das blieb vom Doppeladler. Auf den Spuren der versunkenen Donaumonarchie*, Wien 1966, p. 15.

# INDEPENDENT FINLAND BETWEEN EAST AND WEST

## Jukka Nevakivi

On the wall of the Civil Guards' hall in my home village stood the following text: 'Neither East nor West can force you, O Land, into thrall while your sons ever on guard do stand!' This patriotic text, painted in white on a blue background, depicted in its own simple way the position of the newly-independent Finnish state, lying between Russian and Swedish 'thraldom'.

This sentence could also be construed as describing the position of Finland in even broader terms: under pressure on the one hand from the Soviet Union and on the other from Germany and the Western powers. This interpretation sees Finland not as the 'outpost of Western civilisation' but on the contrary asserts that Finland can remain itself only by ensuring that neither Eastern nor Western influence sets its imprint on the country. Read in this way, the motto could even be regarded as a suitable declaration of the Paasikivi line of neutrality, developed after 1944.

An awareness that their country would have no future so long as it remained at the mercy of outsiders as a pawn between Russia and its adversaries had taken root among the Finns as early as the eighteenth century. Experiences during the period of autonomy from the mid-nineteenth century onwards strengthened this view. It thus comes as no particular surprise that it was planned to include a statement of neutrality in the declaration of Finnish independence in 1917 — the fourth year of the world war — and an address was drawn up in consequence for despatch to the national assembly convened to prepare a constitution for Russia.[1]

The recently renewed controversy in Finland over what Lenin intended when he recognised Finnish independence at the end of 1917 prompts another question: what would have happened if the Finns invited to Petrograd in December 1917 to request recognition had been delayed by, say, a month? The Soviet government would no longer have had the opportunity to 'grant' Finland independence before the conclusion of peace at Dorpat in 1920, and recognition would have taken on a completely different tone.

This question also raises another point, for it is a reminder of who in the end offered Lenin this opportunity. As Professor Georg von Wendt, the representative of the Finnish government in Stockholm in December 1917,

128

The White victory parade, 16 May 1918. General C.G. Mannerheim receives a bouquet; behind him stand the regent P.E. Svinhufvud, officers of the White army and German officers. *F*

recalled, V.V. Vorovsky, the representative of the Bolshevik government in Sweden, treated Finland in practice like an independent state immediately after the declaration of independence on 6 December, for example urging his countrymen who were travelling out or back through Finland to ask for a Finnish transit visa. It was Vorovsky who arranged for an invitation to be sent to P.E. Svinhufvud, the head of the Finnish government, to travel to Petrograd. Svinhufvud also came under pressure from Berlin: Germany did not want to recognise Finland's independence before Finland's former motherland had done so.[2]

Svinhufvud, for his own part, would have preferred to have nothing to do with the Bolsheviks. In his opinion the Finns had to exploit the opportunity that had opened up 'of its own accord' to break free from Russia, contenting themselves solely with recognition by foreign countries. It was his belief that Finland needed to have no more to do with Russia but would henceforth orient itself towards the Western world.

As a civilian, completely cut off from the realities of military and political life, at least during his exile in Siberia between 1914 and 1917, Svinhufvud tended to pay insufficient attention to Finland's strategic position beside the then capital of Russia. Although he was clearly aware of this problem throughout the period leading up to the attainment of independence, he made no gesture whatsoever to show readiness to offer guarantees that an independent Finland would not allow its territory to be used against Soviet Russia.[3]

Although the advice given to Helsinki from Berlin — that the Finns should first request recognition of their independence from Petrograd — corresponded to international practice, the primary aim of the Germans was to place their eastern relations on a good.footing, with Finland as a buffer against Soviet Russia. However, in the course of the next three months military and political developments gave Finland a more active role than hitherto as a vassal in the territory between Germany and Soviet Russia.

After realising that Russia was not going to be constrained by the peace terms concluded at Brest–Litovsk, the German supreme headquarters decided as early as March 1918 that the Bolshevik revolutionary movement was aimed primarily at Germany: 'A strong military power should therefore be created on the Russian frontier, the more so because the supreme army command is trying constantly to send forces to the west in ever increasing numbers . . . For this reason it is particularly desirable to obtain freedom from responsibility for an Eastern Front. Finland offers this possibility.'[4]

It was not known at first in Helsinki that Germany had not the slightest intention of supporting Finnish attempts to expand to the east of the old frontier of the grand duchy. In encouraging the Finns to send expeditions to Archangel, Karelia and Petsamo in the winter of 1918, German military headquarters had nothing more remarkable in mind than using them against the Entente forces dug in at Murmansk. Thus independent Finland had managed by the summer of 1918 to develop into a useful instrument of German military policy directed against both the Soviet government and the Allied intervention in North Russia.[5]

Instead of being able to pursue a neutral course, Finland was brought dangerously close to involvement in the world war as a result of the inter-

Three young ladies admire the knight (and his horse) who slew the fearsome Red dragon. Outside German headquarters in Helsinki, spring 1918. *E*

vention of German troops during the civil war, and the influence subsequently wielded by Germany over the Finnish government. An immediate consequence was that Finland was not able to foster its relations with the Western powers or — after grain deliveries from Russia had ceased — to procure food from the West. The famine of 1918 can be regarded as the first concrete reminder of Finland's vulnerable position between East and West.

That White Finland seemed ready barely a year later to put itself at the disposal of the Western powers for use against the Soviet government arose from a belief, strengthened by experience in the Finnish civil war, that the Bolsheviks offered Finland neither economic nor political security. The victorious commander of the White Finnish forces, General Carl Gustaf Mannerheim, now replaced Svinhufvud as regent of the country. Mannerheim's intention was to help into power in Russia, with the support of the Western countries, a government which would have made an end of the Bolsheviks, restored the old order, opened the doors once more to Finland's trade with the East, and confirmed Finnish independence, possibly even with extended frontiers (in Eastern Karelia).

Although Petrograd was not threatened through Finland in 1919 other than by a single British naval attack launched from Terijoki against Kronstadt, the attempt had in itself awakened in that city earlier frightening memories from the time of the Crimean war. The leading article published in *The Times* on 17 April 1919 caught the eye of V.P. Potemkin, author of the official Soviet history of diplomacy: 'So far as stamping out the Bolshevik is concerned, we might as well send expeditions to Honolulu as to the White Sea. If we look at the map we shall find that the shortest and easiest route is through Finland . . . Finland is the key to Petrograd and Petrograd is the key to Moscow.'[6]

After the Bolsheviks had established their position and the Western powers had finally withdrawn from Russia, the Finns had to get accustomed to the idea that they themselves had to arrange their relations with the Soviet government. The task seemed impossible because the other side was regarded as a virtually proscribed state committed to the attainment of world revolution. The situation was eased in that Soviet Russia was alone, isolated and, as the war with Poland in 1920 was to demonstrate, militarily weak.

The concessions obtained from Moscow when the peace treaty of Dorpat was concluded in 1920 even aroused in Finland the dangerous illusion that the Soviet government would agree to give up permanently what the imperial government had regarded as essential for national defence, namely the bases in the Gulf of Finland, the southern part of the Karelian Isthmus and even Petsamo.

The paradox of the Dorpat treaty lay in its being simultaneously too favourable to Finland and yet branded by Finnish right-wing circles as a 'shameful peace'. Although only a very small group was in fact responsible for using the Dorpat frontiers as a pretext for exerting pressure on Finnish foreign policy, this aroused in the Soviet Union the idea of a revanchist Finland which, like many new European countries after the First World War, was ready to pursue hazardous policies to satisfy its irredentist demands.

The traditional German orientation of Finnish military and cultural circles was thus a liability as far as foreign policy was concerned. That, as well as a right-wing radicalism that was exceptionally strong by Scandinavian standards, and relations with Berlin that continued to grow closer even after 1933, naturally aroused unease in the Soviet Union, as too among the Western powers. There were indeed grounds for fear: as research has shown, Hitler had stated at the beginning of the 1930s that Finland would be a possible ally against the East.[7]

Be that as it may, Finland was classified as part of the Soviet sphere of influence in the secret protocol accompanying the Molotov-Ribbentrop pact concluded on the eve of the Second World War. There is no indication of whether Hitler even contemplated how Finland, abandoned to the Soviet Union in the division of North-eastern Europe into two spheres of influence, could ever remain as it was. As regards Finland's status in relation to the Soviet Union, the pact seemed with a single stroke of the pen to have restored the position as it had been at the beginning of 1918 before German intervention. It remains a mystery whether Stalin wanted to reunite Finland to Russia with a firmer hand than Lenin had wanted or been able to use.

The concessions demanded of Finland by Moscow in 1937 and repeated during negotiations between the two countries in the autumn of 1939 may be regarded as minimal demands in order to restore Russia's earlier strategic opportunities for action along the frontier with Finland. The territorial demands were the primary and fundamental element of these claims, limited during the final phase of negotiation to the islands near Hanko, the outer islands in the Gulf of Finland, the coast of the Gulf of Finland south of Koivisto and the western part of the Rybachy peninsula. The secondary element was a non-aggression pact, whereby each party would bind itself not to join groupings or alliances which were directly or indirectly hostile to the other party. This was a considerably less severe demand than the mutual assistance treaty previously sought by Russia.

The arguments put forward by the Soviet leaders in support of their demands as they appear in the Finnish Blue-White Book and in Paasikivi's memoirs repay the trouble of re-reading. Their military origins were clear: if, for example, 16-inch coastal artillery were located on Finnish territory at Koivisto, it would be able to close off the entry of the Red Fleet into the Gulf of Finland from the Kronstadt naval base. On the other hand Molotov's transparent assertions that the presence of Soviet troops on Finnish territory would no more violate Finland's security and neutrality than it had endangered the independence of the Baltic states to the south of the Gulf of Finland left the Finns cold. The last document sent to the Finnish negotiators by the Soviet foreign minister on 9 November 1939 ended with the sentence, 'It is clear that if the Hanko district or the islands to the east of Hanko are sold or exchanged for a corresponding area in the

Soviet Foreign Minister V.M. Molotov signing treaties at his desk: *top*, flanked by
Ribbentrop and Stalin in August 1939; *centre*, signing the treaty of assistance and friend-
ship with the Finnish Democratic Republic in December 1939 (O.V. Kuusinen,
Zhdanov, Voroshilov and Stalin are looking on); and, *bottom*, signing another treaty of
friendship, cooperation and mutual assistance in 1948, this time with representatives of the
Republic of Finland. *B, G*

Soviet Union, they could no longer be Finnish territory or within the frontiers of Finland.' This caused Paasikivi to burst out that this was 'pettifoggery'.[8]

Paasikivi drew attention to the fact that in the memorandum presented to him by the Soviet leaders at the beginning of the negotiations, the aim of the Soviet Union was defined as not only to ensure the security of Leningrad but also 'to bring Finland into a firm association with the Soviet Union on the basis of friendly relations'. The Finnish government regarded this as the next direct objective of the Soviet Union's policy towards Finland.[9]

It must be concluded even from the context of the memorandum that the Russians were more concerned with Finland than with its government. In the same way as Lenin was prepared in 1918, despite recognising Finnish independence, to support the Finnish People's Commissariat and conclude a treaty with it,[10] Stalin was ready to by-pass the lawful Finnish government. On 2 December 1939 the Soviet Union concluded a treaty of friendship and mutual assistance with the 'Provisional People's Government of Finland' led by O.V. Kuusinen. Besides fulfilling the Soviet Union's territorial demands by exchanging the areas at issue for a sizeable part of Soviet Karelia, this treaty also met the desire for a military alliance. Mannerheim drew attention in his memoirs to the proclamation made by the Kuusinen government which referred to 'the century-old desire of the Finnish people', subsequently accomplished by the treaty: 'the reunion of the Karelian people with the Finnish people, incorporating the Karelians in a united and independent Finnish state'.[11] Paasikivi for his part seized on the mutual assistance pact included in the subsequent treaty; according to this, the Finns were freed from the obligation of taking part in military operations outside their own frontiers. He regarded this as so significant that he showed it, as originally published in the paper *Bolshevik*, to Colonel-General Zhdanov in 1945, when a similar Finnish–Soviet treaty was discussed in Helsinki![12]

Thus if White Finland had attempted with Western support to expand into Eastern Karelia, the Soviets had been prepared twice over to join this area to a 'People's Finland' which was firmly linked with the Soviet Union. The relationship between the Finnish and Karelian peoples was subsequently recognised once again with the foundation, under the chairmanship of O.V. Kuusinen, of the 'Karelian–Finnish Soviet Socialist Republic' (1940–56), which some feared as the embryo of a Finnish soviet republic.

The Winter War proved a decisive stage in Finno-Soviet relations in that Moscow has never subsequently attempted to interfere with Finland's sovereign rights through by-passing its official government. The Soviet government's maintenance of the conventions of normal international relations is shown particularly in its readiness in 1944 to negotiate a new peace with much the same 'inner circle' as had been in power in 1940 and 1941. This fact seems even more remarkable because the Finnish leadership had never entered into such close contact with the enemies of the Soviet Union as during those years.

If Finland had refused to negotiate peace in March 1940 and had accepted the intervention forces offered by the Western powers, its history might have turned out very differently: there need have been no war between the Soviet Union and the Western powers, but Germany would probably have

A Soviet transport column, caught in the snow during the Winter War. *D*

attacked in the north even more rapidly than it actually did, and an isolated Finland would have suffered even more severely.

On the other hand, it must have been known to the Soviet government that Finland's war aims were limited and that the country had no wish to become mixed up in the great war then in progress, and in consequence did not want to let itself be used as a stepping-stone against any great power, the Soviet Union included. This was probably clear to the Soviet government, for example, from the fact that Mannerheim had rejected offers of White Russian volunteers whose acceptance by the Finnish army could have been interpreted as supporting anti-Soviet ideology.[13]

During preparations for the Continuation War and during the war itself, as Professor Jokipii has now comprehensively shown,[14] Finland was undeniably guilty of measures which could be regarded as offensive in character, and even aimed at the total destruction of the Soviet Union. Moreover, the future frontiers of Finland were also to be delineated in the light of the final solution of Germany's eastern question. We may suppose, too, that considerable diplomatic difficulties would have arisen later for Finland if Finnish troops under the command of General Falkenhorst had succeeded in cutting the northern part of the Murmansk railway, or if the Finnish and German offensive spearheads had succeeded in 'shaking hands' on the Svir, to say nothing of what would have happened if the Finns had participated more vigorously in the siege and destruction of Leningrad.[15]

The acceptance of Mannerheim, then president and commander-in-chief, as a negotiating partner in 1944 could even be interpreted as a sign that he had not gone too far in accommodating the wishes of his German 'brothers-in-arms'. A second, politically important motive was plainly the view that the Finns had nobody with authority comparable to Mannerheim's to lead Finland towards peace and ultimately into a third war, this time against the Germans. Mannerheim was the most conservative person possible to pilot Finland along the new political course that corresponded with the interests of the Soviet Union. In 1944 he occupied the same position as Paasikivi during the years that followed. It was of no consequence that in their time both had supported the West with all their might; Paasikivi the Germans in 1918, Mannerheim the Entente in 1919!

The mildness of the Soviet Union's policy towards Finland in 1944 may be partly explained by the fact that Moscow had no need at that time to worry about foreign intervention in the affairs of that corner of the world. At the end of the previous year Great Britain had been ready to agree to the Soviet proposal to demand Finland's unconditional surrender! There was no need for Stalin to listen to the United States which had broken off relations with Finland but had not declared war. If at that point the Soviet government abandoned its original demand and accepted that it could negotiate peace terms with Finland, this happened without pressure from the Allies. However, with the future in mind, the most important reason for the change may have been the strengthening resistance of the Finnish armed forces at the decisive moment in July 1944. The Soviet army's offensive was halted and Finland was never occupied.

The fact that Finland preserved its identity, did not let itself be carried along by the current, and looked after its own affairs with self-restraint up to the end of the armistice period has provoked many questions and explanations. One of the most decisive factors in this miracle must be the way the nation's moral fibre withstood the test, although even Paasikivi had doubts about this on many occasions. No vendetta, terror or any other kind of political disorder worth mentioning occurred after the leftists had come back from underground, from the camps and prisons, and after those members of the armed forces who had not reconciled themselves to the armistic had been transferred to civil life. The nation held together.

No post-war revolution or coup d'état — or even an attempted one — took place in Finland, although the possibility of one taking place was used as a scare tactic in the skirmishing of Finnish internal politics. Nor was an anti-war opposition movement born in which the communists would have found allies among anti-fascist social democrats and non-socialists.

In circumstances such as these, an attempted revolution would probably have led to a scenario approximating to a civil war. There were in the country about 400,000 trained and battle-tried soldiers, of whom a small minority were communists. A significant proportion of the arms hidden secretly at the end of the war and also of the weapons that had vanished when the Civil Guards were disbanded, as well as weapons taken home from the front as 'souvenirs', had disappeared without trace; and both the army and the police were under tight government surveillance. The frontiers with Sweden and Norway were difficult to control and this would have facilitated foreign intervention in the conflict, perhaps even by the Western powers after 1948.

The most powerful argument that the Finnish communists could not even have been expected to attempt a revolution is the strong influence of the Communist Party of the Soviet Union over the Finnish Communist Party and the fact that violent change in Finland did not accord with Soviet interests. Reasons for this were the uninterrupted course of war reparations deliveries, the willingness of the Finnish government to accommodate Soviet vital interests such as the defensive needs of Russia's north-western frontier, the need not to provoke Sweden into alliance with the West, and perhaps even the views of the Western powers themselves.

It is clear that no firm agreement between the Soviet Union and the Western powers had been reached about the future position of Finland. It had already moved away to the sidelines of military activity by the time of the Yalta conference in February 1945, so there was no reason to put it on the agenda. Instead Finland had the honour of organising the first free elections in accordance with the Declaration on Liberated Europe approved by the conference, and thus became for a little while a model for Germany's former allies which had begun a new life in the democratic spirit of the United Nations.[16]

Although an Allied Control Commission was established in 1944 to supervise the carrying out of the terms of the armistice, up to the end of 1945 Finland had to make its way entirely alone in settling with the Soviet Union not only its final wartime accounts but also its political relations. Finland's sole economic backer at this time was Sweden which for a year after the armistice continued its wartime relief work and the granting of credits. On the other hand, no aid worth mentioning was received from the United States during the first year of peace, although the official desire for aid had already been put forward during preparations for the armistice negotiations.[17]

Despite the possibility that the Americans may have known that Stalin had encouraged Finland to ask the West for economic aid,[18] the United States refrained from granting any credits until December 1945. This seems to have been an attempt to avoid all possible causes of friction with the Soviet Union which could upset its war effort; Stalin had promised to join the war against Japan as well, and this phase came to an end only three months after the end of the war in Europe.

A second significant reason was an American unwillingness in principle to assist countries falling within the Soviet sphere of influence, particularly when they had to pay war reparations to their former enemy. However, in November 1945 a fundamental change occurred in this respect. When the Americans received Finnish negotiators seeking credit in Washington the following month, they told them that credit would be given solely on the express condition that it was not used to finance war reparations. Although this principle was maintained in future and the embassy in Helsinki scrutinised in detail the credits given to Finland and the use of export licences, the impression remains that the Americans knew very well that these credits indirectly, and perhaps decisively, eased the fulfilment of war reparations.

The possibility that arose in the summer of 1947 of participating in the European reconstruction programme started by the Americans put the new Finnish foreign policy through a real baptism of fire. The Marshall Plan aroused public expectations in Finland, perhaps because it was regarded as a possible means of loosening the frightening ties that had developed in relations with the East and gaining support, at any rate in economic respects, from the West.

President Paasikivi seems quickly to have perceived the political implications of the offer but, as a banker, to have hoped to the last that Finland, too, would be able to get its hands on the promised free dollars. It could no longer be said that Finland had a real need for foreign currency. Demand for paper products had grown steeply and Finnish production was working at full speed on exports to the west. 'Export industry is now earning terribly well,' Paasikivi noted in his diary on 8 June. 'Exports this year will possibly rise to 250 million dollars.'[19]

As is well known, the Soviet Union refused to take part in the aid programme, which it interpreted as part of United States attempts at domination, nor did in allow participation by the countries in its sphere of influence. Understanding that acceptance of the Western powers' invitation to take part could lead to the collapse of relations with the east, rebuilt with difficulty, and perhaps also to postponement of ratification of the final peace treaty signed the previous February (and which would mean the Allied Control Commission staying on in Helsinki), the president dictated the government's decision to reject the offer. The decision about Marshall aid gave direction to later comparable decisions in Finnish foreign policy. It has become a principle to conduct economic relations with the West in such a way that they have not strained political relations with the East, which have taken priority.

An unpredictable consideration when Paasikivi was making this decision in 1947 had been the possibility that the Western powers would respond to Finland's refusal by breaking off economic relations and freezing dollar credits already granted. However, the Finnish minister in London, Eero A. Wuori, had been able to obtain reliable information, before matters had been decided, that no retaliatory measures were to be expected.[20]

The Western powers had a categorical interest in keeping Finland within the sphere of their economic aid in spite of the fact that the country could not formally approve of the Marshall Plan because of its special position. Despite the losses it had suffered during the war, Finland was the most important producer of newsprint in Europe and a particularly notable producer of cellulose. Because its war reparations deliveries were largely based on metal industry production, paper and wood products were saved for export and acted at a critical phase as a real trump card in developing economic relations with the West. The State Department was still claiming in 1948 that Finland's exports were of great importance in implementing the European reconstruction programme, and that Finland was taking an active part in trade with Western Europe and the United States to the mutual benefit of all the countries concerned.[21]

Paasikivi found that the most difficult problem in preparing for negotiations about the Treaty of Friendship, Cooperation and Mutual Assistance proposed by Stalin in 1948 was once more the question of how the Western powers would react to a military pact. The decision was not eased by the pressure exerted by the United States' representatives in Helsinki, which included economic threats. Although the Finns thought they noticed that the Americans were making exports to Finland difficult, for example by delaying licences for the Westinghouse turbines intended for the Karihaara power station, this was a misconception.[22]

Even before the parliamentary elections of July 1948 the State Department issued general instructions that Finland was to be treated differently from the so-called satellite countries because the Americans hoped not only to maintain but also to increase the independence of the Finns as far as opportunities allowed. For this reason the United States favoured measures aimed at assisting Finland in fulfilling its obligations, and thus depriving the Soviet Union of the possibility of increased control over the country which could result from applying the penalty clauses in the Finno-Soviet compensation agreement.[23]

Competition between the Americans and the Soviets for the sympathy of the Finns intensified as the elections approached. Dollar credits obtained from the United States alone since the war amounted to well over $100 million by the beginning of July, at which point — a week before the elections — one half of the total $300 million (at 1938 prices) required in Finnish war reparations deliveries had been accomplished. Moreover the Soviet Union had stated in June that it was cutting by one half the amount of outstanding war reparations deliveries. At the same time the Western embassies in Helsinki — even the British, who were then being moved out of the leading position among Western powers by the Americans — intensified their propaganda activity. With the help of Finns opposed to the People's Democrats they spread reports giving warnings about the Communists, referring for example to events in Czechoslovakia.[24]

After the general election, only three months after Finland had concluded the Treaty of Friendship, Cooperation and Mutual Assistance with
the Soviet Union, the defeated People's Democrats were dropped from the
Finnish government. This occurrence conflicted completely with the
course of events in other countries on the western borders of the Soviet
Union, and the world considered it sensational. Although the decision was
condemned in the Soviet press, even as contrary to the spirit of the Friendship Treaty, the Soviet government did not intervene in events. By the
same token the People's Democrats had to manage without foreign
support. They had to get used to the fact that even though they had the
opportunity, after a long period in opposition, to share the responsibility
of government between 1966 and 1981, they were no longer entrusted
with the most important portfolios.[25]

Disentanglement from the Communists also determined finally the attitude of Britain and the United States towards the position of Finland. In
October 1948 Paasikivi noted in his diary that Wuori had reported that
Finland was no longer classified as a 'satellite state'. Nine months after the
signature of the Treaty of Friendship, Cooperation and Mutual Assistance,
the State Department was already prepared to classify Finland once more as
a Scandinavian instead of an 'East European' country.[26]

In the early 1950s, it was not just Washington that contemplated the
possibility of Finland sliding into the Western camp. The Soviet mass
media also artfully made clear their fear that the Fagerholm government
then in office would prepare the country to join the Marshall aid organisation and perhaps even the newly-founded Atlantic alliance. During succeeding governments dominated by Urho Kekkonen, however, the exact
opposite was predicted. The commercial treaties concluded with the Soviet
Union after war reparations had ended, and long-range economic cooperation in particular, aroused questions as to whether Finland was becoming
imprudently dependent on the East.[27]

Finland's credibility underwent a particular trial in 1958 when the
communist-led People's Democratic League, which had won in the elections, was kept out of the government by President Kekkonen's appoint-
ment of a cabinet dominated by the social democrats and the conservatives.
During the ensuing 'night frost crisis' the United States ambassador in
Helsinki offered Finland the opportunity of obtaining economic aid in the
event of the Soviet Union cutting off its exports altogether.

Although this encouraging gesture does not seem even to have been discussed, Washington was convinced that the Finns would stay afloat. In its
policy paper on Finland the National Security Council emphasised that the

Finns had maintained their democratic institutions intact. Despite Soviet pressure, they had skilfully avoided participation in Soviet-backed endeavours such as the Warsaw Pact. Moreover, the Finns had so far maintained and to some extent strengthened their economic links with the Western powers.[28]

Confidence in Finland's ability to maintain its own position in the future and its way of life between east and west was increased in particular by the continued attempts Finland deliberately made in the early 1960s to strengthen its commercial interests in the west, while simultaneously placing added emphasis on its neutral position and beginning to modernise and strengthen its armed forces with the support of Great Britain and the Soviet Union as signatories of the peace treaty. On the other hand doubts arose because of the frighteningly strong development of trading ties with the Soviet Union, the strengthened position of the communists, and President Kekkonen's well-known peace initiatives to the Scandinavian countries, which the Americans regarded as aimed expressly at weakening NATO.

The view of Finland prevailing at that time in the National Security Council was favourable, if hesitant and distant:

The measures which can be taken in support of Finland are limited because of the danger of Soviet counter-measures and Finland's determination to attempt to avoid that danger. While there is thus little possibility, short of a situation in which Finland's independence is endangered, of bringing about a dramatic or major change in the Finnish situation, it is clearly in the interest of the United States, as well as the Free World in general, to continue efforts to strengthen Finland's independence and Free World orientation.[29]

This analysis, together with many of the American confidential documents previously cited, shows that the position of Finland between east and west was not so self-evident even after the Second World War as many pessimists have imagined. Undoubtedly the neutral road is a lonely one, so much so that even the other neutral European countries do not offer lasting company; all of these have in their status and policies their own individual character, needs and independence.

The neutrality policy, characterised as 'active peace-seeking', which Finland has pursued since the beginning of the 1970s has nevertheless obtained results which could not even have been dreamed about in the 1950s and 1960s. It has increased Finland's international standing and strengthened its position between East and West. In contrast with earlier times, when Finland drifted into dependence on either East or West if it

was confronted by danger, it is at present at a safe distance from both — as
distant as it is possible to be in the modern world. And Finland is correspondingly more independent than ever before.

## NOTES

1. Sven Lindman, *Eduskunnan aseman muuttuminen 1917–1919*, Suomen kansanedustuslaitoksen historia, 6, Helsinki 1968, p. 206.
2. G. v. Wendt, 'Finlands inträde som erkänd stat in staternas krets — Utdrag ur anteckningar från december–januari 1917–18', *Hufvudstadsbladet*, 4 Jan. 1938. Tuomo Polvinen, *Venäjän vallankumous ja Suomi 1917–1920*, Porvoo and Helsinki 1967, pp. 174–7.
3. Cf. Polvinen, p. 173, and T. Torvinen, *Autonomian ajan senaatti* (Valtioneuvoston historia 1917–1966, 1), Helsinki 1978, p. 181.
4. Cf. Jukka Nevakivi, *Muurmannin legioona — suomalaiset ja liittoutuneiden interventio Pohjois-Venäjälle*, Helsinki 1970, p. 16 footnote, and the source mentioned there.
5. Cf. Mauno Jääskeläinen, *Itä-Karjalan kysymys*, Porvoo and Helsinki 1961, pp. 148–57.
6. See V.P. Potiemkine, *Histoire de la diplomatie*, 3, Paris, 19, p. 67, where the author quotes word for word the final sentence of *The Times*'s leading article.
7. Jukka Nevakivi, 'The Great Powers and Finland's Winter War. Aspects of Security — the Case of Independent Finland', *Revue Internationale d'Histoire Militaire*, 62, 1985, p. 59, and the source mentioned there.
8. V.V. Tanner, *Olin ulkoministerinä talvisodan aikana*, Helsinki 1951, p. 128.
9. J.K. Paasikivi, *Toimintani Moskovassa ja Suomessa 1939–41*, Porvoo and Helsinki 1958, p. 51.
10. On Lenin's demand the 'Republic of Finland' was changed in the treaty to 'the Socialist Workers' Republic of Finland', although this constitutional change was not implemented in Red Finland. See Osmo Rinta-Tassi, *Kansanvaltuuskunta punaisen Suomen hallituksena*, Helsinki 1986, p. 423.
11. G. Mannerheim, *Muistelmat*, Helsinki 1952, II, p. 143.
12. *J.K. Paasikiven päiväkirjat 1944–1956*, edited by Yrjö Blomstedt and Matti Klinge, Porvoo, Helsinki and Juva 1985, p. 153.
13. See Jukka Nevakivi, *The Appeal That Was Never Made: The Allies, Scandinavia and the Finnish Winter War, 1939–1940*, London 1976, p. 174 footnote.
14. Mauno Jokipii, *Jatkosodan synty — Tutkimuksia Saksan ja Suomen sotilaallisesta yhteistyöstä 1940–41*, Helsinki 1987.
15. Jukka Nevakivi, *Ystävistä vihollisiksi — Suomi Englannin politiikassa 1940–1941*, Helsinki 1976, p. 187.
16. Cf. Tuomo Polvinen, *Suomi kansainvälisessä politiikassa 2: 1945–1947 — Jaltasta Pariisin rauhaan*, Porvoo, Helsinki and Juva 1961, pp. 15 and 48–9.
17. See the author's article in *Suomen Kuvalehti*, 5 Dec. 1986: 'Suomi — vähäosaisten vapauden patsas', p. 20. Unless otherwise mentioned, the following interpretation is based on the material cited in that article.
18. Cf *Paasikiven päiväkirjat*, I, p. 119.
19. *Ibid.*, p. 461.
20. Jukka Nevakivi, *Maanalaista diplomatiaa vuosilta 1944–1948 jolloin kylmä sota teki tuloaan Pohjolaan*, Helsinki 1983, p. 81, and in the following source.
21. Commercial Counsellor Willis C. Armstrong to Leonard Morey, Morey Machinery Co. Inc., New York, 23.6.1948; doc. 611.60 D/15/5 2248, National Archives [NA], Washington.
22. See *Paasikiven päiväkirjat*, I, p. 604. On the Treaty of Friendship, Cooperation and Mutual

Assistance in general and its consequences, see the author's paper to the Swedish Royal Academy of Military Science (Kungl. Krigsvetenskapsakademien) on 13 May 1986: 'J.K. Paasikivi och VSB-pakten', published in *Kungl. Krigsvetenskapsakademiens handlingar och tidskrift*, 4, 1986, pp. 231–9.

23. Daily Staff Officers Summary 19 June 1948; RG 59: General Records of the Office of the Executive Secretariat (box 6), NA.

24. See Nevakivi 1983, p. 138.

25. See the author's article in the collection entitled *Paasikiven hirmuiset vuodet — Suomi 1944–1948*, Helsinki 1986, p. 174.

26. Memorandum of the State Department representatives to the Chairman: R Procedure Subcommittee of the Department of Commerce; doc. no. R/ROC/COC M–33, RG 151: General files, Trade export 21–1 Finland, NA. For Wuori's observation see *Paasikiven päiväkirjat*, I, p. 667.

27. As appears from the author's research on the reports of the U.S. embassy in Helsinki in general.

28. National Security Council, 'U.S. Policy Toward Finland', NSC 6024, 30 Dec. 1960 (p. 5); Eisenhower Library, Abilene, Kansas.

29. Ibid., p. 6.

Faces in the crowd. The revolutionary events of the national strike in November 1905 brought politics into the street. Here, a revealing cross-section of Finnish society has been captured by the photographer in Senate Square, Helsinki. *E*

# THE INTELLIGENTSIA, THE STATE
# AND THE NATION

## Risto Alapuro

It can be argued that populism and a fixation with the state have been the predominant themes of Finnish intellectual history from the latter half of the nineteenth century, when the opening up of political life helped shape the conditions for the emergence of intellectuals as moulders of ideology. A central question till after the Second World War has been the standing of the educated class as a representative of the nation in relation to the state, as a listener and formulator of the nation's voice, and as an intermediary between nation and state.

Compared to this, the liberal strain has clearly been secondary — both as a struggle for the widening of the individual's political rights and the strengthening of representative institutions against the state, and as the critical intellectual tradition emphasising its own autonomy.

Liberation from political dependence was at the heart of the nationalism of Europe's small nationalities in the nineteenth century. The demands of autonomist nationalism were in many cases liberal. They aimed at broader political rights and the guarantee of fundamental laws against repressive ruling nations and foreign or local bureaucracies. The Czechs' freedom movement is often referred to as 'bourgeois nationalism' and the same holds true for the movements of many other minority nationalities of the Habsburg empire. An example closer to Finland is that of the liberal Young Estonian Movement at the beginning of the twentieth century.

Liberal political demands were however of secondary importance in the Finnish nationalist movement, although it too is usually regarded as dedicated to the cause of autonomist nationalism. The main wing of the movement, known as *Fennomani*, did not demand liberation from the state's suffocating structure, but was focused on the state. Its anti-bureaucratic tendency was above all inspired by the need to attack Swedish, the language of the bureaucrats.

For the Finnish nationalists the nation became synonymous with the state; the development of the former would be realised through the latter. As a good Hegelian J.V. Snellman, the formulator of the movement's ideals, saw the state as an area where individuals behave according to a moral code and work to promote the good of all. 'Political man or 'a citizen of a state' was for Snellman the kind of practitioner of free civil

147

action who regards the wellbeing of everyone as his responsibility, and identifies with the nation.[1] Snellman's intellectual idea was thus state-centred. His most important successor, Z. Yrjö-Koskinen, saw the state as not only 'an association founded for purposes of utility' but 'the very frame of the nation's life, created by the nation according to its power and needs in order to fulfil some unique purpose in the world'.[2] The Finnish nationalist movement, which he led, saw itself as 'a state party' and aimed at strengthening the 'nation-state'.

This ideology correlated well with the situation in Finland. Unlike almost all other minority nationality areas, Finland *already was* a state, or at least possessed advanced administrative and political institutions in a period of growing public awareness and involvement. The emperor Alexander I had created a grand duchy out of the Finnish-speaking areas he had conquered in the course of the Napoleonic wars. The administration and economic structures of the grand duchy of Finland were strengthened during the nineteenth century. The nationalist movement there did not need to fight to bring about a separate political status; its task lay in reinforcing the existing institutions *vis-à-vis* Russia and in the creation of a nation and ideology corresponding to a state.

A central issue was the building of a cultural connection between the educated class and the nation. 'The people' meant above all an independent peasantry. The Finnish nationalists sought to form an alliance with the 'Finnish people', in other words to create a system of values in which the Finnish-speaking educated class took the central role and which was founded on a prosperous peasantry. A nation had to be created by replacing the Swedish and bilingual upper class which Finland inherited from the times of Swedish rule with a Finnish-speaking upper class, linked to the people by language and outlook, and by advancing and cultivating the nation's cultural strength. Because the nationality struggle was in the first place about culture, it was the cultural affiliations of individuals in power which became the focus of attention rather than the bureaucratic power structure as such. Although the Swedish-language bureaucrats were attacked, there was no assault on the existing set-up itself.

In this struggle the nationalist intellectuals endeavoured to promote the nation's affairs by appropriating the existing state. In many cases it was only a short step from the intellectual hotbed of Helsinki University to the top echelons of political life. Both Snellman and Yrjö-Koskinen made the transition from the University to membership of the Senate, the government of the grand duchy. Both were also ennobled.

The course pursued by the intellectuals can be explained by the fact that

The intellectuals meeting the people. Two students buying 'national' costumes from a festively-dressed farmer and his wife. Painted in Düsseldorf by Arvid Liljelund, 1878. *B*

not only the intelligentsia but also the entire upper class lacked a strong base outside the structures of state. A true land-owning upper class like that of Hungary or the Baltic provinces did not exist. It was the civil service, the administrative machinery of the grand duchy, which provided employment and sustenance for 'persons of quality' in Finland. The peasants owned the land and were therefore the dominant land-owning class. The class structure was the same type as in Scandinavia. A responsiveness towards the demands of the peasantry or an attempt to win their loyalty was just as natural as an overwhelming concern with the state. From the foregoing it follows that many intellectuals were linguistic converts. The entire *Fennomani* movement was drawn from the Swedish-speaking educated class.

The basic political outlook of *Fennomani* was conservative. In the Finnish four-estate parliament, which had evolved during the Swedish period and existed right up to the beginning of the twentieth century, the independent peasantry was represented as one estate alongside the nobility, the clergy and the burghers. Although according to Snellman the political power of the peasantry should increase, 'in fact' Finland was already 'a democratic country'. 'This follows simply from the fact that the soil is owned by the peasant. . . . What has been achieved in most other European countries by centuries of effort or by revolution — the freeing of the mass of the people to give them an independent social position — has always existed . . . in Finland,' Snellman wrote in 1862.[3] Yrjö-Koskinen did not regard political representation as a combination of political interests, but stood for the theory of virtual representation. There existed a general will which was not created out of the clash of particular wills, and so the extent of political rights was not for him a central problem.

The national task of the intellectuals was both populist and patriarchal. It was populist in the sense that the educated class had to be culturally at one with the nation; *Fennomani* had a certain 'love of the masses'. But at the same time it was patriarchal in the sense that intellectuals had to raise the nation to maturity and do so explicitly through the state. Both notions were to be found in the concept of the unity of the state and nation.

The dependence on Russia also makes this task understandable. The right way to make the country's position stronger was to strengthen the nation, to develop Finnish culture and so ensure the country's existence. The wrong way was to raise a racket by aspiring for political freedom or — just as damaging — to drift into open conflict with the Russian empire. A certain kind of internally structured self-control was required. Realism was part and parcel of building the state and being responsible for it. It was a realism which looked out for anything that might threaten the basic interest — the development of the nation. The contrast with Polish nationalism is very striking; it too was subordinated to Russia, but it produced a heroic struggle for freedom and even the idea of redeeming nations through sacrifice.

The largely Swedish-speaking liberal intelligentsia in nineteenth-century Finland were also not without significance. But their liberalism was of an economic and aristocratic nature and not politically radical. The premise for opposing a bureaucratic conservatism did not arise because, first, the bureaucracy participated in the creation of national coherence and, secondly, the liberals penetrated the leading positions in the state administration with very little difficulty. In Finland the liberals did not need to organise an oppositional group activity in which wide civic circles might have used constitutional arguments. They simply did not need the support of popular movements as in many other countries. As a consequence, existing institutions were defended on constitutional grounds and, when relations with Russia became strained, this line of defence tended to see demands for social reforms as detrimental. As a result, that section of civil society which is generally capable of independent organisation and critical discussion remained weak in nineteenth-century Finland.

Rather than promote the extension of political rights, the Finnish nationalists tried to serve the good of the nation by organising mass movements in order to educate and elevate the peasantry to become useful members of society. In these associations were united 'a patriarchal-conservative conception of society and the new idea of free civic activity' — a description given to the Finnish nationalists' first organisation founded in 1874 with the aim of providing wide education, the Society for the Advancement of Popular Education for the People.[4] These societies performed a kind of administrative function and were a mainstay of the prevailing social order. They also offered the peasantry the possibility to shape their own demands and interests.

Both aspects were important in the temperance movement, the largest formally organised movement at the end of the nineteenth century. It received state aid, Finnish-nationalist intellectuals served in its top echelons, and the local leadership consisted mostly of teachers, the clergy and freehold farmers. Country people, workers in industry and craftsmen formed the greater part of the membership. It embodied the central ideals of Finnish nationalism in that it was an attempt to promote organisations within the sphere of the state, to educate the people, and to push demands for legislative reforms.[5]

But the ideology of the temperance movement also corresponded to the peasants' requirements and needs; it was rooted in the peasants' own set of values and was thus familiar to wide groups. At the same time, it helped politicise distress and suffering, because it proposed steps to combat drunkenness, which gave the common people the opportunity to think of their own problems as social problems. The temperance movement was also directly linked to the creation of the workers' movement in Finland. It was probably more important in the initial stages of the socialist workers' movement than the workers' associations founded by the liberals.[6]

These nationalist-inspired popular movements opened the way to the politicisation of the common people, but they also had a moderating influence on the process of organisation. A graphic example is provided by Tampere, the country's largest industrial centre. There the temperance movement was the workers' first and only mass movement in the nineteenth century. 'The *Fennomani* of the working people' was evident as early as the 1860s, and the Tampere working men's association was for a long time a cultural movement, a continuation of working-class *Fennomani*.[7] At the beginning of the twentieth century, the socialist workers' movement was small in Finland, and the nationalist-inspired awakening of the people was to prove significant for its development.

At this time, then, the intelligentsia's vision of the solidarity between itself — the educated class — and the people was still strong. No serious conflicts had disturbed this image in any way, but the years 1905–7 dented that image. The Russian government's momentary loss of strength in the 1905 revolution led to a national strike and a great wave of activity in Finland. The workers' movement increased its membership many times over, and one of Europe's most backward political systems was transformed at a stroke into a unicameral parliament elected by a general franchise. The social democrats became the largest party in the new parliament. The end-result of these events was the shattering of the image of the 'people'; fear, doubt and uncertainty began to creep in, as the people seemed to step for the first time outside the intellectuals' defined notion. As this did not correspond to the idealised vision of the intellectuals, so the intelligentsia's picture of themselves became bruised.

However, it is easy to exaggerate the potency of the change. Viewed with the benefit of hindsight, the challenge was more constrained than it seemed in the confusion. The magnitude of the change was also due to the exceedingly tight constraints and the backwardness of the political and civic superstructure of the grand duchy. A long stride was taken in the reform of the political system, but nonetheless it was only the completion of the work of organisation set in motion by the Finnish nationals and the liberals. Many young liberals regarded most forms of activity in the workers' movement favourably because, in its own way, the workers' movement had participated in completing the political structure of the country from a base which had already been laid down. 'The socialist workers' movement continued the same line as the Finnish nationalists in educating the people but drew the line at a bourgeois society.' The originality of working-class culture was not so much its content as 'the fact that while assembling at the workers' hall, the poor folk collectively shaped their own place in the community and in society'.[8]

It is enlightening to compare the case of the Baltic lands. In 1905 the power-vacuum led to the eruption there of violence in the countryside. Churches were looted and nobles murdered. In Livonia and Courland more than one-third of the manor houses were destroyed or suffered serious damage. In Finland the same power-vacuum in Russia led to the creation of parties, unions and associations, the 'nationalising' of political life and the evolution of lawful norms. The Social Democratic Party's few intellectuals came mostly from the Finnish nationalist intelligentsia, and its political activity was concentrated within the framework of a political system. In relations with Russia it was more resolute than most other parties. In 1913 J.K. Paasikivi of the Old Finn party, a leading Finnish nationalist and later Finland's seventh president, reflected that in due course the social democrats would evolve as 'a radical progressive party'.[9]

The breakthrough achieved by bourgeois cultural liberalism at the beginning of the century helped to make the abruptness of the change easier for the intellectuals to bear. Debate about sexual morality and marriage as an institution was more passionate than ever before, and in the period following the Great Strike, Swedish-speaking cultural radicals and Finnish-speaking liberals made proposals for separating church and state. The Great Strike thereby instigated debate about cultural changes and about a new kind of ideological structure among the intellectuals.

However, the Great Strike crisis did not produce a political liberal challenge. Finland did not have to undergo the kind of lengthy struggle for extending political rights such as that which — in Scandinavia, for example — united the liberals and the workers' movement. Thanks to the 1905 revolution, political reform was achieved with relative ease, and without the liberals and social democrats ever actually forming a united front. In the nineteenth century a critical intellectual tradition independent or critical of the state did not arise because the essential question was the strengthening of the state in relation to Russia. Moreover, it was easy for the intellectuals to penetrate the state structure. No such tradition was generated at the beginning of the twentieth century either, because internal democratisation occurred painlessly without a struggle against the state lasting many decades. In both instances, Finland's dependence on the Russian empire played a decisive part.

When the First World War broke out, the nationalists' assumptions about the alliance of the intelligentsia and the people, with the intelligentsia acting as the spiritual leaders of the nation, still remained largely relevant. They were part of the ideology of the nation which the intelligentsia had created during the preceding half-century.

Equipped with this view of their role in society, the intelligentsia were unusually poorly prepared for the blow they received in 1918. In January the Social Democratic Party staged an attempted revolution, which was defeated three months later. 'The people', who were supposed to share the aspirations of the educated class, seemed to have planted a knife in its back.

Fraternity and liberty. Russian troops in Helsinki during the summer of 1917. The banner
on the left hails free Finland and Russia, the Finnish-language banner on the right greets
the free Finnish people and urges all peoples to unite in what would seem to be the free
workers' state.

The insurrection was incomprehensible and at the same time a terrible
violation. It was a shock particularly for the Finnish-speaking educated
class; all that it stood for seemed to come into question. The experience
undoubtedly explains an important part of the excesses of the White terror
at the end of the war and the extreme distress in prison camps after it.

The incomprehensibility of the insurrection might be due to the fact that
the conflicts that preceded the war never really came to a head. The
workers' movement in Finland was far removed from the kind of revolutionary inclination such as was present in the Russian workers' movement.
In fact the years 1917 and 1918 severed the political development which
fundamentally had a close resemblance to that of Scandinavia. The two
sides drifted into war — explicitly drifted — for no other reason (putting
it briefly) than the fact that the state of Finland had no coercive mechanism
in 1917. Because of the Russian revolution, the basic protection given by
Russia to the prevailing social order was lost — as was the domestic

authority, the 'russianised' police. In these circumstances and with a majority in parliament and in government, the workers' movement could not be brushed aside without it forming an alternative centre of power. This gave those conflicts which existed the possibility of becoming critical. Ultimately the war came about because the workers' movement did not voluntarily consent to resign in 1917 and give up the position it had won. Already the advantages gained and the defence of its own power centre drove relatively moderate social democrats into becoming reluctant revolutionaries.

The Finnish revolution was not preceded by a ruling culture in decay, as was the case with the French and Russian revolutions. These were indeed also cultural revolutions which set up completely different ideological structures. In contrast to Finland, strong subversive patterns of thinking had already developed in these countries before the upheavals, and finally in the revolution itself the legitimacy of the old system was swept away. The entire system of values, which defined social reality and social relations, collapsed. A new symbolic system, which had been developed earlier by the intellectuals, was thrust to the fore. It made a new order seem reasonable and in part even self-evidently necessary.

In Finland almost the opposite situation prevailed. A relatively new national system of values was apparent in intellectual circles. Therefore an analysis of the crisis that had taken place was impossible, because the intellectuals lacked the necessary conceptual arsenal. A critical study of the war was not made for many decades. The Finnish revolution was different from many others in that practically the entire intelligentsia opposed it.

The main legacy of the civil war for everyone concerned was a bad conscience which nothing could entirely wipe clean. The unavoidable fact of the 'people' taking part in an insurrection and the victor's bloody revenge was an impediment to an unambiguous heroic interpretation taking shape. The war did not produce anything authentically positive, as a struggle justified in terms of a prevalent system of values could have done.

The problem was exacerbated by the fact that just before the civil war Finland had proclaimed its independence, and relations with Soviet Russia brought into focus the need for close cooperation between the nation and the state. National unity was depressingly shattered just at the moment when it seemed more essential than ever before.

The activities of the educated class in the inter-war period and for a long time after the Second World War can be seen as a reaction to the traumatic shattering of their nationalistic-populist self-image in 1918, and as attempts to reconstruct their lost contact with the people. The conflict itself was not always evident; it was, rather, imperceptible and unexpressed, a fundamental fact just beneath the surface, which could not make or was incapable of making a direct encounter. It was the inability of the ruling culture to face up to this that loaded it with significance.

Practically the only area in which this cultural malaise could be expressed and the experience of the civil war dealt with openly was in literature, which had traditionally been the chronicler of the sensitive relations between the educated echelon and the people. The best analysis of society in the inter-war period is to be found in its pages. The most important works turn repeatedly to themes of the agrarian people or the working class and their relations with others, often with members of the educated class. If the picture of the people is not always pretty, neither is it so of Finland's young educated class, 'the transferees from the backwoods' as one of the writers, Joel Lehtonen, depicted their members. Identifying with the people was problematical, but so also was support for the ruling nationalistic ideology. Irony, disappointment or self-critical overtones were commonly resorted to by many writers.

In lyric poetry the new generation's most essential experience after 1918 was one of 'a state of intellectual bankruptcy'. The poetry of the 1920s was almost totally unhistorical and rejected the immediate past — a revealing choice. It wanted to start a new page: 'the young poets did not want to or could not be on the side of the victors or losers' but steered a course away from everyday reality towards a fraternal ideal with no national borders and illusions, which was thought to have positive values.[10]

But political reaction to the events of 1918 could only begin from the existing base of nationalistic ideology; once more, the attempt was made to unite the people and the educated class. Now the legacy of the nineteenth century acted quite unambiguously against the working class. Entrapped by an 'un-national' ideal, the working people were in fact excluded from the nation. The 1918 attempt at revolution became a war of liberation against Russia, in which a large section of the working class had declared in favour of the principal enemy, Bolshevik Russia.

The old precepts of Finnish nationalism did however spawn a variety of attitudes. Conservative, national patriotism was prevalent among the older generation and, for example, in the universities. The Finnish Civil Guard became a central national institution actively supported by all non-socialist groups, an armed class-based organisation alongside the army. The most important response of the young Finnish-speaking educated class drew upon the populist line of the nationalist legacy. The activists in the Academic Karelian Society (AKS), the principal student movement of the period, wanted to wash away the 'bad dream' of 1918. In many ways they duplicated themes of the nineteenth century. They too resolved to construct a united 'Finnish national state' and to legitimise a system of values which would give the Finnish-speaking educated class a central role in it. In the 1920s, as before, the way forward was perceived through the idealisation of the peasants and in the name of the peasantry. And like the Finnish nationalists of the nineteenth century the AKS criticised those in power but ignored the structure of power as such. In the 1920s impassioned attempts to find a connection with the 'people' were based above all on the Agrarian Party, at the time the largest non-socialist party. The AKS wanted to win the working class over to the populist-nationalist system of values and, in the 1920s at least, supported social reforms. They even sought connections with the social democrats. After Hitler's coming to power in the 1930s their aims took on a fascist tinge. They wanted to construct an integrated nation by common consent — the Finnish equivalent of *Volksgemeinschaft* — by changing the state in a corporative direction.

At the beginning of the 1930s the semi-fascist Lapua movement — which was regarded as a movement of farmers — also propelled young educated people towards fascism. When this movement seemed to be returning to the kind of White solidarity of 1918, the longed-for unity with the people seemed to have arrived. The greater part of the AKS followed it with enthusiasm.

Finland lacked the basic preconditions for the kind of reaction spawned at the end of the First World War by the threat of revolution in several East European countries. In the country's peasant-dominated social structure, the upper class occupied a weaker position than in countries with a feudal past; the continued serious threat from the East also guaranteed that the question of the nation's solidarity continued to be a genuine and painful problem. Reaction thus lacked a proper structural base. But the experience of the civil war had driven the educated people to attempt a reconciliation, with resources which were insufficient for solving the problem.

The outcome of the Second World War meant that the question of relations between the educated class and the people had to be tackled anew. The armistice agreement with the Soviet Union banned organisations such as the Civil Guard and the AKS. The communists were to be permitted to function openly, and they became a strong political force. The compromised wartime political leaders had to go, and openly anti-Soviet activity, which had been linked to anti-communism at home, was no longer possible.

*Above*, swearing the sacred oath at a meeting of the Academic Karelian Society in 1935. *B Below*, a left-wing view of an AKS meeting. The speaker declares: 'Yes, brothers and comrades, Finland ought to be great! Here's a map, but it's far too small . . . If I had a globe, I'd show you, boys, our fatherland's natural frontiers!' (*Kurikka*, Helsinki 1926)

But in Finland, unlike the other Western neighbours of the Soviet Union, where communist parties had been banned between the world wars, the political system survived intact, as did the groups which dominated cultural life. Bourgeois hegemony was strong in the important cultural institutions, particularly the University, where the leading figures were students in the 1920s and 1930s. The first reaction to the politics of reconciliation with the communists and the Soviet Union was one of prickly defensiveness.

The 1930s-style small left-wing groupings which were revived in the immediate post-war period suffered a rapid demise. At first, left-wing cultural activity was spirited but it had already faded by the end of the 1940s. Those left-wing intellectuals who tried to establish relations with the people by seeking a connection through the national line of the nineteenth century received no sympathy from the educated class. For Raoul Palmgren, a left-wing intellectual of the 1930s, the welcoming of the educated class into the left-wing workers' movement meant the educated returning to the service of the nation becoming in some respects its spiritual leaders. In his book *Suuri Linja* (1948) Palmgren deliberated on this problem, as had the young nationalistic educated class of the inter-war period, but his solution took a socialist form. Gradually the left-wing intellectuals also fell into disfavour with the Communist Party.

The old nationalist culture began to disintegrate from within in the 1950s. For the young generation of writers after the war — known as the fifties modernists — the great ideologies of the 1930s were empty bastions, whether they were patriotic or left-wing. 'The poets did not launch an attack, but in choosing to site their observation post on the sidelines, they did however keep their eyes open. Gradually, from this quietly critical position, they began to undermine a great deal. By refraining from taking sides, and by focussing attention on linguistic and artistic problems, they brought about a new kind of cultural climate. Many cherished national myths began to crumble, and there emerged no new defenders of such myths.'[11]

The content of the literature was less important than the new vision of the role of literature, an understanding of its autonomy. There was no justification for criticising literature on the grounds that it did not reflect the well-established way of thinking.[12] This modern notion of separating the different spheres of life brought into question the basic cornerstone of conservative nationalism, i.e. that culture as a whole should represent a uniform system of values. A similar emphasis on intellectual freedom and autonomy was also evident among scholars in the social sciences.

The healing of the trauma and the partial return to the Scandinavian course, from which Finland had been cut off in 1918, did not however begin in earnest till the 1960s. The break-up of the pack-ice which occurred in that decade was both a breakthrough for cultural liberalisation and the completion of the old line of nationalist populism.

The time was ripe for such a breakthrough. In the 1960s Finland finally became an industrialised society. The social change was more tumultous than in almost any other Western European country: the number of university students multiplied, the farming community collapsed, the surviving farmers — including those with small acreages — finally entered the market economy, people moved *en masse* to the towns and to Sweden, the standard of living rose, and technical modernisation destroyed earlier group relations and bonds of solidarity in the industrial arena. The societal context in which the intelligentsia acted underwent a change. All this severely weakened the traditional base of class divisions, both the separate working-class culture which had been a vital force since the civil war and the agrarian foundation of national culture. The traditional 'peasant/small farmer nation' was irrevocably disappearing.

An intellectual storm, which in the 1960s took the form of a new swing to the left among all the young Western intelligentsia, left its mark on the breakthrough. At the beginning of the 1960s Finland's educated class was still, practically speaking, anti-communist. The intellectuals simply had no connections with social democratic movements and even less with the communist working-class ones. The communists in Finland 'have an insignificant active leadership, a non-existent support among the educated class and an enormous passive mass following, which indeed sounds fine but the practical value of which is relatively minor' — thus a pamphlet anticipating changes at the beginning of the 1960s.[13] The traditional nationalistic culture was scooped out hollow but was not being replaced by anything new.

In this situation *cultural* concepts, and therefore the intellectuals also, attained an exceptionally pronounced role. The new values and ideas aroused considerable enthusiasm. There was a hazy feeling that the old ways of thinking did not answer the question 'What really is happening?', the title of a collection of verse by the archetypal poet of the 1960s, Pentti Saarikoski, published in 1962. Irony worked well, the least nuance giving rise to great dramatic suspense.

It was in this atmosphere that literature, however apolitical, provided a political sounding-board. Literature made an important contribution to the erosion of the world-view created by the events of 1918 by transferring interpretations to paper and not leaving them merely in the collective memory. When for example the 1950s modernists Paavo Haavikko and Veijo Meri each published a novel in 1960 which happened to be set in the year 1918,[14] they in their individual ways planted there a seemingly non-ideological course of events. They placed civil war and all its implications into history from a new angle, away from the immediate area of the trauma. Their other output can be similarly evaluated. It was a positive step with a clear social and historical importance.

The changing 1960s also saw head-on clashes over literature. The right of literature to remain within its own separate sphere, without taking any stance with regard to traditional nationalistic values, was questioned. These conflicts were a continuation of the redefinition of literary values which had taken place in the 1950s.

Most important, this literary debate had radical political repercussions. In 1960 the second part of Väinö Linna's trilogy *Here under the Northern Star* was published. This book opened more locked doors than any other work. It showed the intellectuals and the entire bourgeois readership how the insurgent side in the civil war could also be seen as part of the nation. In presenting the insurgents as activists and as sensitive people who acted worthily and responsibly, it legitimised them as Finns and, as it were, gave them back their rights of citizenship.

The significance of Linna's work was that at the same time as he presented the revolutionaries as revolutionaries, he did so in a way which the educated class could approve *in their own terms*. He made the insurgents *understandable* to the educated. Many critics classed the work as being in the tradition of the working-class novel, but in fact Linna's heroes were not workers but small farmers, and their sons had all the characteristics of the peasantry.[15] In the final analysis they were not too far from the cherished picture of the people traditionally held by the educated class. For the first time the war came to be generally accepted as a class-conflict. Linna effectively dismantled the trauma of many decades and showed the intellectuals how to find a new way of reaching the 'people'; although the people had rebelled, they had also striven for the nation's best interests.

The intellectuals could embrace this notion because it linked up with the old. At the same time it signified a change in their system of values. The meaning of the nation widened; disagreements could now be incorporated in it; particular kinds of conflict could be seen as having a positive force.

The ideal of pluralism burst to the fore in the 1960s. Linna's book fitted in with this trend and strengthened it. Because the burden of the past had been so heavy, the breakthrough of liberalism was impressive. The cultural radicalism of the 1960s was consciously opposed to the uniform culture of nationalism and proclaimed tolerance of differences and disagreements and the victory of rationality. It endorsed freedom, the recognition of the rights of the individual, the right to hold divergent views — in a word the declaration of human rights associated with the French revolution.[16] The rights of prisoners and the homeless were defended, there were demands for the acceptance of pacifism and equal rights for women, and there was a call for the separation of the church from the state. The entire cultural scene was in a state of ferment.

A new ideological structure was laid down by the intellectuals, of which many features have become everyday realities. It is perhaps not by chance that the demands and opinions of the 1960s were in many ways reminiscent of those demands raised in the crisis provoked by the 1905 strike. It was as if the shroud of 1918 was lifted and the legacy of 1905–6 was given new life.[17] Those liberal impulses released by the liberating effect of the Great Strike only began to evoke a resonant echo when the shadow of the civil war receded.

Attitudes towards the communists were transformed in this new situation. The intellectuals found it possible to embrace them too in their concept of the nation. This stand was seen as 'reasonable' in a society based on pluralism. It was *rational* to treat communists the same as others, because they would thereby accept the general political fundamental rules. The communists began to be increasingly seen as on a par with other Finns. In 1966 they entered government and remained in it, apart from small breaks, for the ensuing fifteen years.

The cultural and political breakthrough in Finland in the 1960s seems to have been unusually abrupt. Its most dramatic feature is indeed this integration of a sizeable communist movement, which seems to have been made possible because the kind of structural features which have fostered sharp social and political cleavages in Western European countries where the communist party has been strong do not exist to the same degree in Finland. Italy and France, and to some extent Portugal and Spain, are examples; they experienced fascism much more painfully than Finland ever did, and the status of the upper class in these countries has been much more powerful than in agrarian Finland. The legacy of the civil war, even linked to fear of the Soviet Union, could not be repeated interminably. In the 1960s Finland began to return culturally and politically to that Scandinavian mainstream of which it had always been a part in terms of the country's social and administrative structure.

This does not, however, mean that the intellectual tradition of nation-

Changing times. In 1968, left-wing students occupied the Old Student House, scene of many AKS meetings in the 1930s. The young man with the loudhailer is Ulf Sundqvist, who later rose to prominence as a social democratic minister and bank director. *H*

alistic populism disappeared entirely. Certain basic features survived in changed form, and reappeared at the end of the 1960s and the beginning of the 1970s.

Building a bridge to the working class did not remain a liberal prerogative; it went much further. When the educated class finally encountered the workers' movement, the atmosphere was electric. For an appreciable number of the young intellectuals, the discovery of the people in the guise of the working class was a genuine revelation which swiftly led them into the Communist Party and in particular its minority hard-line wing. For a time, hard-line communists controlled the strongest student organisation; there is no comparable phenomenon is other countries. The hard-liners took an unreservedly favourable view of the Soviet Union, leaving little or no room for Maoist or Trotskyite tendencies.

This reaction speaks volumes about how deep-seated was the desire for solidarity with the people among the Finnish intelligentsia. Identification with the people carried with it a degree of moral compassion and idealisation of the people as represented by the party, and it implied service to that ideal. Many of the national themes which seemed to express the creative power of the people, such as folk songs, underwent a renaissance.

In the long term, the revolutionary enthusiasm of the 1960s turned out to be a false dawn. Finding a new form of solidarity between the educated class and the people was in fact a part of the phase begun after the civil war and not a new beginning. After the trauma in culture had been identified, its significance faded both in educated and in working-class circles. The communist movement split in the 1970s and began to decline. Most intellectuals drew away from the party's minority wing and no-one took their place.

What remains is the political aspect of the tradition. In contrast to the countries of Western Europe, the left-wing intellectuals in Finland soon found their way into the institutions of the state, often as civil servants or in other politically influential positions. Becoming involved in the working-class parties was in fact part of this phenomenon. As we have seen, the intellectuals had always seen the way ahead in terms of influencing the state; it was the state which would resolve social problems and meet the needs of the nation.

This state-centred tradition of political action had reaped the victory which it might have won in the modern state in any case. In the 1960s and 1970s, the state's sphere of activity widened in Finland with the creation of an extensive welfare state. But it is obvious that this development corresponded well to the long-term orientation of the intellectuals.

## NOTES

1. Tuija Pulkkinen, 'Kansalaisyhteiskunta ja valtio' in Risto Alapuro *et al.* (*eds*), *Kansa liikkeessä*, Helsinki 1987, p. 66.
2. Yrjö-Koskinen, *Kansallisia ja yhteiskunnallisia kirjoituksia* II, Suomalaisen Kirjallisuuden Seuran toimituksia 108:2, Helsinki 1904–6, p. 51, as cited in Roberta Gifford Selleck, 'The Language Issue in Finnish Political Discussion: 1809–1863', unpubl. Ph. D. thesis, Radcliffe College, Cambridge, Mass., 1961, p. 184.
3. J. V. Snellman, *Samlade arbetem—VI*, Helsingfors 1895, p. 65–6, as cited in Selleck, 'The Language Issue', pp. 172–3.
4. Ilkka Liikanen, 'Kansanvalistajien kansakunta', *Kansa liikkeessä*, p. 132.
5. Irma Sulkunen, *Raittius kansalaisuskontona, Raittiusliike ja järjestytyminen 1870-luvulta suurlakon jälkeisiin vuosiin*, Historiallisia tutkimuksia 134, Helsinki 1986, pp. 95–204.
6. Sulkunen, *Raittius kansalaisuskontona*, p. 270.
7. Pertti Haapala, *Tehtaan valossa. Teollistuminen ia työväestön muodostuminen Tampereella 1820–1920*, Historiallisia tutkimuksia 133, Helsinki 1986, pp. 185–96.

8. Pauli Kettunen,'Missä mielessä vanha työväenliike oli poliittinen liike?', *Kansa liikkeessä*, p. 250.
9. *Paasikiven muistelmia sortovuosilta*, I, Porvoo-Helsinki 1957, p. 180.
10. Pertti Lassila, *Uuden aikakauden runous*, Helsinki 1987, pp. 78, 104, 122–3, 128, 132.
11. Kai Laitinen, *Suomen Kirjallisuus 1917–1967*, Helsinki 1967, p. 173.
12. This idea has been put forward by Matti Viikari; see Johan von Bonsdorff, *Kun Vanha vallattiin*, Helsinki 1986, p. 44.
13. Kalervo Siikala, *Kansallinen realismi*, Jyväskylä 1960, p. 96.
14. Paavo Haavikko, *Yksityisiä asioita*, Helsinki 1960, and Veijo Meri, *Vuoden 1918 tapahtumat*, Helsinki 1960.
15. Matti Peltonen, 'Väinö Linnan torpparitrilogian 'Täällä Pohjantähden alla' sanoma eli talonpoikaisuus ia työläisyys Väinö Linnan torpparikuvauksessa', unpublished 1986.
16. Matti Viikari in von Bonsdorff, *Kun Vanha vallattiin*, p. 47.
17. Pauli Kettunen, 'Vuoden 1906 Suomi, vuoden 1918 Suomi, Nyky-Suomi', *Kansa liikkeessä*, p. 286

# THE GERMANOPHIL UNIVERSITY

## Matti Klinge

The difficult and dramatic periods in Finland's recent history can be described as a function of the rivalry between the two leading great powers in the Baltic area, Russia and Germany. The foundation-stone for this period of rivalry was laid in 1870–1 when Germany became a great power after crushing France, hitherto the most powerful continental state apart from Russia. The new German empire was also the immediate neighbour of the Russian empire.

The Germany of 1871 was not yet the strong and united empire it came to be. Skillful diplomacy and dynastic ties held Russia and Germany together as allies as long as Alexander II and Prince Gorchakov on the one side and Kaiser Wilhelm I and Otto von Bismarck on the other were at the helm. Relations began to deteriorate in the 1880s, and in the early 1890s Russia concluded an alliance with France directed against Germany. Both Russia and France wished to protect themselves against Germany's growing strength and capacity for expansion. The alliance gave France guarantees of support in the event of a defensive or a revanchist war with Germany, while Russia obtained great economic advantages from the link. There was heavy French investment, not least in the remarkable expansion of the Russian railway network, a development whose military, economic and national importance for Russia cannot be exaggerated.

However, French investment did not affect Finland. In the 1880s Finland's cultural orientation had been towards France, but Berlin and Vienna began to exercise a strong influence in the 1890s. As French and British influences grew in Russia, Finland began to be drawn culturally and economically towards Germany. After the conclusion of the Franco-Russian alliance this trend attracted attention and then caused unease within influential circles in Russia. An important background factor consisted of developments in Russia's Baltic provinces where, especially during the 1880s, the imperial government had pushed through a series of reforms designed to reduce the political and social importance of the German-speaking upper class. This led to the Russian language being favoured, but it also stimulated the emergence of local, national cultures, not least in Estonia. The imperial government sought to reinforce the ties between the Baltic provinces and Russia by weakening the German

The New Student House, designed by Armas Lindgren.

element, but also wished to promote a social renewal which would favour the non-German population of the provinces in all respects.

In Finland too a Finnish-patriotic and Finnish-national form of the culture had gradually emerged, largely with the government's blessing, since the country's incorporation into the Russian empire in 1809. The rising Finnish-speaking middle classes began to play an increasingly active political role, especially after the accession of Alexander III in 1881.

The central role of the University in Finnish life arose out of an 'accumulation of cultural capital', which also mainfested itself politically, especially at those times when the Diet was not in session (it met in principle every third year during the latter part of the nineteenth century and up till 1905). The political division of the four estates into two (the nobility and the burghers) which supported liberalism and two (the clergy and the farmers) in which Finnish nationalism dominated was reproduced within the University, above all within the student body, which was sometimes torn by heated party struggles. The teachers there were more sophisticated in their political activities; both liberalism and Finnish nationalism derived many of their most important ideologues and leaders from among the professors. When parties in the proper sense were formed during the governor-generalship of N.I. Bobrikov (1899–1904), it became clear that only a minority inside the University regarded themselves as supporters of the governing Old Finn Party, while a majority of teachers and students adhered to various groupings or tendencies within the oppostion.

The essential cause of the Finnish-Russian conflict while Bobrikov was governor-general lay in Russian military policy: the imperial government felt obliged to secure its hold on Finland in view of the possibility of German invasion. The Russians naturally regarded a potential German invasion of Finland, then as later, as a threat to the security of the imperial capital, St Petersburg.

Finnish resistance to the measures of russification introduced by the Russians therefore had an important international dimension, especially since immediately after the outbreak of the dispute in 1899 the resisters turned abroad and attempted to rouse foreign opinion against Russia and its policies in Finland. A central role in these Finnish efforts to attract foreign support was played by members of the University.

Many opportunities were provided by the personal contacts which so many Finnish scholars had acquired during their years of study abroad. Germans played a leading part in the great international address signed by prominent foreign scholars and cultural figures (even though Italian signatories were more numerous than German, and British only slightly less so). The Finns largely appealed to French and British opinion in the name of general principles of freedom, which they did not believe were sustained in the same way by the German tradition. However, it soon became apparent that the French tradition of human rights provided little real support for the Finnish case in the dispute, and the Finns increasingly turned their thoughts from ideals of justice towards the realities of power. The marked growth of Germany's economic, political and military strength began to

A group of Swedish-speaking students preparing to set off to collect signatures for the Great Address in 1899. More than half a million names were collected within a short time, although the emperor politely declined to accept the volumes of the address presented to him. The man who shot Governor-General Bobrikov in 1904, Eugen Schauman, is fourth from the right. *B*

make an impact, not least after·Russia's defeat by Japan and the events inside the Russian empire (including Finland) in 1905-7.

The idea that a European or world war was imminent was quite widespread for many years before the assassination at Sarajevo. It arose essentially from a change in outlook on the world. From the 1890s the positivist-optimistic way of thinking with its faith in material expansion gave way to a new mode of thought based on pessimism and individualism in art, repudiation of the dominant symmetrical forms and a greatly increased interest in the religious, especially the theosophical and occult, dimensions of human life. At the same time, radical political groups placed great expectations in the potential of a future great war for creating social and political revolution. Nor were the expectations in industrial circles without importance. As with the revolutionaries, their expectations were fulfilled, though perhaps in a way and in a sequence which they had not anticipated.

A central aspect of Finnish activity around 1900 was the attempt to publicise Finland's problems abroad through a deliberate appeal to foreign opinion over an internal crisis within the Russian empire. Part of the background for this development was the general optimism at the time about the force of law, which found expression, for example, in the establishment of the International Court of Arbitration at the Hague on the initiative of Nicholas II. The peace movement, represented by such well-known names as Bertha von Suttner and Frédéric Passy, was a significant force in Europe in the 1880s and 1890s, and in Finland attracted the support above all of Zachris Topelius. The works of his declining years, not least *Stjärnornas Kungabarn*, were devoted to the cause of peace. The Dreyfus affair and the Boer war also served strongly to reinforce anti-militaristic and anti-imperialistic tendencies. In addition to more self-interested calculations, this optimism about the force of law must be seen as an important motive or at least justification for the Finnish appeal to 'enlightened' European opinion.

However, optimism concerning peace and the force of law suffered a number of decisive setbacks during the first years of the new century. One reason for this was the growth of terrorism and political assassination, above all in Russia but soon also in Finland. Even more important were events outside Europe, namely the British victory in the Boer war and especially the Russian defeat in the war against Japan. Power and force, not negotiation, had proved decisive. Finnish appeals to Britain, the oppressor of the Irish and the Boers, or to France, whose alliance with Russia continued and grew stronger, seemed increasingly inappropriate. European opinion had had no effect, but the Japanese war and internal pressure had produced changes throughout the whole Russian empire, including Finland.

Interest in international politics appears to have been slight in Finland between 1899 and 1914. No detailed studies of this subject seem to have been undertaken, but it is likely that the country's inability to conduct an independent foreign policy, the lack of a network of foreign correspondents abroad and the absence of interest in political science at the University, combined with the preoccupation of Finnish politicians with Finnish-Russian questions and internal party political problems, produced a situation in which there was little expertise in foreign policy matters. There were on the other hand highly developed economic, cultural and intellectual ties with other countries. The importance of Germany for Finland increased throughout this period, and in the years immediately before the First World War so did that of Finland for Germany.

The economic, cultural and military rise of Germany after unification in 1870–1 began to be clearly apparent around the turn of the century.

Germany's population grew from 41 million in 1871 to 68 million in 1914. (In contrast, the population of France only increased by 3.5 million during the same period.) By the outbreak of the First World War Germany was producing twice as much steel as Britain and four times as much as France; production of coal, iron etc. had increased more rapidly there than in any other country; and Germany was undoubtedly the leading country with regard not only to production but also to training and research in the chemical and electrical industries, both areas of the most advanced modern technology. Germany had also become a colonial power during the 1880s and 1890s, and between 1898 and 1908 a large and powerful modern fleet was constructed to ensure it a first-rank position in world politics and colonial questions.

In the realm of ideas, this growth was matched by an expansionist ideology of Germanism, which was sustained above all by the *Alldeutscher Verband* (1891) and the racist *Gobineau-Vereinung* (1894). These organisations sought to emphasise Germanism, *Deutschum*, in all its aspects. In Finland, as in some other foreign countries, this was reflected in the growing importance of the German language. The point is well illustrated by changes in the language in which academic dissertations were published. In 1885 out of a total of ten doctoral theses defended at the Imperial Alexander University, three were written in German. By 1914 eighteen out of thirty-seven were in German, and one each in French and English, and the proportion had steadily risen throughout the years in between.[1] Thus the scholarly world in Finland had gradually been drawn into the German cultural empire.

This is hardly surprising in view of the potential represented by German scholarship and the German universities. Germany had developed a strong university system which, in comparison with France and Britain, was both modern and oriented towards research. For Finnish scholars there was no alternative, at least close at hand, since both Russia and Sweden were just as German in their orientation in several disciplines, above all in chemistry. In medicine, too, Germany (and Austria) had also outstripped the rest of the field and put an end to the earlier orientation towards France. The self-portrait given by a Finnish scholar in 1914 may be taken as typical: 'I speak both our native languages equally well — or equally badly, if you prefer — but German is my mother-tongue when it comes to scholarly matters.'

The outbreak of the world war forced the Finnish public to speculate about what the future might hold, both in general terms and specifically in relation to Finland. An important and insufficiently emphasised factor is that since the time of Bobrikov there had been no conscription in Finland and the Finns therefore had no troops of their own. As a result, they were not psychologically involved in the war in the same way as other inhabitants of the belligerent countries and instead were able, like the neutrals, to turn their minds to speculation and how best to react to such situations as might arise.

It is clear that during 1914 the conduct of the Germans, not least in Belgium, aroused some antipathy in Finland, and that there was also a resurgence of traditional loyalty towards Russia and the imperial family. However, the Russians failed to exploit such currents of opinion either psychologically or in their propaganda, and the Russian defeats in East Prussia soon created a situation in which pro-German sentiment began to gain ground.

It was often claimed during and after the war in reports and statements emanating from Finland to the Entente powers that German agitation in Finland began immediately after its outbreak. Reports to this effect were produced during the war by a Frenchman resident in Helsinki, Dr Jean Poirot, who had particularly good contacts there, and after the war the same view was advanced, and defended in the press, by Professor Yrjö Hirn. There would appear to be no written sources describing German agitation in Finland, but this is inherent in the nature of such activity. We know that the German minister in Stockholm was ordered immediately after the outbreak of war to attempt to organise seditious activity in Finland, in the same way as the Germans tried to do this in India, Ireland and other sensitive parts of the British empire. We also know that an organisation whose aim was an uprising against Russian rule in Finland was set up in 1915, and that the potential leaders of this revolt soon received military training.

In this connection, a central role was played by the University, by some of its teachers and some of its students. The most senior local administrator at the University, the Vice-Chancellor Edvard Hjelt, was the first and most influential of the older persons to lend support to the activities which eventually led to the formation of a Finnish *Jäger* battalion in Germany. Hjelt was strongly oriented towards Germany in two particular ways. First, he was a chemist, and chemistry was the discipline under the strongest German influence. As a young man, he had studied in Germany and he returned there regularly on visits. In contrast, to judge from his private papers, he did not know Russian or English and had only a limited command of French. Hjelt was not only tied to Germany by his scholarly contacts, but like his father and both his brothers, he belonged to the circle around the German church in Helsinki.

The German community in Helsinki also provided the two young students, Walter Horn and Bertel Paulig, who established contact between the German legation in Stockholm and the activists among the student body in Helsinki. With Herman Gummerus, an anti-Russian Finnish academic who was sent from Rome to Stockholm by the Germans, Horn and Paulig drew up the document which set out the guidelines for the military training of Finnish students in Germany. The former German consul in Helsinki, Goldbeck-Löwe, who served as the chief contact in Stockholm to the naval attaché Fischer-Lossainen, was one of the pillars of the German colony and the German church in Helsinki.

A central role in the movement of opinion in favour of Germany was played by students, particularly that group among them which had recently adopted a Germanistic ideology. This was true of the young, active circle among Swedish-speaking students, especially those who belonged to the *Nylands nation* student association and, to some extent, the *Vasa nation* student association. The ideology of Swedishness that was developed within this circle was clearly racist in tendency, and in contrast to the pessimistic emphasis on idleness of the preceding generation, its proponents adopted a view of life which emphasised action (*Tataktivismus*) and manliness as displayed through military or sporting skills. The first Finns who travelled to Germany were recruited from this group, and they subsequently provided the Finnish commissioned and non-commissioned officers of the *Jäger* battalion. This first contingent of Finnish troops in German service were disguised as Boy Scouts, *Pfadfinder*, and they are known by this name.

The social background of the *Pfadfinder* group was an elevated one both in comparison with the student body as a whole (most of them were students) and especially in comparison with the troops who served in the later 27th Royal Prussian *Jäger* battalion as a whole. The dangerous choice made by these young men and the sense of self-sacrifice they displayed had an important psychological effect on their parents and other relatives, and thus helped to shape the attitudes of influential circles. The actions of the *Pfadfinder* group therefore created something concrete to which other Finns with German sympathies ultimately had to react, and to react in a positive manner.

It is of some significance that the idea of armed rebellion under the leadership of Finns trained in Germany aroused a response not only among Swedish-speaking but also among Finnish-speaking students. There had been quite an amount of pro-Russian enthusiasm for the war in August and September 1914 among Finnish-speaking students, but opinion changed after the great Russian defeats in the early stages of the war. In

Finnish minds, and not least in Finnish-speaking circles, Germany's military successes were associated with the religious and scientific impulses from Germany that were so much admired in Finland. During the war political contacts between Finland and Germany were channelled through Sweden, where a strong body of pro-German opinion was only too happy to assist in a variety of ways. It is noteworthy in this connection that just before the war activist circles in Sweden exercised on important influence on the development of opinion among Finnish students. During the spring of 1914 the chairman of the Uppsala Students' Union, Dr Olof Palme, succeeded in winning over a number of Finnish-speaking student leaders to a pro-German line and in bringing about a political rapprochement between Swedish-speaking and Finnish-speaking student circles with the express purpose of resisting Russia more effectively.

The opposition which in Bobrikov's time had had a legalistic and political basis re-emerged during the second decade of the century in a new guise. Changes in general attitudes to the world had led to less emphasis on formal and analytical modes of thought and greater sympathy for explanations resting on concepts like intuition, race, struggle and will. The earlier form of opposition gave way among the new generation to an ideology of action and struggle, which found significant expression in the publication *Svenskt i Finland, utgiven av Svenska Studenters partidelegation* (Helsinki 1914).

In addition to Russia, the socialist working class now constituted a new threat to the values of the circles which the *Pfadfinder* group represented in social terms. It has become common in school textbooks and in many general accounts to regard the Bobrikov years, 1899–1905, and the period after 1909 or 1912 as the first and second 'periods of oppression'. However, it has been convincingly demonstrated that there were differences between Russian policy in these two periods, and in addition another fundamental difference was the changed nature of relationships betwen social groups in Finland.

It is understandable and natural that those who served in the *Jäger* battalion, and the body of opinion which supported them, indignantly rejected the accusation that they had prepared themselves in advance for the civil war which broke out in the unforeseeable circumstances of 1918. However, the circles which sustained the idea of rebellion and the *Jäger* movement were deeply concerned by the way society had developed in Finland since 1906. The threat to the continuance of the social order and to the legalistic tradition that was central above all to the Swedish-speaking educated class no longer came in the first instance from Russia and the

Russian government but from socialists and the proletariat. The possibility that the Russian government could not in the long run keep the masses under control was often discussed. It was therefore consistent to seek external support for the maintenance of the 'Germanic' social order against the threat from the Finnish and Russian masses, given that the point of departure consisted of the theories of race and cultural formation that were so prevalent during these years.

The period of conflict in Bobrikov's time was an internal Russo-Finnish matter. There were appeals to European opinion, but their purpose was to restore the '*status quo ante Bobrikov*', not to detach Finland from the Russian empire. During the second decade of the century and especially after the outbreak of war, the question at issue was whether Finland should move from the Russian to the 'Germanic' cultural and political sphere. It was not a question, at least in the first instance, of laws and Finland's formal status, but of the country's social identity in the future: it was regarded as a question of race and cultural psychology.

Such patterns of thought were common in young Swedish-speaking circles at the University. The ideological development of these circles was largely determined by impulses from Uppsala (Kjellén and his supporters) and from Gothenburg (W. Lundström and his Riksförening för svenskhetens bevarande i utlandet [National association for preservation of 'Swedishness' abroad]), two centres which in their turn were greatly influenced by Germany. In this connection, P. Rohrbach's book *Russland und wir* attracted a great deal of attention in Sweden.

Despite the new feelings of linguistic and racial identity experienced by Swedish-speaking students, Germanism nonetheless created bridges between them and Finnish-speaking circles, since it pushed the legalistic aspect, which had previously been of such central importance, into the background. Swedish-speakers came to accept something of the outlook previously asserted by the *Fennomani*, who had created their own political doctrine on the basis of Hegelian ideas about cultural formations. Their doctrines had concentrated on the nation and its cultural strength, not on the state and law. The Finnish-language nationalists had applied this ideology in relation to Russia when they argued that the decisive goal was to preserve the nation, not its laws. Swedish-speaking youth had now come to the same conclusion via another route and had accepted that what was decisive was not the form, namely the law, but culture and its strength and power, which in extreme cases would mean its *physical* strength and power. The old theological and more recent economic contacts of the Finnish-language nationalists produced a more traditional but no less strong Germanophilia. In times of crisis, it was possible for these two brands of Germanophilia to find each other, and this created the pro-German front which ruled Finland from the autumn of 1917 to the autumn of 1918.

The academic world played an important role in this confluence of various pro-German currents. Traditionally, the University occupied a central place in the formation of opinion in Finland, and its role was accentuated when parliament was prevented from functioning or was not summoned and when strict press censorship was imposed. During the second decade of the twentieth century the authority of the University in this respect had only increased, since the Finnish Senate, as a 'government of civil servants', did not enjoy the confidence of either parliament or the public. In contrast, the University, which still retained its full autonomy in relation to the Senate and the Governor-General, experienced a period of general growth and of external and internal development.

The Swedish- and Finnish-language student newspapers, *Studentbladet* and *Ylioppilaslehti* founded in 1912 and 1913 respectively, the new student union building, and the University's scholarly activities bear witness to a spirit of enterprise and faith in the future within the academic world. During the first decade of the century the University's position was improved by the creation of a great number of new posts and scholarly institutions, increased salaries for academic staff and the modernisation of the examinations system. The personal links between the University and the highest levels of the administration had been close for several decades and during the period of reform between 1905 and 1909 the leading men in the Senate were either active or former professors. The voice of the University was therefore something Finns were accustomed to listening to, and this was particularly so during periods of wartime censorship.

Against this background, it is easy to understand the low spirits of the Entente over the situation in Finland. In his precise reports to Aristide Briand and other French leaders, Dr Poirot pointed out that only one in six of the professors could be regarded as friends of the Entente and the majority of them did not dare to declare their sympathies openly before their Germanophil colleagues. All the students' associations, especially *Nylands nation*, were pro-German, as were those newspapers which were closest to the young intelligentsia.

After the declaration of independence on 6 December 1917 and its recognition on 4 January 1918, the University felt it desirable to mark what had been achieved with a magnificent academic celebration in January 1918. The festivities were purely pro-German in nature, and the singing of

*Die Wacht am Rhein* obliged the French consul to leave the hall. The fact that France alone among the Western powers had recognised Finland's independence was not noted in any way. The academic festivities after the spring of 1918 were even more pro-German, and even after Germany's collapse in November 1918 the University and its students long continued to manifest their German sympathies. From a Finnish point of view, Germany was and would remain a great power, even if it were temporarily defeated and weakened, and no other great power had emerged to replace it in the Baltic area. After the world war, it was the traditional Germany — the Germany of theology, medicine and chemistry; the Germany that the University had always known — which remained, even if Germany in its economic and military manifestations had not been regarded, especially during a world war, as something independent from the German cultural entity.

## NOTES

1. For a fuller account, see *Historisk Tidskrift för Finland*, 3 (1987), pp. 528–9.

# THE WOMEN'S MOVEMENT

## Irma Sulkunen

In 1906 Finland's four-estate Diet was abolished and replaced by a uni-cameral legislature (*Eduskunta*). When it met for the first time in 1907, nineteen of the 200 elected members were women. Miina Sillanpää was one of the nine who belonged to the Social Democratic Party, which had the greatest representation in parliament with eighty seats. Having been a servant herself at one time, Sillanpää was the prominent leader of the Association of Domestic Servants. Alongside her were Hilja Pärssinen, a teacher, and Ida Ahlstedt, a seamstress, both of whom were active in the women workers' movement. Among the ten women members on the right were such veterans of the women's rights movement as the nobly-born Alexandra Gripenberg and Lucina Hagman, a headmistress. This nineteen-strong female presence constituted only 9.5 per cent of parliamentary membership; nevertheless, these women were in a unique position. They were the first women in Europe to whom universal and equal suffrage had opened the door to the state legislature.

But how is it that the forerunners of female suffrage reform were to emerge from a country as peripheral as Finland, and with relatively little fuss at that? This question has often been asked. Why were Finnish women so easily granted a civil right for which women in many other countries fought in vain for years? And why were Finnish men prepared to stand alongside them in the demand for a radical extension of the franchise? Universal and equal suffrage had been included in the social democrats' manifesto right from the party's inception, and by the early twentieth century the other, recently-formed parties also took a firm stand in support of women's entitlement to the same voting rights as men.

A number of explanations have been offered for this phenomenon. That the suffrage reform represented a show of strength, as a unanimous and cohesive nation defended its rights and identity, has been the argument favoured particularly by early historians, who saw it as a decisive factor in Finland's struggle against Russian oppression. Women, like working-class men, were felt to have salvaged their right to full citizenship, within that struggle.

More recent interpretations have also placed the suffrage reform within the broader context of Russian-Finnish relations and the ensuing political tensions. However, they emphasise the role played by Governor-General

178

*The awakened.* Painting of peasant women at a religious meeting by Venny Soldan-
Brofeldt (1901). *A*

Obolensky, the imperial appointee, rather than that of the Finns themselves, in the achievement of universal and equal suffrage. The entire
reform has even been ascribed to the skilful tactics employed by Obolensky
in his attempt to pacify the striking 'masses' and to prevent the general
unrest from expanding into a large-scale rebellion. This line of argument
would suggest that it was thanks to Obolensky's tactics that women in
Finland also won the vote, but that they did so more or less by accident as a
by-product of a greater issue.

The third way of dealing with the subject has been to focus on the
politics of equality — a view prevalent among the public at large rather
than among specialists. This approach uses the early achievement of
universal and equal suffrage as an argument in present-day gender discussions, rather than examining it as a problem in itself. The franchise is
viewed simply as evidence of the fact that Finland has traditionally enjoyed
a relatively great degree of equality between the sexes. In support of this
view, it is argued that Finnish women have always been exceptionally
active with regard to work alongside men, and this tradition has survived
up to the present.

'The power of women continues to grow in our country. They have won 23 seats'in parliament, and now there are 15 women conductors in the service of the Helsinki tram company.' (*Suomen Kuvalehti*, 1917a) *B*

These interpretations are undoubtedly valid as far as they go. However, they leave certain important questions unasked. In what way, for example, did female suffrage become a political issue in the mobilisation which culminated in the national strike of 1905? What does the fact that it was brought into the political arena, and attained with relative ease, tell us about male-female relations in Finland at the beginning of the twentieth century? And, to go a step further, what was it about male-female relations in Finland that made possible the extraordinary transition straight from a patriarchal system of representation, based on social rank, to a system in which full citizen status was held by every man and woman?

It may be that these questions cannot be answered fully, at least not if we examine the subject against the background of national unification or national politics. Neither, surely, will the mere application of present-day values to the past bring us any closer to the root of the matter. For example, to apply modern concepts of equality to the suffrage reform of 1906 and to the period leading up to it must be inappropriate, not to say misleading. On the contrary, we must assume that the early achievement of female suffrage was in no way related to an equality that had traditionally existed between the sexes. It is truer to say that the whole modern notion of equality was practically unknown in Finland at that time, as was today's 'contra-positional' methodology for the study of male-female relations.

In what follows I hope to demonstrate this, as well as to introduce a fresh perspective into the study of gender relations and women's suffrage. My starting-point is the development of organised movements and groups. This point is particularly relevant because it is in the very process of social organisation that the actions of individuals or groups of individuals come into contact with the structure of society. It is here that people's common interaction, modes of thinking and societal spheres of influence take shape. Moreover, cultural developments are linked to this process. Thus it is also possible to trace the nature and evolution of society's gender classification through the organisation process. In addition, we may examine more generally the question of male and female identity within the sense of citizenship, and look at the division of duty which asserted itself in the construction of political democracy.

The 1906 parliamentary reform drew Finland closer to Western patterns of state and society. One of Europe's most anachronistic systems of representation was suddenly abandoned in favour of modern democracy. Although the swiftness with which this took place was unprecedented, the transition did not lack the necessary preliminary groundwork. The development in the legislative system was a logical conclusion in Finland, as elsewhere, or perhaps it is more accurate to say that it exemplified one juncture in the long and multi-stage chain of events which led to the gradual collapse of the old society and the materialisation of the new. The transition took a different form in different countries. Variations in social, occupational and cultural patterns of life determined the nature of the transition at a local level. In each quarter, old and new confronted each other in an unprecedented way.

Despite regional and chronological differences, we can nonetheless make certain generalisations about the nature and development of this transition. If we take social organisation as our focal point, we can divide the development into three basic periods: the revivalist movement, the emergence of formally co-ordinated social groups, and finally the emergence of party political organisation. It is out of these three stages of mobilisation that the chief characteristics of modern society were created.

Revivalist movements are widely considered to be obsolete relics from a period in history when religion held a prominent place not only in defining community relations and affairs of state, but also in creating the world view and very identity of the individual. They are happily dismissed as an unstable and irrational phenomenon for which there is no longer any room in the modern world, or if there is, then only as a cohort of political conservatism.

However, one can also consider the role of religious revivals from another perspective. They can be seen as the first fracture in the old hierarchical social structure, and thus the first to clear the way towards a new, modern era. They symbolise the first fragmentation of a world view which could not cater for different spheres of life. They mark the burgeoning disintegration of the collective concept of human existence in favour of one of self-reliance and self-accountability as an individual. The validity of this interpretation is born out by the fact that in all Protestant countries in the West, powerful religious revivals preceded political organisation — if not directly, then at least as an element of organised popular movements. Similarly, revivalism preceded the emergence of industrialisation and the 'capitalist ideal'.

In Finland, revivalist movements sprang up in the middle of the eighteenth century around the coastal regions, which were economically advanced. From there, they spread to the marginal areas of the country, where they reached a peak at the end of the nineteenth century, in other words precisely at the dawn of the new era of politicisation.

It is from this perspective that it is interesting to examine not only women's role in the revivalist movement, but also women's activities as indicators of gender relations in eighteenth- and nineteenth-century agrarian Finland. The issue is a provocative one particularly because, almost without exception, it was women who sparked off the revivalist movements with their experiences of religious conversion and ecstasy. This is what happened during the early stages of revivalism, when a young shepherdess from Kalanti called Liisa inspired religious awakening in southwestern Finland. It is also what happened a little later in the area around Pori, when a whole group of women, from servant girls to farmer's wives and daughters of the well-to-do, even found themselves in court as a result of the commotion caused by their preaching. Likewise, a little further north, in and around Merikarvia, it was another woman, a farmer's daughter Anna Rogel, who acted as the catalyst to revivalism. People gathered from far and wide to hear her impressive trance-like preaching, and she operated over a broad area as a self-appointed revivalist leader. During the eighteenth century groups sprang up around women who practised fervent preaching and other spiritual works. In the same way, in the nineteenth century, women acted as the spark that ignited the revivalist movements of the distant eastern and northern regions of

Finland. And at the beginning of the twentieth century one Saara Malinen generated a sequence of evangelistic movements as a result of her trance-like sermons and her healing ability.

All surviving data on the early religious revival indicate that female leaders enjoyed firm support and respect in their community. Their preaching and spiritual works did not provoke opposition at a popular level. On the contrary, both men and women came to hear them, and to ask for help over both spiritual and material problems. Documents describing the revivals give the strong impression that the basic stratum of society did not consider the role of religious leader at all unsuitable for women. Their large numbers in this position demonstrate rather that it was an office considered particularly appropriate for them.

Furthermore, these early records illustrate that although clerical and secular officialdom kept a close eye on the movements, this was not because their chief organisers were women, but above all because of the generally destructive influence they had on the patriarchal hierarchy. Revivalist movements were after all the first to place individual will on a level which threatened to destroy not only the patriarchal traditions of the household, but also the whole hierarchical structure of a society based on rank. Revivalist movements were moreover the first to furnish the new model of social organisation with its physical form, as like-minded members gathered together to promote their personal faith, breaking the barriers set by household, village or even parish. Indeed, it was as a result of this type of voluntary coming together through faith that those who participated in the revivalist meetings provided the groundwork for the future shape of society and state.

So what does women's role in early revivals reveal about the relationship between the sexes? The obvious, and apparently reasonable, answer would be to interpret revivalist movements as an early stage of female emancipation, one which enabled women to transcend the private sphere into the public, to break out of a condition of subordination into one where they held social sway. This sort of interpretation conceivably allows that, by their own actions, these women broke radically free of the limits of the traditional female role, and took the first step towards the equality of the sexes. This interpretation raises problems, however, because it imposes an almost unequivocally modern outlook on the past. It regards women as independent actors in history in a situation where individualism had not yet become an established frame of reference for the concept of human existence. It raises problems on another level too, because it uses this individualistic world-view to trace what it understands to be the traditional role of women. It attributes to the female identity certain qualities which have issued from the thought-processes of modern society, rather than from the conditions of the period in question.

Personally, I am inclined to see women's active role in revivalism as evidence not so much of women's emancipation potential but of the 'old-world spirit' or absence of conflict which characterised gender relations during the early stages of social organisation. Despite the fundamental patriarchal structure and the manifest division of labour, the 'subjection of women' was not at that time a governing principle of rural society. Rather, in keeping with the collective concept of human existence, the bond between man and woman was also continuous and unbreakable. The fact that, within this whole, men and woman both had their distinctive role and area of activity did not mean that a woman's sphere was any simpler, or valued any less, than a man's. Except within a small minority, men and women were equally powerless in the realm of public influence, and, given this, the basic principles of life had more to do with class differentiation than sex differentiation. The opposite sex was viewed as a part of one's self rather than as the oppressor or the oppressed, as an essential counterpart rather than as a contradiction. Thus, while the areas of activity were different, this cannot be taken primarily as evidence that a strategy of sexist subordination existed at the basic stratum of society, but must in fact be seen as the division of labour within a given unit, whose chief purpose was to maintain the efficiency and productiveness of the whole collective community.

Women in revivalist movements thus perpetuated, rather than challenged, the traditional role-division of the old social order. And it is apparent that in the allocation of responsibilities, being the agent of redemption and spiritual solace belonged just as much to the woman's sphere as to the man's and maybe even more so. It is possible to draw an interesting comparison here between the women revivalists and the witches of former times, who functioned as the healers in their communities. Moreover, the concept of a 'spiritual mother' is surely not a modern one.

However, what was new and liberating with regard to gender classification was that the revivalist movements caused the relationship between man and woman to be cast in a completely new light. Despite the collective and traditional features of revivalism, it was an individualistic experience. It was a personal resolution, and one which radically altered the nature of human relationships. It is true that religious enlightenment was capable of forming a barrier between husband and wife. On the other hand, it was also capable of uniting them with the renewed bonds of their personal faith. In this sense, revivalist movements did indeed play a key role in initiating the development of an individualistic outlook which fore-shadowed the emergent gender division. It was an outlook in which both men and women were forced to accommodate their sense of identity to a new concept of human existence which took the atoms, and not just the universe as a whole, into account. Thus it is not simply a question of women discovering their individuality and freeing themselves from the patriarchal aegis, as is often claimed, but more a question of the collapse of the whole collectivist ideology and the birth of a new one. At the same time, by distinguishing between the spiritual and the material, revivalism triggered a differentiation between life-spheres which, in the following decades, drew a sharp distinction between the public and the private, between masculine and feminine.

At the time that universal and equal suffrage was achieved in Finland, revivalist movements were still fairly influential, especially in rural areas. The ascetic movement started by L.L. Laestadius (1800–61) in Scandinavia had spread to Northern Finland, and like the revivalism in Ostrobothnia and Savo, it reached its peak as a popular movement in the decades leading up to the franchise reform. During this period, revivalist movements also took on distinctly pre-political characteristics. They even associated directly with political organisations, particularly with the Old Finn Party, which was founded on the ideals of an agrarian society. At the same time, leadership began to limit itself either to the priesthood or to male members of the laity. However, women still represented an important section among the followers.

Just when revivalist movements were reaching their peak in marginal areas, the overall character of organised groups began to change. A new wave of organised activity was set in motion in the coastal regions, where the loosely co-ordinated revivalist movements had begun to disappear towards the end of the nineteenth century. This second stage in the process of organisation, which in Finland lasted on the whole from the 1880s to the parliamentary reform of 1906, was marked by the emergence of formally organised groups of citizens.

During the 1880s, which has been labelled as the age of ideas and organised activity that had not been seen hitherto, widespread social organisation mushroomed on every level of society. Almost simul-taneously, with the temperance movement leading the way, the first workers' associations were founded, as well as the first youth clubs and women's societies. In addition, the old revivalist movements began to

On the way to a temperance meeting, 1890. *T*

consolidate their organisations, Free Church evangelical associations spread across the country, and co-operative enterprises began to establish themselves.

This almost simultaneous emergence of different types of groups and societies indicates that at this stage social organisation was still very indiscriminate. It was not a behavioural model which had filtered down from the ruling to the lower classes. On the contrary, all were driven in their own way towards group co-operation more or less at the same time, starting with the south and west of Finland, and stretching to the marginal areas. The types of organisation may have differed, but the fundamental mechanics of the process were the same.

The lack of discrimination also indicates that gender differences had no essential significance during this second phase either, at least in its early stages. Women worked alongside men as organisers in local societies. Their participation in temperance societies, workers' associations, youth groups and Free Church organisations was mostly as active as that of men. For example, women constituted almost half the membership in temperance movements and youth clubs at the end of the nineteenth century.

This was particularly so in the countryside, where the emergence of organised social movements coincided with, and was often related to, deep-rooted revivalism.

In addition to the fact that men and women were more or less equally active in the organisation process, absence of sex discrimination within the newly-established organisations themselves was a particular characteristic of the situation in Finland. Men and women tended to belong to the same societies. It was only at the beginning of the twentieth century that this pattern of co-operation began to break down. At this point, specific women's associations started to gain a firmer foothold, as women gradually became involved with religious-ethical societies and with the Martha Association (Martta Yhdistys), which promoted the ideology of family and motherhood. Actual women's rights organisations, by contrast, remained even at this stage a mere thread in the whole fabric of organised activity.

The fact that men and women worked side by side in the same organised social groups speaks for itself: a strong sense of unity still existed in the relationship between the sexes at the turn of the century in Finland. Apart from within the narrow stratum of the privileged classes, male and female interests and identities were not yet divisive. In keeping with the tenets of traditional agricultural society, the predominant feature of the social gender classification continued to be the essential harmony between masculine and feminine.

This does not, however, mean that this concept of human existence, stemming from the collective nature of agricultural society and culture, and the view of male and female unity along with it, would not have disintegrated in Finland with the dawn of the new century. This process had already begun when the comprehensive cultural outlook had broken down, and the consequent shift in world-view had channelled itself firmly into the revivalist movements. During the following stage of the organisation process, it was precisely groups like the temperance and youth movements which encouraged and defined this transformation. At the same time they also made a natural transition from old-fashioned peasant communities to a modern society of citizens. These movements enabled men and women to understand the rights and conditions of their new status as citizens. They also helped to create the theory and practice of the newly-developed male and female identities. Thus, in the ideologies of these organisations the concept of human existence began to take shape against the background of a new and antagonistic gender division. Man and woman began to separate and take up opposing stances, and their

Members of the Martha Association on a course in fruit-preserving in the 1920s. Founded in 1899, the association soon became the largest and most powerful women's organisation in Finland, with some 64,000 members in 1924. The movement was largely inspired by patriotic anxiety at a time of crisis, and endeavoured through an intensive educational programme to combine the basic principles of hygiene and household economy with patriotic duty. *J*

identities began to conform to those divisions in their life-spheres which industrialised society had brought with it. Femininity gradually became identified with the private sphere, and masculinity with the public.

It was in fact the emergence of these organised social groups which caused the hierarchical sense of identity, based on rank, to be replaced by a sense of the individual's citizenship, equally applicable to every sector of society. Although the demand for equality was one of the terms of democratic citizenship from an early stage, the substance of the concept was nonetheless far from unambiguous and consistent. For example, the conditions which applied to a working-class citizen were differently defined from those which applied to the more privileged classes. Likewise, what was expected of male and female citizens started to be sharply categorised according to the new type of gender division. Just as her identity had been, so the demands made of woman as a citizen were soon associated with privacy and the family, in contrast to man's public and working life. Taken together, these two spheres were apparently shaping the emergent, 'democratic' citizenship.

Although these organisations, which called themselves progressive movements, fiercely promoted these modern male and female identities, the unfamiliar dogma and codes of conduct did not easily penetrate the basic stratum of society. The unity between the sexes and the, albeit weakened, sense of solidarity continued to typify the concept of human existence. Evidence of this can be found in organised activity since, well into the twentieth century, Finland firmly adhered to a pattern of organisation which was not sexually divisive. By contrast, evenly-distributed, cooperative work in organisations which were not sex-discriminating was no longer a common model in the industrialised countries of Western Europe, not to mention America. By this time, it was more likely to have been quite rare. For example the temperance movement in England and America was sharply divided between the sexes as early as the 1870s. Moreover, by this stage women in these countries had for the most part formed their own women's rights, suffragist and housewife associations, moral and philanthropic societies, or women's sections within political parties.

If we are to draw a specific comparison with industrialised Western Europe and North America, then the special nature of organised institutions and of women's social role in Finland must of course be largely attributed to the slow and late development of industrialisation. Agriculture, which for most of the country meant smallholdings, survived in Finland as the major method of production well into the first half of the twentieth century. It is significant, for example, that just after the turn of the century 90 per cent of Finland's population still lived in the countryside, and the majority earned their living through agriculture or other closely-related sources of livelihood. Another feature of circumstances in Finland was that the most important branch of industrialisation, the forest industries, was concentrated in the countryside and employed much the same sector of the population as agriculture.

Given this economic background, it was not surprising that the social and ideological nature of organised activity should strongly reflect the values and customs of agrarian society. As a result, the concept of human existence, as well as gender relations remained 'behind-the-times' in Finland for a good deal longer than in Western Europe, which experienced rapid industrialisation and urbanisation.

Compared to Western Europe, then, Finland lagged several decades behind in developing an antagonism and dichotomy within the notion of citizens' roles. These features only seem to have taken root at the third, or party-political, stage of the process of organisation. Then the whole machinery of the democratic system, from party groups to other rapidly-politicised interest groups, stood firmly in support of the recently-established gender division, and undertook to exercise that division in social and political life.

Another characteristic of developments in Finland was that this new gender division only emerged fully after universal and equal suffrage had been achieved. It is perhaps extraordinary that a key role in this was played precisely by the legislative system; this was the area which ultimately defined the separate identities of male and female citizenship, based on the differences in life-spheres.

This was reflected in parliamentary activity, in that both right-wing and socialist women limited their spheres of interest right from the start to questions of household management, education and family, and the position of women and children. In the years that followed, they guarded this 'feminine' domain closely, often with recourse to feminist arguments. Thus the fact that women identified themselves with the feminine and the private did not mean that they were marginalised in social and political life. Rather, they were allocated their own carefully-defined place in the democratic order from the most basic stratum of society to the pinnacles of the legislative body.

All this brings us to the conclusion that, when the suffrage reform became the order of the day and acquired a symbolic value in Finnish-Russian relations, the question of separate, inherently male or female qualities was still of secondary importance to the majority of the population. It is significant that it was precisely those organisations which were not sexually divisive that supported universal and equal suffrage, such as the temperance movement, youth groups and workers' associations. Women's right to the vote was not analysed or presented as a specific issue within the demands of these organisations, but simply seemed as natural as the right of disfranchised men to participate in the legislative system. It is also significant that of the social ranks, it was notably the peasant estate that lent the most unqualified support to women's right of franchise, while the only formal arguments against women's suffrage were put forward by the Swedish-speaking parliamentary members, who represented the educated classes and the heads of industry. Only middle-class women defended women's voting rights as a separate issue, and even they claimed the minimum of conditions by basing their demands, right up to the last minute, on the criteria of wealth and status within the old order of rank.

It seems easier to understand the untroubled early success for women's suffrage in Finland if we examine it from this angle. In short, we can say that the whole question of female suffrage reached the Finnish parliament well before its time. There was simply no place in Finland's strongly agrarian society for the kind of militant suffragist movement and polemic over equality which spread across English political life at the turn of the century. The distinctions between the private and public spheres were still blurred, and similarly the new male and female concepts of citizenship were only just becoming established. As a result, the suffrage debate was dealt with according to a concept of human existence and to life-experiences which were, in a sense, a legacy from the collectivist agricultural society. It was the same world-view which had first become introduced into the revivalist movements, then carried over to organised social activity, and finally, though by now less forcefully, to party-political organisation. And just as it had made possible the radical transition from a corporate hierarchy to modern democracy, this development is precisely what made the fulfilment of female suffrage unusually accessible in Finland.

## NOTES

1. Cf. O. Seitkari, *Eduskuntalaitoksen uudistus 1906* (Suomen kansanedustuslaitoksen historia, 5), Helsinki 1958. U. Tuominen, *Säätyedustuslaitos 1880-luvun alusta vuoteen 1906* (Suomen kansanedustuslaitoksen historia, 3), Helsinki 1964.
2. O. Jussila, *Nationalismi ja vallankumous venäläis-suomalaisissa suhteissa 1899–1914*, Helsinki 1979.
3. E. Haavio-Mannila *et al.* (eds), *Keskeneräinen kansanvalta. Naiset Pohjoismaiden politiikassa*, Stockholm 1983.
4. This essay is part of a larger research project, funded by the Finnish Academy: 'The organisation of women in Finland from the eighteenth century to 1917'. The first report on this project appeared in R. Alapuro *et al.* (eds), *Kansa liikkeessä*, Helsinki 1987, pp. 157–75 (I. Sulkunen 'Naisten järjestäytyminen ja kaksijakoinen kansalaisuus').
5. I. Sulkunen, 'Väckelserörelserna som ett förskede i organiseringens historia', *Historisk Tidskrift för Finland*, 69 (1983), pp. 1–14.
6. H. Stenius, *Frivilligt — jämtlikt — samfällt. Föreningsväsendets utveckling i Finland fram till 1900-talets början med speciell hänsyn till massorganisationsprincipens genombrott*, Helsingfors 1987. I. Sulkunen, *Raittius kansalaisuskontona. Raittiusliike ja järjestäytyminen 1870-luvulta suurlakkoon*, Helsinki 1986.
7. I. Sulkunen, 'Naisten järjestäytyminen ja naisasialiike vuosisadan vaihteessa' in, K. Eskola, E. Haavio-Mannila, R. Jallinoja (eds), *Naisnäkökulmia*, Juva 1979.
8. A. Innala, *Suomen naisen alkutaival lainsäätäjänä*, Joensuu 1967.

The pride and joy of the workers' movement was the wooden house in which members of the workers' association could meet and indulge in a variety of uplifting activities, from debating circles to drama groups. Here, members of the Ylänaa workers' association are about to put the roof on their house (1913). *R*

# THE LABOUR MOVEMENT

*David Kirby*

During the 1880s and 1890s, Finnish workers were active in a variety of organisations such as the temperance movement and the bourgeois-philanthropic workers' associations; but it was not till 1899 that an independent Workers' Party came into being, and another four years were to elapse before the adoption of the title and basic tenets of Marxist social democracy. Within four years, the small and rather insignificant Social Democratic Party had been transformed into a mass movement. In the months immediately following the 1905 revolution, party membership touched 100,000. The first elections to the new unicameral legislature in 1907 gave the party eighty out of 200 seats. This success was to be repeated in subsequent elections: in 1916, the party even secured an absolute majority of 103 seats.

The spectacular rise of a social democratic party whose ideology closely followed that of the German Marxist Karl Kautsky, in an overwhelmingly agrarian part of the Russian empire, is something of a puzzle which still intrigues historians. I would like to range a little wider here than the perimeter of Finnish national development and consider the Finnish experience in the light of developments elsewhere in Europe. Seen in this broader context, two aspects of the development of the labour movement in Finland are particularly striking. The first is the amazing speed at which a relative latecomer to the ranks of social democracy became a mass-based national party; the second is the comparative absence of political tradition or experience upon which such a movement could be built. Recent studies have suggested that the labour movement was an outgrowth of the national movement, an integral part of the process of mass mobilisation and organisation of the Finnish people. It did not have to undergo decades of struggle against reactionary industrialists and landowners in order to achieve recognition. On the contrary, the Finnish nationalists, lacking a powerful and potentially supportive middle class, had to turn to 'the people' in order to build up a movement capable of inheriting the state, once control had slipped from the hands of imperial Russia. Thus it was that the labour movement came into being under bourgeois tutelage, with the demands of labour channelled into safe reformist activity. There was little opposition in 1906 to the main demand of the labour movement,

193

universal suffrage, and there was also a wide measure of support for land reform in bourgeois circles.

The relatively painless birth of the labour movement within the cradle of Finnish nationalism, which took place in the last two decades of the nineteenth century, does not however explain why the movement took off so spectacularly in 1905–6. If anything, it tends to reinforce the impression that the 'people' were called into political existence by the nationalists, that the absence of genuine working-class traditions of organisation and protest meant that this bourgeois-liberal phase *had* to take place in order that the working class could derive sufficient experience and self-confidence to strike out independently.

The early years of the Finnish labour movement tended to follow the pattern of development in other Northern European countries. There is an interesting parallel in the case of Norway, where the Labour Party (DNA)

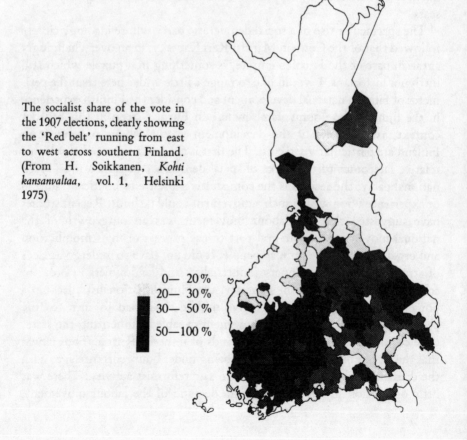

The socialist share of the vote in the 1907 elections, clearly showing the 'Red belt' running from east to west across southern Finland. (From H. Soikkanen, *Kohti kansanvaltaa*, vol. 1, Helsinki 1975)

0— 20%
20— 30%
30— 50%
50—100%

grew to maturity during a period dominated by the suffrage question and
the union with Sweden. The DNA, like its Finnish counterpart, initially
drew its support largely from the artisans and skilled workers in traditional
small-scale industries. The liberals of the Venstre party played an active
part in promoting workers' organisations, which they hoped to use in the
struggle against royal prerogative and ultimately against the union. The
alliance with Venstre continued after the formation of an independent
labour party in 1887, although there was also a more overtly 'socialist'
wing around Knudsen and Jeppesen. At the turn of the century, the party
adopted a noticeably broader, reformist programme. In the words of the
party newspaper *Social-Demokraten*:

With the growth of the workers' political organisation, it became involved in
day-to-day politics and was made familiar with the process of social development.
This had a moderating effect. Initially, it had remained on the outside, and had
constructed theoretical models of its ideal society. Now it is getting involved in
practical work and is beginning to gain independent experience. From being an
out-and-out class party, it is becoming a universal organisation, which invites all
classes to join and set the religion of fairness on the throne . . . and thus it is that
social democracy, from being a strictly limited workers' party, is becoming a
people's party.[1]

This reformist phase came to an end after the break-up of the union in
1905. The DNA, no longer needed as an ally by Venstre, became increasingly isolated in the system, and was forced to look after its own interests.
The electoral system worked against the party; in 1915, for example, in
spite of increasing its share of the vote from 26.5 to 32 per cent, it lost four
seats in the Storting elections. The radicalisation of the DNA during the
first fifteen years of independence has been attributed to the sudden and
massive creation of a 'new' unskilled proletariat, more receptive to a
radical ideology, and more willing to resort to militant industrial action to
remedy grievances which a blocked parliamentary system seemed unable to
resolve. This interpretation, first put forward in 1922 by Edvard Bull, has
been subjected to much criticism, but the salient facts are not in dispute,
namely that rapid industrial development after 1905 did engender a new
spirit of trade union militancy, and that the DNA did adopt a radical line
which was ultimately to take it into the Communist International.[2]

The break-up of the Swedish-Norwegian union and the patriotic protest
strike which was the Finnish response to the revolution of 1905 in Russia
may be seen as turning-points in the period of broad collaboration between
a national-minded, reformist-inclined bourgeoisie and a relatively weak
reformist labour movement. The working classes of both countries,

aroused to political activity in the period of political crisis, failed to perceive any material improvement in their conditions, and were indeed made uncomfortably aware of the shortcomings of their position in society. In Norway, rapid industrial development after 1905 and the failure of the DNA to make much headway in Storting elections undermined the tactic of parliamentary reformism and made militant trade unionism, under vigorous leadership, a more attractive proposition. In Finland, the relative lack of industrial development and the rapid advances by the socialists in parliamentary elections gave the labour movement an excessively political character. As early as 1918, Edvard Gylling commented on this fact, which he attributed to the large numbers of rural supporters of the Social Democratic Party, for whom political activity was the means of resolving the land question.[3] Gylling was however also aware of the revolutionary impulse which had brought so many of the rural poor into the party, and which surfaced once more during the revolution of 1917.

The degree of rural support for the Social Democratic Party, which persisted long after the civil war, is a remarkable phenomenon, particularly in the light of the failure of other socialist parties to attract support in the countryside. In France, support for socialism was confined to certain areas which had been 'Red' since the revolution of 1848. French 'peasant socialism' was also a good deal more autonomous in its orientation than was rural socialism in Finland. What is particularly striking about the Finnish case is the degree of organisation of rural workers within a party more reminiscent in structure and ideology of the German Social Democratic Party (SPD) than of the decentralised, ideologically heterogenous French socialist movement. There was moreover no 'Red' tradition to build on, nor were there any tendencies towards 'natural anarchism' in the Finnish rural population.

The labour movement was not, however, sowing its seed on virgin soil when it began to spread into the countryside. From the 1880s onwards, a variety of organisations had begun to recruit more broadly than had the earlier élitist nationalist institutions, such as the Finnish Literature Society. In particular, the temperance and youth club movements often provided the initial impetus for the founding of a workers' association.[4] The setting up of a workers' association, especially in the heady days of 1905–6, is often described in the memoirs and reminiscences of party veterans as a momentous parting of the ways between workers and bourgeoisie. In many instances, however, the workers' associations were set up by committees of citizens, including local worthies, and the often-repeated story of workers triumphing in debate with their bourgeois opponents and immediately setting about founding their 'own' association may be part of the mythology of the movement rather than an accurate reflection of the truth. The parting of the ways was often a gradual process; many, if not most workers' associations retained a distinctly non-proletarian character for several years after their foundation.

After 1906, however, there is a noticeable scission. The workers' associations withdrew more and more into their own world, rejecting and spurning the perceived evils of bourgeois society. What was in effect a sub-culture was created, centred on the workers' hall (*työväentalo*). This thriving sub-culture was created in a remarkably short space of time, rather late in the day in comparison with the rest of Europe, and it undoubtedly gave the movement a sense of solidarity and an enthusiasm which elsewhere showed signs of waning by 1914. The syndicalist militants of France, for example, frequently complained that workers preferred to play cards or read comics, and the falling rate of subscriptions for *La Bataille Syndicaliste* would seem to substantiate their complaints. In Germany, in Carl Schorske's words, a *Parteiverdrossenheit* (literally 'party sulkiness') was palpably evident on the eve of war. In the urbanised countries of the West, there were also more attractions for the worker — pubs, cafés, music-halls, football matches, as well as a great variety of non-socialist organisations which actively sought to recruit working-class support. The Finnish worker, especially in rural areas, had rather fewer temptations. In the workers' hall, of which there were over 1,000 by 1917, the worker was in the company of his peers, and might indulge without fear of patronage or scorn from his social superiors in that doggedly earnest version of self-improvement which socialism represented for the rank-and-file activist in Protestant Europe.[5]

The everyday life of the Finnish workers' associations was in many respects similar to that charted by Claude Willard in his massive study of Guesdism in France. There was little discussion of national or theoretical issues. Practical matters, such as the collection of dues, admission of new members and the creation of an infrastructure of committees (of which the entertainments committee was often the most important), predominated. Support for the local socialist newspaper was one of the chief tasks: as the federal secretary of the Gard reported in 1898, the principal obligation of members of the group was to order the newspaper which represented the organisation and the socialist doctrine in the region.[6] Support for left-socialist papers was also one of the main concerns of the workers' associations which affiliated to the Finnish Socialist Workers' Party after 1920. Some workers' associations did attempt to build up libraries, though lack

May Day demonstration, led by a brass band, in the forecourt of the workers' house at Nokia. *K*

of funds usually brought such noble aspirations to a premature end. A thorough study of the workers' libraries would be a rewarding exercise, although the purchase of a book is no guarantee that it will find favour among the readers. As in other countries, workers preferred easy-to-read literature, often with striking or moralising titles. A certain amount of pamphlet literature was produced by the party, but relatively few of the classic Marxist works were available in translation.

The members of the workers' associations were imbued with a strong sense of morality, even self-righteousness, which at times assumed religious characteristics. Consider, for example, the protest of the Jurva workers' association in 1921, directed at the refusal of local shopkeepers to advertise in the left-socialist newspaper *Vapaa Sana*. The bourgeoisie abused and insulted socialist workers at will, 'for in this society made foul by bourgeois arrogance, we are of no more consequence than birds of passage, which in the summer-time set off to see the world in a neighbouring land, on condition that we are grateful for the crumbs which happen to fall from the table of our merciful masters.'[7]

The temptations of the demon drink prompted an even more eloquent flood of moralising on the part of the righteous minority. There were also attempts to prevent card games and dancing on the premises of the workers' association. The Socialist Workers' Party devoted a good deal of time to discussing means of combating the 'spiritual decay'which beset rural workers' associations, who were often obliged to put on dances as a means of raising money. 'Drunkenness, immorality and other vices flourish precisely in those places where dances are the only form of evening entertainment,' declared one delegate at a district meeting of the party organisation in northern Finland: 'This is anything but favourable for the revolutionary mass activity of the proletariat.'[8]

What does this dour morality, with its distinct echoes of 'awakened' Christianity, say about the spiritual roots of the Finnish labour movement? Irma Sulkunen has recently suggested that, at a time when large numbers of people were beginning to turn away from the church, the temperance movement offered workers a kind of religious substitute as a means of coping with the harsh realities of everyday life. On the other hand, Sven Rydenfelt and Jaakko Nousiainen were careful to avoid drawing conclusions about the possible connection between backwoods communism and fundamentalist religion in areas where both enjoyed wide support, such as northern Savo. In his study of Swedish communism, however, Rydenfelt did suggest that earlier religious radicalism might have left its traces, as in the village of Tvärån in Norrbotten, a stronghold of anti-clerical fundamentalism at the beginning of the century, where the communists took 63 per cent of the vote in 1952.[9] In the absence of firm evidence, it is probably wise not to draw any conclusions about the influence of religious revivalism , though it is worth noting that the rise of the labour movement in Finland coincided with a sharp decline in formal religious observance, and the weakening of the authority of the clergy.

The workers' association also offered the opportunity for those who had acquired a modicum of elementary education to practise their skills. The labour movement did indeed provide a channel for the talented to rise above the ranks of the manual labouring class, although the hardships endured by many working-class activists should be a reminder that considerable sacrifices often had to be made on the way to party or parliamentary office. At its lowest echelons, the Finnish labour movement was overwhelmingly proletarian. Village schoolteachers, who were often socialists in Italy or France, rarely joined the movement in Finland. A strong desire for independence from bourgeois tutelage is palpably evident in the ill-written pages of the minute-books of the associations. At the same time, however, these pages breathe a spirit of bourgeois rectitude, especially in matters of behaviour. One of the purposes of youth clubs and temperance associations had been to curb uncouth behaviour, to 'civilise' the rough peasant. The workers' associations were founded on the same assumptions, with the difference that workers themselves should exercise a collective or 'comradely' discipline, and not be told what to do by their social superiors.

Studies of elementary education in France have suggested that the inculcation of two sets of republican values — fraternal, pacifist and internationalist on the one hand, bellicose and nationalistic on the other — had a deep impact on the collective psyche of the French working class. It has also been argued that the intensity of nationalist propaganda in imperial Germany tended to create a framework of assumptions and notions in which the social democrats were also trapped. To date, rather little work has been done on the diffusion of nationalist ideas in Finland through the medium of education. The records of the annual meetings of elementary schoolteachers clearly reveal that they regarded themselves as being at the forefront in the battle to bring national values to the populace at large. It is also clear that they had grave doubts about the degree to which they were succeeding. This was especially noticeable in the peripheral areas of Karelia and Northern Finland, but in areas where the labour movement had struck deep roots, there were many who would have echoed the sentiments of H. Pulkkinen, speaking to the Tampere district meeting of elementary schoolteachers in 1921:

Seen in terms of our social conditions, the opportunities for inculcating love of the fatherland are not good, because the great majority of the pupils in the elementary schools come from the working class, a very mixed crowd of people who live in wretched conditions. We ought to influence this crowd too; but how?[10]

Pulkkinen was of course speaking in the aftermath of the civil war, when the defeated 'Reds' were widely regarded as unreliable and unpatriotic elements. Before 1917, however, there is little to suggest that social democratic party members were lacking in patriotism. Many workers' associations were prepared to protest about violations of national integrity during the last years of imperial rule, though it is curious that there seems to have been so little discussion at grassroots level of the major national issue of Finland's relationship with Russia in 1917. Without further detailed study of how the ordinary Finnish socialist regarded the complex question of nationality and national interest (not necessarily the same thing), it would be unwise to make rash judgements. However, I would suggest that there did exist a strong but passive sense of national identity, which was channelled into national political activity, not in the first instance to preserve the constitutional contours of the state from Russian encroachments, nor to erect a specifically Finnish-language state, but to use an existing state structure for the reform of society. In other words, I do not believe that working-class political activity was fuelled by the desire to *defend* a notional or putative state, which at the turn of the century was the impelling force behind bourgeois politics.

To return to the question of why socialism spread so rapidly into the countryside after 1905, the sudden political awakening which culminated in the strike week at the end of October 1905, and which was sustained by the prospects of a dramatic breakthrough on the question of suffrage reform, is of crucial importance. The extension of the franchise had never generated the kind of organised political pressure in Finland that it had in Sweden or Belgium, and it was conceded virtually without a struggle in 1906. The nationalists were in effect taken by surprise. They had to organise themselves into parties capable of contesting elections, whereas the Social Democratic Party was already prepared for this eventuality. The only other 'popular' party, the Agrarian Union (*Maalaisliitto*) was slow to organise, and then remained a regional party until independence. To a certain extent, therefore, the electoral success of the social democrats was a victory for the one party which had a genuine base in the populace at large, and was, as it were, prepared for parliamentary activity. The nationalists had no tradition of mass political mobilisation to draw upon, as had the Irish nationalist party, which could build on Daniel O'Connell's early nineteenth-century campaigns for Catholic emancipation. Moreover, the language issue — still the central plank of the Finnish nationalist platform — did not arouse much enthusiasm in large areas of the hinterland where Swedish was not seen as a hindrance or threat to the lives of working men and women.

The Swedish minority, on the other hand, were far more impervious to the appeal of social democracy. The Swedish-speaking urban worker tended to be more skilled, and could also enjoy the reflected status of the language of the urban class; the rural worker in the south was hostile to the landowners who sought to undercut their labour by employing Finnish-speakers at lower rates, but was also resentful of this competition. Finnish linguistic nationalism was also present in the Social Democratic Party, and this too may have been an inhibiting factor for the Swedish-speaking proletariat.

The events of 1905, which gave the youthful labour movement an opportunity to direct events via strike committees, were thus an important catalyst, and the Social Democratic Party was firmly identified with the

A group of loggers in the 1920s. *K*

demand for thorough reform of an outmoded parliamentary system. The party also succeeded in capturing the mood of protest among the working population. During the period 1905–7, a great range of occupational groups, from railwaymen to tenant-farmers, organised themselves within the camp of labour. Above all, those who earned their livelihood on the land rallied in large numbers to the party. I would suggest that they did so, not because of a deep desire for land, but for more immediate reasons. The ultimate settlement of the vexed question of leasehold tenure was of importance for the tenant farmers, certainly, but they were also anxious to improve their existing contractual position, which in many instances had noticeably worsened since the 1870s. Those who had to sell their labour, either as farm hands or as seasonal workers in the forests and log-floats, also had many grievances, which could not easily be resolved by localised collective action, as Gylling noted in 1918.[11]

The impact on the rural population of the passive resistance after 1899, and the perceived success of the strike of 1905 which seemed to have overthrown authority, proved to be the necessary incentive for collective organisation, much as the Boulangist crisis inspired the woodcutters of the Cher and Nièvre. In his pioneering study, the sociologist L.N. Roblin suggested that militant strike action in this region in 1891–2 owed much to three preconditions: the political impact of Boulangism; the coming together of poor peasants to work in the forests during the winter months, when group solidarity was created; and a realisation that they could not easily be replaced once the work had begun. Roblin also pointed out the difficulties of syndical organisation among seasonal workers, once the initial momentum for action began to decline. *Mutatis mutandis*, many of his observations may be applied to these who worked in the Finnish forests. Seasonal work could afford an opportunity for collective solidarity, but this could not be sustained because of the transient nature of the work performed.[12]

The real heartland of the pre-1918 labour movement was in precisely those areas where leaseholders were to be found in large numbers. Although the commitment of the leasehold farmers to the movement is a matter of some debate, they often fulfilled a kind of leadership role. Examination of the minute-books and accounts of rural workers' associations shows that it was invariably the leasehold farmer and his family who were the backbone of the movement. They had a more independent status than the farmhands and labourers, who were often compelled to go outside the parish in search for work. Meetings could be held in their houses, and they were often sufficiently skilled and motivated to become office-holders. During the years when party membership swelled, they tended to be in a small minority — of the 121 members of the Nurmijärvi workers' association in 1917, for example, leaseholders and their children constituted less than one-fifth — but they tended to stay loyal and keep the association in being during the lean years.

Leasehold farmers had their own particular grievances, but they were also in the forefront of social conflict. Small farmers in practice, they were nevertheless placed outside the ranks of village society by virtue of their insecure status, which made them dependent on the whims of a landlord. There were many with farms large enough for them to employ labour, but there were many more whose holdings were insufficient to provide a living, who were obliged to seek work where they could.

The 'land question' was essentially one of work opportunities for the great majority of those who lived in the countryside, and the experience of work in groups outside the family unit undoubtedly gave an impetus to collective action. This was often primitive and limited in scope, and did not lead to effective organisation. It is perhaps here that we may speak of a fusion of the early traditions of collective organisation for patriotic or morally uplifting purposes and the desire for radical reform which the political organisation of the social democratic party articulated. Many of the norms and values of the youth club and temperance movements were maintained by the organised workers; sobriety, self-discipline, duty, even patriotism shine through in the pages of the minute-books and annual reports. The organised labour movement inherited many of the ethical features of the popular movements of late-nineteenth century nationalism, but rejected the bourgeois society which had spawned them. The degree to which workers' associations rejected the bourgeois world is striking. One explanation may be that opportunities for sharing the pleasures of bourgeois life were strictly limited, especially in the countryside. There were few places of entertainment where the classes could freely mix, such as the music-hall, nor were there any commercially-organised sporting events such as horse-racing or boxing, which persuaded the British worker, for example, that he shared the same tastes as the aristocracy. Similarly, the circumstances which might produce deference, or even a strong desire to ape the middle classes, were virtually absent in Finland. Indeed, it might be asked to what extent the Finnish worker was aware of the urban phenomenon of 'bourgeois culture'. The hostility towards the bourgeois society so frequently displayed was directed largely against the '*herrat*', the upholders of a stratified social system which was already beginning to crumble. In a rural context, this was often highly personalised and subjective, for the '*herrat*' or those who aspired to be members of that select circle were easily identified — as indeed were those who joined the workers' association.

The sense of class antagonism which was evident in the labour movement was also fostered by the lack of mediating agencies which might smooth social frictions, and by the failure of the political system. Whereas the demands of Finnish nationalism had been largely accommodated, those of the rural poor and industrial working class were not. This is not to say that the labour movement faced an obdurate and reactionary ruling class, which set its face against all reform. The evidence of the 1920s would argue to the contrary, especially if one compares the situation in post-civil war Finland with that of Hungary after the crushing of the Soviet regime in 1919. But the great breakthrough of 1905–7, which seemed to offer so much, simply failed to produce results. The Social Democratic Party was the greatest beneficiary of parliamentary reform, but the parliamentary system did not function. The result was internecine feuding between the parties, and the erosion of any likelihood of collaboration between socialist and radical bourgeois groupings to push through reform. The Social Democratic Party adopted a position of revolutionary passivity, and retreated to its own class-conscious corner because there was little alternative. In a sense, all the parties had to adopt an attitude of waiting for a decisive change within the Russian empire, which they were unable to influence in any meaningful way.

Red Guards posing for the camera shortly before the outbreak of the civil war. It is thought that between 75,000 and 100,000 Finns joined the Red Guards in 1917–18, although no more than 50,000 were involved in actual combat. *B*

The sudden collapse of the empire in the midst of revolution did not solve the problem, for the interim inheritor of the powers of the ruler was unwilling to concede the full exercise of authority in the former grand duchy to Finnish institutions alone. The Finnish political parties failed to work together to achieve a settlement of the relationship with Russia, and in the end they fought over the inheritance. The Finnish Social Democratic Party preserved its unity throughout the civil war. There was a strong sense of loyalty within the party, which persuaded even those who opposed the seizure of power in January 1918 to serve in some capacity in the Red administration. Moreover, party members had not been called upon to define their attitudes towards the European war. It was this issue which provoked division and dissent within the parties of the belligerent countries, but it was one which Finnish social democracy simply did not experience.

The isolation of Finnish social democracy from the mainstream of European socialist thought and action is particularly striking, as is the lack of antecedents for a socialist party. Finland not only failed to produce any native variety of socialism; it also remained singularly immune to outside influences. The revolutionary movement in Russia had virtually no impact in Finland. Russian Populists from Bessarabia gave the first major impetus to socialism in Romania, for example, but one looks in vain for similar impulses in Finland. Even when certain Finns did become active in the Russian underground movement towards the end of the century, this seems not to have had any major repercussions in Finland. Radical intellectuals in Eastern Europe were attracted to the ideas of Marx as a means of approaching the problems of backwardness in their own countries, but again, Finns are conspicuous by their absence in the voluminous correspondence of Engels and Kautsky. A recent study has even cast doubt on the Marxist credentials of the man popularly held to be the father-figure of Finnish socialism, and has suggested — in my view, convincingly — that he was essentially a rather muddled nationalist.[13] After 1905, it is true, the party leadership aligned themselves with orthodox Marxism, and sought through the press and party schools to put across those ideas. Nevertheless, the major issues which occupied European Marxists during the years before the outbreak of war — militarism, imperialism, the threat of war — were remote from the Finnish experience, and were never discussed in any serious fashion. Essentially, the 'Marxism' of the party was at best imitative. At an everyday level, it was reduced to the simplest of deterministic formulae, as elsewhere in Europe. It was a faith rather than an analytical tool.

The relative absence of any kind of socialism or labour collectivism does not in itself *explain* the peculiar course of development after 1905, but it does suggest that the mass movement called into existence very rapidly as a result of the events of 1905 rested on very shallow ideological foundations. Even the rather unstable parties which came into existence in the Balkan countries had a more impressive past to which they could refer. Teodor Diamant, for example, had attempted to establish a Fourierist 'phalanstery' in Romania as early as 1835, and student socialists put out a short-lived paper, *Socialistul*, in 1877. Students in Serbia and Bulgaria were also attracted to socialism in the 1870s.

On the other hand, the popular roots of the Finnish Social Democratic Party were a good deal stronger than those of the parties of Eastern Europe, which were strong in terms of intellectual leadership, but very weak in popular support. If we see social democracy as an outgrowth of the popular nationalist movement, as the political preference of the 'deep masses', then its durability, and even its success, becomes more comprehensible. And one might dare to suggest that the strict orthodoxy which the leadership endorsed may also have been a further development of mainstream nationalist thinking, a deterministic world-view which was also favoured by the climate of political stagnation in which the party achieved its greatest measure of support. There is more than a passing resemblance between the exhortations of Snellman and Yrjö-Koskinen to the Finnish nation to build up its strength — preserving its identity unsullied in the struggle with the Swedish-speaking élite, and biding its time until the collapse of Russian imperialism opened the way for final victory — and the doctrine of class struggle as espoused by the socialist leadership, many of whom came to the movement via Old Finn nationalism.

The post-civil war split in Finnish social democracy is interesting in a number of ways. First, the foundation of the Communist Party in August 1918, with a programme which in many ways was a classic statement of the 'infantile disease' which Lenin was to attack two years later, was a reflection of the bitterness and ideological confusion of a significant section of the old party leadership. Seen against the background of splits elsewhere in Europe, it was also somewhat premature, and it had little immediate effect in Finland. To be sure, party agents were sent secretly to Finland, but by the party's own admission they were rather ineffective. The principal concern of the defeated working class was to regroup and strive for some amelioration in the condition of those in the prison camps, and in these circumstances the Social Democratic Party, set back on its feet by right-wingers, was undoubtedly the best bet. It was only when the revived party showed itself, in the eyes of many, to be accommodating rather than uncompromising in its dealings with the White bourgeoisie that opposition began to emerge within the ranks. The real split in the Finnish labour movement did not occur till 1919–20, after the left socialists had failed to capture control of the Social Democratic Party machine. And even then, the Socialist Workers' Party which emerged cannot be seen merely as a legal front for the Finnish Communist Party: it was essentially a continuation of the radical tradition of the old party.

Support for the Socialist Workers' Party, which enjoyed a precarious existence until 1923 when it was effectively smashed up by the police, fell into two broad categories. The left socialists were dominant in towns with a relatively high proportion of large industrial concerns, such as Turku and Helsinki, though they failed to make much headway in Tampere among the largely female workforce in the textile mills, or in towns where small-scale industry was the norm. Left socialism virtually obliterated social democracy in large areas of Northern and Eastern Finland, such as Kainuu and around Kuopio, though the revived Social Democratic Party retained the loyalty of its supporters in the eastern half of Kuopio province and in the old 'Red belt' stretching across Southern Finland. There are several striking features of this division. It was almost always very sharp: voters tended to express a clear preference for one of the two left-wing parties, and with certain exceptions (such as the Turku electoral circle, where the initial left socialist gains were soon clawed back by the social democrats), this preference established a pattern which re-emerged with the formal legalisation of the Communist Party in 1944. Pre-civil war political proclivities do not appear to have exercised a decisive role — the local party in Kuopio West had a markedly moderate reputation, for instance, which that of Uusimaa adopted a radical position on many issues. The experience of civil war does not appear to have shaped preferences, either, for those areas which suffered most through the loss of active members remained loyal to the Social Democratic Party (although it may be that the absence of a radical local leadership at a crucial time — 1919–20 — may have had a marginal effect in determining choice).

The adherence of the majority of workers' associations to the new party in that part of Finland which had been under White control throughout the civil war requires some explanation. One possible interpretation is that the local leadership, left relatively untouched by the war and subsequent White terror, continued to support the radical traditions of the old party, which they believed the new leadership had abandoned. There is evidence to support this argument in the recorded debates which took place in the workers' associations on the question of affiliation to the Socialist Workers' Party; certainly, it is difficult to detect any fundamental shift of attitudes towards an appreciation of the principles of Bolshevism, although there is much criticism of the social democratic leadership for its inability to pursue the 'workers' cause' with vigour. It is also worth noting that the left socialists enjoyed something of an upsurge in activity in areas where pre-war social democracy had not struck deep roots — in the villages of the remote and impoverished region of Kainuu, for example, or in the White heartland of Ostrobothnia. In a sense, the early 1920s can be characterised as the last stage of the process whereby socialism spread into the countryside, as the belated response of the periphery. It is significant also that it was precisely in such areas that the one rival to the Social Democratic Party as a genuinely popular political movement — the Agrarian Union — had established itself between 1906 and 1917, although to what extent the agrarians had creamed off potential socialist support, or blocked the efforts of social democracy to establish itself in these areas, is a matter for conjecture. In these relatively undeveloped regions, there were fewer sharp social divisions than in the south. The life and social habits of the small farmers of these regions did not markedly differ from those of the landless, and there were relatively few members of the educated class seeking to foster Finnish culture and its concomitant social values.

In her study of the origins of French communism, Annie Kriegel suggested that peasants rallied to the Third International in 1920 not because they were attracted by communist theories about the land but because the break-up of closed peasant societies by the war had led to social disorientation and political radicalisation. Claude Pennetier, in his study of communism in the Cher, has pointed to the youth of communist militants; many SFIO veterans simply withdrew from political activity. Philippe Gratton has also suggested that the indifference of SFIO leaders to the problems of remote rural areas such as Corrèze may have prompted many to adhere to communism.[14] Although the circumstances are different, and one should not make too much of points of similarity, I would suggest that these elements are also present in Northern and Eastern Finland. The purchase of large tracts of forest and watercourses by speculators acting for the timber companies, often at knockdown prices, caused much bitterness among the local people. The effects of the intensive exploitation of these resources after the war upon the local economy and social structure have yet to be fully studied, but the fact that the secret police devoted an inordinate amount of space to reporting labour conflicts in the northern forests indicates that it was unsettling, to say the least. Large numbers of men seeking work crowded on to northbound trains, where they found themselves in competition with local small farmers who had been forced by crop failure and general impoverishment to look for work in the forests. An organiser of the northern trade union district (PAP) estimated in 1929 that in normal years around 20,000 men were employed in the forests of the far north in winter. In these sparsely-populated, remote regions, the integrative features which held together the social structure in the south were largely missing. Police reports convey a deep sense of alienation among the local people. A report from Rovaniemi in May 1922 speaks of a hostility towards the army and Civil Guard frontier patrols:

The populace appear to be indifferent to the government and local officials, and indeed to the affairs of the country, of which they have little knowledge, largely because of the limited circulation and demand for newspapers and literature . . . The population in the villages are very uneducated, and the language used by the women is positively crude, so that their receptivity towards the communist agitation which has been conducted among them is entirely understandable.[15]

The local authorities were acutely aware that the lack of schools and roads was a serious obstacle to national integration, and that the backwardness and isolation of the northern and eastern frontier regions created a breeding-ground for discontent, which communism might feed upon. On the other hand, the left socialists were also isolated within those self-same remote regions, where the Agrarian Party became the dominant political force in the 1920s. The sudden upsurge of activity in districts such as Kainuu could not be sustained; dozens of small workers' associations folded or lapsed into inactivity. Trade union and party organisers, already harassed by the police, found their work increasingly difficult as apathy set in. Social democratic associations further south also faced the problem of declining membership, but to an extent were able to draw upon their resources to survive; the workers' association might install a cinema screen, for example, or stage dances to raise funds.

'Backwoods communism' may be characterised as essentially a protest movement by workers living on the margins, lacking any deep traditions of organisation or activity, but ready to resort to direct action to resolve their economic grievances. The communism of the urban worker is more complex, and has been little studied. Undoubtedly, a number of young skilled machinists and engineers were radicalised as a result of the experiences of war and revolution, as in Germany or Britain, and it was from this sector of the workforce that many of the later communist militants were to come. The outdoor trades also proved to be a fertile recruiting-ground for communists. In both cases, the shop-floor and the work site, rather than the workers' associations, were the focus of activities, and the young communists received their schooling in labour struggles rather than in political activity geared towards parliamentary elections. The composition of communist cadres was even more 'proletarian' than the Social Democratic Party had been before 1918; not until the 1960s did significant numbers of intellectuals in Finland begin to flirt with the extreme left. The degree to which the new generation of working-class radicals imbibed Marxism in its communist form perhaps owed less to education — for books were expensive and hard to obtain, and party schools were difficult to organise — than to experience at the workplace and in prison. The ultimate school, of course, was the Soviet Union, though not all who found their way there in the inter-war years survived to return after 1944.

The peculiarly 'rural' tinge to socialism in Finland is unusual, and for this reason, much of this chapter is devoted to the phenomenon. Although parallels are drawn with the experience of other countries, most notably France, firm conclusions should not be made on the basis of these comparisons. The development of the labour movement in each country must to a large extent depend upon national circumstances. French socialism, for instance, had a vibrant revolutionary tradition; this was entirely lacking in Finland. Finnish socialism took root in the soil of national awakening, but we suggest that it drew sustenance from popular, perhaps even quasi-religious perceptions of society which merit further study, rather than from the vision of a Finnish-culture state proffered by the national movement.

## NOTES

1. H. Lange, *Fra sekt til parti. Det norske arbeiderpartiets organisasjonsmessige og politiske utvikling fra 1891 til 1901*, Oslo 1962, p. 195.
2. E. Bull, 'Die Entwicklung der Arbeiterbewegung in den drei skandinavischen Länder 1914–1920', *Archiv für Geschichte des Sozialismus*, 10 (1922).
3. J. Hodgson (*ed.*), *Edvard Gylling ja Otto W Kuusinen asiakirjojen valossa 1918–1920*, Helsinki 1974, p. 30.
4. R. Alapuro *et al.* (eds), *Kansa liikkeessä*, Helsinki 1987.
5. C. Schorske, *German social democracy 1905–1917*, Cambridge, Mass. 1955; S. Hentilä, *Suomen työläisurheilun historia*, vol. 1, Hämeenlinna 1982.
6. C. Willard, *Le mouvement socialiste en France (1893–1905)*, Paris 1965, p. 101.
7. 'Jurvan kirkonkylän työväenyhdistyksen pöytäkirja', 2 Jan. 1921. Labour archives, Helsinki.
8. *Pöytäkirja Oulun läänin pohjoisen vaalipiirin sosialistisen piirijärjestön kokouksesta 7–8.5.1923*, Kemi 1923, p, 29.
9. I. Sulkunen and R. Alapuro, 'Raittiusliike ja työväen järjestäytyminen' in *Kansa liikkeessä*, p. 152.
10. 'Pöytäkirja kirjoitettu Tampereen tarkastuspiirin kansakoulu-opettajiston piirikokouksessa Kangasalan kansakoulussa', 22–23 Aug. 1921. Kouluhallitus, Kansanopetusosasto. File En 8. National archives, Helsinki.
11. Hodgson, p. 29.
12. L. N. Roblin, *Les bûcherons du Cher et de la Nièvre*, Paris 1903.
13. M. Rahikainen, *N.R. af Ursin. Aaatelismies Suomen työväenliikkeessä*, Helsinki 1986.
14. A. Kriegel, *Aux origines du communisme français*, 2 vols, Paris 1964; J. Girault (*ed.*), *Sur l'implantation du PCF dans l'entre deux guerres*, Paris 1977; P. Gratton, *Les paysans français contre l'agrarisme*, Paris 1972.
15. J. H. Vennola collection, file 7: 'Etsivän keskuspoliisin tilannekatsaus', 8 May 1922. National archives, Helsinki.

# FINLAND AS A NORDIC SOCIETY

## Erik Allardt

Finland is a Nordic society not only because Nordic cooperation has been so far-reaching in the cultural, political and economic fields, but also because of the nature of its social system. Such categorical statements are not particularly interesting from a more analytical point of view. The real question is in what respects Finland as a society exhibits Nordic features and attributes. If Finland is compared with the other Nordic countries, the results vary depending on whether the point of departure is social institutions, culture or the social structure. In institutional terms, Finland is particularly Nordic in character, and is also quite strongly Nordic in terms of social structure. It is in the cultural sphere that Finland diverges most clearly from the other countries of the Nordic region, even if Finnish culture and cultural life also contain many striking Nordic elements.

The institutions of a society include its laws and administrative system as well as the rules and customs which apply within large spheres of society like the family, education, the economy and so on. In institutional terms, Finland is very Nordic in character and above all very similar to Sweden.

A quite central feature is that Finland, like the other Nordic countries, is a parliamentary democracy. All the Nordic states now have unicameral parliaments, and governments are based on the political groupings which can construct a majority in these parliaments. In other words, the government requires a parliamentary foundation.

If these matters are viewed in a historical perspective, it is naturally important that for about 700 years from the Middle Ages until 1809 Finland was a part of the Swedish kingdom. Finland constituted the eastern 'half of the realm' within that kingdom and was as such subject to the same legal and institutional principles as all its other parts. When, as a result of the war of 1808–9, Finland was attached to the Russian empire, the country became an autonomous grand duchy with the Russian emperor as grand duke. An element of the country's autonomous status was that the Swedish legal system and the law code of 1734 were still to apply there. In consequence, the country retained its institutional structure from the period of union with Sweden. Indeed, the social institutions of Sweden and Finland are so similar that specialists on administrative history like Gustaf Petrén usually speak of the two countries as the eastern Nordic region in contrast to the western Nordic region, consisting of Denmark, Norway and Iceland.[1]

This picture, taken at Smedsby on the Ostrobothnian coast in 1976, symbolises the shift from a rural, self-sufficient society to the modern, urban and post-industrial world. Photograph by Mikael Herrgård.

In administrative matters, Denmark and Sweden are in many respects opposites within the Nordic system. Finland is close to Sweden, while Iceland and Norway are closer to Denmark. However, the principles of government and administration have converged in many ways and, as a result the similarities between the five countries are greater today than during earlier periods.

One difference between the two Nordic systems has been the degree of administrative centralisation. A conspicuous feature of the Danish system has been a rigorous centralisation of executive power, a feature that has its historical roots in the long period of political absolutism, which was based on the principle that crucial decisions needed to be under government control. The Danish central administration has been linked to the government, and the great departments of state have dealt with both national and detailed regional questions. The development of regional self-government in Denmark has been comparatively weak. In contrast, county governors for example have had considerably more power and influence in Sweden than in Denmark. Local self-government has also historically been under

strong central control in Denmark, although it has recently been significantly extended through, for example, the important municipal reforms of
1970. Decision-making has been more decentralised in Sweden, where in
principle the government has only been responsible for decisions affecting
the whole country while, as we have seen, the country governors have
possessed important decision-making powers.

The degree of centralisation in the other Nordic countries lies somewhere in between the contrasting traditions represented by Denmark and
Sweden. Iceland has essentially followed the Danish system, while Finland
has resembled Sweden. Finland has had and still has county governors and
central administrative bodies organised along the same lines as in Sweden.
Norway has been influenced by both Denmark and Sweden and lies
roughly in the middle of the spectrum. At all events, there are clear differences between the eastern Nordic and the western Nordic administrative
systems. In Sweden and Finland, a large part of the central administration
is carried out by bodies which are not part of the government. There are
many bodies of this kind in Finland, like the organisations responsible for
schools, shipping, waterways and the environment, agriculture and social
affairs. In contrast, decisions which in Finland and Sweden are made by
such extra-governmental bodies are taken in Denmark by the ministries of
state, often in the minister's name, even if in practice questions are often
delegated to junior officials. Another difference between the eastern and
western Nordic regions is that complaints against administrative decisions
can be made in ordinary courts in Denmark, Norway and Iceland, whereas
in Finland and Sweden such appeals must be heard by special administrative
courts.

The way in which the principle of open government has been applied is
of special interest. Documents relating to court proceedings have in principle been public in all the Nordic countries, including Finland, but historically the principle of open government in relation to the administration
proper has had a much stronger position in Sweden than in Denmark. In
Sweden, which included Finland at the time, the status of administrative
papers as documents open to public inspection was regulated for the first
time in 1766. Every document in the possession of a public institution has
in principle been available to the general public, especially in Sweden,
while in Denmark such documents have been regarded as the tools of their
trade by officials who have largely been able to determine which of them
should be made accessible to the public. The same fundamental principle
has applied in Finland as in the case of Sweden, but it has been applied much
less consistently than in Sweden because Finland has been subject to more

disturbed internal conditions, a more sensitive international position, wars and so on. Developments over the last few decades have produced an increasingly similar situation in all the Nordic countries regarding the principle of open government, and the essential rule in all of them nowadays is that important administrative documents ought to be open to the public.

The institutional similarities between Finland and the other Nordic countries, especially Sweden, are by no means restricted to the administrative sphere. The institutional structure is almost identical in Sweden and Finland within large areas of society like education, and this is true of both the schools and the universities. For example, there are many similarities between the examination systems in the two countries.

An important consideration is that the essential features of the economic institutions of the Nordic countries are very similar. All five are capitalist societies with strong elements of the mixed economy. Major economic decisions are usually taken after consultation between governments, organisations representing management and labour, political parties and the business world. The principles of the market economy prevail, but considerable attention is given to socio-political considerations when fundamental decisions are made.

Structurally, that is with regard to the dominant groupings in society, Finland resembles the other Nordic countries in many important ways. All are homogeneous states in race and religion, and all are Nordic welfare states whose social policies have had a levelling effect and have reduced the differences between the various social groups. An important factor in the modern history of all the Nordic countries is that industrialisation has created a very homogeneous working class which is not, as in many other countries, divided by religion or by conflicting regional loyalties. Class differences have not been particularly deep in the Nordic countries, but they have been evident nonetheless, and have constituted the primary basis for political consciousness. Until the 1970s, class-based voting, which involved the working class voting for the socialist parties while other voters supported the non-socialist parties, was more pronounced, especially in Finland and Sweden, than in continental Western Europe. The reasons for these phenomena are historical. In comparison with the continental countries of Western and Eastern Europe, the feudal system was not fully developed in the Nordic region, including Finland. The aristocracy never became sufficiently strong to be dominant, while the peasantry not only enjoyed a certain political independence but were also able to exercise a measure of political influence during some periods. The rather weak position traditionally occupied by the nobility has been regarded by the

British scholar Frank Castles as one of the main conditions both for the strength of Nordic social democrary and for the growth of the Nordic welfare state.[2]

Finland's social structure has clearly differed from that of the other Nordic countries in one important respect which emerged in the mid-nineteenth century and persisted for about a century: Finland remained an agrarian society whose economic structure was dominated by agriculture and its ancillary occupations for much longer than the other Nordic countries. In this much, Finland's social structure has much in common with the border-states of Russia like Poland, Hungary, Bulgaria and Romania, not to speak of the Baltic countries of Estonia, Latvia and Lithuania. These border-states long remained very rural and agrarian in comparison with Western Europe; they were peripheral areas and tended to be caught between contending Russian and German pressures.

This agrarian dominance in Finland had two central consequences which from the late nineteenth century differentiated Finland's social structure from that of the other Nordic countries. The first was that freeholding farmers became a particularly important group in the process of nation-building; and the second was the emergence in Finland of a rather large rural proletariat. The economic background to the importance of the free-holding farmers in Finnish politics for about a century up till the mid-1980s was that it was they who owned the country's forests when demand for paper products drew Finland rapidly into the world economy towards the end of the nineteenth century. They became a part of the capitalist world system, and thus it lay in their interests to defend the prevailing social order. The independent farmers were numerically the largest single element in the victorious White army during the Finnish civil war of 1918. When Finland had to adapt to the new conditions which governed its foreign policy after the armistice with the Soviet Union in 1944, the Agrarian Union became the leading and dominant group in Finnish politics.

The existence and nature of the Agrarian Union (renamed the Centre Party in 1965) are symptomatic of Finland's unique position between Eastern and Western Europe. Parties representing the farming interest have not been of any importance in Western Europe, except in Sweden where the earlier Agrarian Union was also renamed the Centre Party. In Finland this party remained a quite central political force at least till the mid-1980s, being represented in more governments than any other party. In many East European countries farmers often supported authoritarian regimes or dictatorships between the two world wars, but in Finland the party of the farmers remained a democratic and above all a parliamentary party. There were, however, attempts in Finland also to introduce authoritarian solutions. In the early 1930s the right-wing Lapua movement, which drew much of its support from the farmers of Ostrobothnia and Western Finland, tried to carry out a coup d'état, but it was ultimately checked with relative ease. In spite of the presence of tensions similar to those of Eastern Europe, Western European political solutions nevertheless prevailed. In nearly all respects, the development of agrarian politics in Finland represents an interesting intermediate form in relation to Western and Eastern Europe.

The emergence of the freeholding farmers as a leading political force is only one side of the coin. At the same time as they were being drawn into the world economy at the end of the nineteenth century, certain social problems in the countryside emerged for the first time, while others which already existed became more acute. A sharp fall in mortality rates in Finland, as in other European countries, led to a rapid increase in the population during the nineteenth century. The resulting problem of overpopulation in its turn produced a rapid growth in the numbers of the landless. The land could not be further subdivided, and farmers could no longer find land for all their children.

The size of the landless population grew in all the Nordic countries, but two factors made the problem much more severe in Finland. There was considerable emigration from Finland to the United States, but it never reached the same order of magnitude as in the other Nordic countries, partly because of certain inhibiting factors which applied to areas within the Russian empire. An even more important reason why the solution of the problem of overpopulation was delayed was that industrialisation began late. There was, simply, too little industry in Finland to absorb and sustain a stream of migrants from the countryside. At the beginning of the twentieth century the landless constituted about half of Finland's rural population, much higher than the proportion in Sweden. The presence of a rapidly growing rural proletariat was also one of the foremost structural reasons for the Finnish civil war of 1918.

Finland represents an intermediate form once again in the nature of the actual and attempted solutions applied to the problems of the landless rural population. The problem was so great in Finland that it could not be solved, as in Western Europe and the other Nordic countries, by market forces. Instead, the Finns sought a solution in great agrarian reforms intended to distribute land to the landless.

The main agrarian reforms were the crofters' law of 1918, the *Lex Kallio*

Evicted leasehold farmers, 1907. The eviction of the leaseholders from the Laukko estate in central Finland was a *cause célèbre* of the time, providing the Social Democratic Party with ample election propaganda. *K*

of 1922 and the land procurement law of 1945, all of which made it possible for various groups among the rural population who did not own land to acquire holdings; the third also sought to provide land for refugees from Karelia and Porkkala displaced by the Second World War. The crofters' law and the *Lex Kallio* led in the early 1920s to the creation of close to 100,000 new agricultural holdings or farmsteads. In the 1940s nearly 120,000 new farms of all sizes were created.

The great agrarian reforms by no means solved all problems. They also produced new difficulties by creating a large number not only of smallholdings (defined as no more than 5 hectares of cultivated land) but also of miniscule holdings (no more than 2 hectares of cultivated land) which were often not economically viable. However, the reforms did eliminate some of the social injustices associated with the existence of a landless rural proletariat and gave a new kind of independence to the weakest and most dependent groups in society. The reforms also had important political effects: the previous members of the rural proletariat began increasingly to accept the prevailing social system as legitimate and worth defending.

The rural proletariat only finally disappeared through an enormous movement of people from the countryside, mainly between 1960 and 1975

Table 1.  DIVISION OF THE FINNISH POPULATION INTO
OCCUPATIONAL CATEGORIES

| Occupational category | 1950 % | 1960 % | 1970 % | 1975 % | 1980 % |
|---|---|---|---|---|---|
| Agriculture and forestry | 41 | 32 | 18 | 12 | 9 |
| Industry | 21 | 19 | 21 | 21 | 21 |
| Building industry | 8 | 10 | 9 | 8 | 6 |
| Transport and communications | 6 | 7 | 7 | 7 | 7 |
| Trade | 8 | 10 | 13 | 13 | 14 |
| Service industry | 9 | 11 | 13 | 15 | 18 |
| Pensioners, students *et al.* | 6 | 11 | 18 | 20 | 24 |
| Unknown | 1 | 0 | 1 | 4 | 1 |
| *Total* | 100 | 100 | 100 | 100 | 100 |

when Finland experienced one of the most rapid periods of structural
change in Europe. In 1960 as many as 32 per cent of the Finnish people still
derived their income from agriculture and its ancillary occupations. By
1975, as table 1 shows, the corresponding figure was down to a mere 12
per cent. There was a great shift of population from agriculture to other
occupations and from the countryside to Southern Finland, the Helsinki
region and Sweden. The changes in the occupational structure in their turn
altered the class structure of Finnish society in an almost dramatic way.
The greatest change undoubtedly lay in the sudden virtual disappearance of
the rural proletariat. In 1950 more than 250,000 people had worked on
smallholdings, i.e. agricultural units no larger than 5 hectares. By 1980
this category had fallen to 16,000 individuals. During the same period agricultural labourers practically disappeared. Between 1960 and 1975 Finland
finally became an industrialised society with a social structure resembling
that of the other Nordic countries.

As a result of these changes, Finnish agriculture became homogeneous
both in its nature and in the size of its farming units. Finnish agriculture is
increasingly based on units which would traditionally be described as
medium-sized, heavily mechanised and farmed without recourse to paid
labour. The 1980 census showed that only 2 per cent of the country's
farmers are employers. The farmers have increasingly come to resemble
small businessmen, and have also become increasingly similar both in the
structure of their industry and in their way of working to farmers in
Western Europe and the other Nordic countries. Change was late but
exceptionally rapid.

It is the Finnish language which has primarily given Finland its unique
cultural features. As is well known, it is not an Indo-European language

An abandoned farmstead in North Karelia. Since the 1960s, this has become a familiar sight in the peripheral eastern and northern parts of the country. G

like Swedish and Russian but a Finno-Ugrian language related linguistically to Hungarian, Estonian and a large number of different languages spoken in the northern part of the Soviet Union. There is a rich and independent tradition of Finnish folktales and folklore. But despite the unique features of Finnish in relation to the other Nordic languages, philologists have emphasised that Swedish and Finnish are semantically rather similar. Each language has many loan words taken from the other. There is a strong purist tendency in Finland which produces attempts to find genuinely Finnish new words, and which has sometimes led observers to overlook the fact that many terms in Finnish are direct translations from Swedish. For example, compound words are often produced by combining existing words in the same way as in Swedish.

Such semantic and conceptual similarities between Finnish and Swedish naturally arise from the long common history of the two countries; there have been Swedish-speakers in Finland since medieval times. The Finnish constitution of 1919 gives the status of national languages to both Finnish and Swedish. Moreover, there have also been a great number of Finnish-speaking groups in various parts of Sweden throughout history, the best known being those who live in the Tornio valley, those who emigrated

to Sweden after the Second World War and those from Savo who settled in
the areas of Sweden known as the 'Finnish forests' during the sixteenth
and seventeenth centuries. However, as the systematic studies of Eric de
Geer have shown, there have been many other such groups throughout
history.[3]

Finnish culture also contains many East European and Baltic elements.
During the period of autonomy (1809–1917), when St Petersburg was a
world metropolis, Finland's urban culture in particular was influenced by ·
that city. Finland has also received important impulses from the south,
especially Germany. In many respects, Finland has been a melting-pot for
independent Finnish, Swedo-Nordic, East European-Baltic and Southern,
primarily German, cultural elements.

Despite the uniqueness of Finland's cultural characteristics in a Nordic
context, the significance of its shared historical heritage with Sweden
should not be underestimated. Finland was a part of the Swedish kingdom
for considerably longer than the southern Swedish provinces of Skåne,
Blekinge, Halland and Bohuslän. Matti Klinge has written of the inner
cultural unity present in the old, pre-1809 Swedish kingdom, which to a
great extent persists to this day.[4] He mentions as examples the homogeneity in certain everyday phenomena like farming methods, types of
building, tools, food and drink. Innovations were disseminated from the
centre in Stockholm first to the cultivated, fertile provinces which remain
favoured by nature to this day — Östergötland, Sörmland, Uppland,
Finland Proper, Satakunta and parts of Tavastia and Nyland — and then
spread later to the heavily forested peripheries in Småland, Dalarna,
Norrland, the interior of Västerbotten and Ostobothnia, Savo, northern
Tavastia, northern Karelia and so on. Klinge also points out, as an explanation for the semantic and conceptual similarities between Finnish and
Swedish, that Finnish as a language of culture was created by people who
always had Swedish in their thoughts and who devised concepts in conformity with the Swedish tradition.

Cultural similarities between Finland and Sweden and in some respects
the other Nordic countries are also to be explained not least by a shared
religion, Lutheranism, and by shared principles governing their judicial
systems. Both religion and law are powerful forces in shaping the ideas,
values and fundamental symbols of a society, and accordingly, even though
Finland differs much more clearly from the other Nordic countries in its
culture than in its institutional structure, it is nonetheless clear that in
many respects Finland is culturally a typically Nordic society.

During the decades immediately following the Second World

War, the Nordic countries were known both for their political stability and for the democratic nature of their political debates, but in this Finland was an exception. Political instability in Finland was manifested in frequent changes of government, and the depth of social conflicts could be seen in such phenomena as frequent disputes on the labour market and the strong support given to the communists, who in the 1950s attracted the votes of about a quarter of the electorate. Four significant types of conflict, each with a structural background, can be observed during various phases of Finland's recent history. The first is *class conflict* between the working class and the middle class, which has been expressed politically in the struggle between the socialist and the non-socialist parties. The second is the *ideological struggle* between the communists and the other political groupings. A central aspect of this struggle has been the conflict inside the labour movement between social democrats and communists. The third is the *tension between town and country*. There has been a clash of interests between the consumers in the towns and the farmers as producers which was expressed politically in the rivalry between the social democrats and the Centre Party. The fourth is the *language conflict* between the Finnish-speaking majority and the Swedish-speaking minority. Swedish-speakers have had their own political representatives in parliament and local government in the form both of the Swedish People's Party and the Swedish-speaking sections in the socialist parties.

These different types of conflict have all been significant and dominant at various times. The class conflicts culminated during the civil war of 1918. Up till then the working class was represented by the social democrats alone, but a final break between social democrats and communists occurred thereafter. This split proved permanent and it has led at times to sharp conflicts within the labour movement.

The language struggle was a central source of conflict in Finnish politics at certain times till the late 1930s; it has ceased to be so since the Second World War. However, its scope was limited because the labour movement refused to participate in the struggle, which consequently was primarily a cultural tug-of-war between the Finnish- and Swedish-speaking middle class.

The reasons why political conflicts in Finland have been so severe can be sought in many interacting factors. The country's position between Eastern and Western Europe, the traditional importance of agriculture during a period of industrialisation, the civil war of 1918 and the bitter memories it left behind, economic inequalities, Finland's cooperation with the losing side in the Second World War and so on — all in different ways contributed to the acerbity of political conflict during the 1950s and 1960s.

However, the political situation in Finland has changed strikingly since around the middle 1970s. Governments have remained in office for longer periods; conflicts have been perceived as less bitter — a point clearly confirmed by public opinion surveys; and the communists have lost much of their electoral support. All the great traditional sources of conflict have gradually developed a more peaceful and less acute character, due not least to the fact that the political forces representing all sides in these traditional conflicts had a seat in the country's governments during the 1980s. Table 2, which gives the number of seats won by the political parties in the three elections between 1979 and 1987, shows the trend of developments clearly.

Table 2. SEATS WON BY THE POLITICAL PARTIES IN THE PARLIAMENTARY ELECTIONS OF 1979, 1983 AND 1987

|  | 1979 | 1983 | 1987 |
|---|---|---|---|
| *Social Democrats | 52 | 57 | 56 |
| *People's Democrats (communists and left-wing socialists) | 35 | 27 | 20 (16 + 4)† |
| *National Coalition (moderate conservatives) | 47 | 44 | 53 |
| *Centre Party | 36 | 38 | 40 |
| *Swedish People's Party | 10 | 11 | 13 |
| *Rural Party | 7 | 17 | 9 |
| Christian Union | 9 | 3 | 5 |
| Liberal People's Party | 4 | — | — |
| Constitutional Conservative Party | — | 1 | — |
| Greens (not an organised party) | — | 2 | 4 |
|  | 200 | 200 | 200 |

*Represented in any of the three governments in office during the 1980s up till the summer of 1987.
†Contested the election as two separate electoral lists.

Once again, these trends can be explained by many interacting factors. The country's economic development has been comparatively favourable; its international position has been stable; economic and social inequalities have been reduced; the traditional agrarian dominance has been broken; the rural proletariat has disappeared; and personal memories of the civil war are fading. Political debate has been based on the assumption that 'consensus' prevails, in itself a remarkable term in view of purist attempts to keep Finnish free from foreign words.

At all events, Finnish politics have evolved in a 'Nordic' direction. This does not mean that all political problems have disappeared; in place of the traditional ones are new sources of conflict like pollution, nuclear power, the position of women, the new poverty, data protection and suchlike, but these are increasingly the same as those of the other Nordic countries.

In order to justify talking about a specifically Nordic type of welfare state, Gösta Esping-Andersen and Walter Korpi employ a distinction well-known in social policy between a *marginal* and an *institutional welfare model*.[5] The marginal model is based on the assumption that welfare and other social measures should only be applied in case of need, that the greater part of the population should attend to their own welfare, and that the state should intervene only when people cannot look after themselves. In the marginal model, welfare measures should be based on the test of need. The institutional model assumes that social measures should include all citizens, that the welfare of the individual is the responsibility of the collective, and that social welfare should be achieved by socio-political means rather than through market mechanisms. The institutional model rejects the test of need because the latter is assumed to discriminate in a negative way.

Neither of these models has ever been realised in a pure form, but the Nordic countries have consistently sought to apply the institutional model. The Nordic welfare systems attempt to cover the whole population; they are institutionalised so that citizens can be guaranteed a reasonable level of welfare and security; and it is assumed that welfare institutions ought also to cover a great many aspects of life like education, housing policy, leisure and political activity.

There are differences in the welfare systems of the Nordic countries, even if all of them, including Finland, have developed in the same direction. These variations reflect historically conditioned differences in their social structures. For example, Denmark has by tradition had proportionally more small businessmen than the other Nordic countries and has never developed a state system of occupational pensions in the same way as the others. Finland also diverges in some respects from the general Nordic welfare model in a way that clearly reflects the country's history and social structure.

First of all, it is the case that Finland became a welfare state at a late stage, later than the other Nordic countries. Matti Alestalo and Hannu Uusitalo have shown how Finland's level of social security and welfare provision was among the lowest in Europe during the 1930s.[6] However, the systematic construction of the Nordic welfare state only began after the Second World War. While the other Nordic countries began to have a fairly well-developed system of welfare and social security towards the end of the 1950s, Finland did not catch up with them till 5–10 years later. In the 1960s Finland's system of social security began to have a scope which approached the generally high level in the rest of the Nordic region. By the 1980s Finland, along with Norway, was close to the average among West

European countries in welfare and social security provision. In 1983 social expenditure as a percentage of gross national product was 22.2 per cent in Norway and 23.5 per cent in Finland as against 30.7 and 35.7 per cent in Denmark and Sweden respectively. Generally, it is Sweden that has taken the lead in social welfare reforms.

However, there are also interesting structural differences between Finland's welfare policies and those of the other Nordic countries, especially Sweden. These differences arise from the relative strength of the various political parties, which in turn are conditioned by differences of social structure. In Sweden, the social democrats in cooperation with the trade unions have been able to push through many reforms shaped in accordance with their own ideas. In the case of Finland, a policy of reform has required cooperation with other groups, above all the Centre Party. In contrast to some of the other non-socialist parties, the Centre Party has systematically supported a policy of reform in social welfare, but in certain essential respects it has taken a different line from the social democrats. The latter, in accordance with the interests of their supporters, have supported a system of social security directly linked to income in which payments would serve as compensation for lost income. On the other hand, the Centre Party, representing the farmers, has strongly emphasised the desirability of equal payments that are independent of normal income. These differences between the social democrats and the Centre Party have made it easier for other interested groups, for example the employers, to influence the policy of reform. The Finnish occupational pensions scheme is a good example of a result based on compromise. In accordance with the Swedish model, the scheme is universal, but in Finland expenditure on social insurance is financed primarily by private insurance companies and not, as in Sweden, by state investment companies. Another consequence of the Centre Party's political strength is that more emphasis has been placed in Finland on housing policy in the countryside and within agriculture, and less on the construction of publicly-owned housing in the towns than in Sweden. Alestalo and Uusitalo point out that the fact of welfare policy being the result of compromise by no means weakens it in some circumstances: when the existing welfare system is the creation of different political groups, demands for reductions in social expenditure tend to be few and ineffective.

As a general conclusion, it can be said that Finland in most essential respects manifests the same basic features as the other Nordic societies. There are divergences, but they can be clearly understood and explained by the particular course of Finland's history and by the special characteristics of the country's social structure. These general conclusions apply not only to welfare policy but also to the whole of Finland's institutional and structural character, culture and politics.

## NOTES

1. G. Petrén, 'Government and central administration', in F. Wisti *et al.* (*eds*), *Nordic democracy*, Copenhagen 1981.
2. F. Castles, *The social democratic image of society: A study of the achievement and origins of Scandinavian social democracy in comparative perspective*, London 1978.
3. E. de Geer, 'Finska och svenska språkgrupper och minoriteter i Sverige och Finland', in S. Huovinen (*ed.*), *Finland i det svenska riket*, Stockholm 1986.
4. M. Klinge, 'Sverige, svensk-Finland, finsk', in Huovinen (*ed.*), *op.cit.*
5. G. Esping-Andersen, W.Korpi, 'From poor relief to institutional welfare states': The development of Scandinavian social policy', in R. Erikson, E. Hansen, S. Ringen, H. Uusitalo (*eds*), *The Scandinavian welfare model. Welfare states and welfare research*, London 1987.
6. M. Alestalo, H. Uusitalo, 'Finland', in P. Flora (*ed.*), *Growth to limits. The Western European welfare states since World War Two*, Berlin-New York, 1986.

# FINLAND: A TYPICAL POST-INDUSTRIAL STATE?

## David Arter

The pace of economic modernisation in post-war Finland has been unique. In no other European democracy has the progression from an essentially agrarian society through a period of accelerated industrialisation to a predominantly service economy been compressed into a mere four decades. Finland, it seems, has become a typical post-industrial state in the lifetime of many Winter War veterans. Contrary to the thrust of much modernisation theory, however, the extremely rapid rate of economic change has not presaged significantly destabilising or radicalising developments in the political arena. The substantial socio-economic changes of the post-war era have occurred within a largely stable political framework, and a basic continuity has been maintained through the institutions of the constitution, the presidential office, the party system and, till recently at least, electoral behaviour.

### Post-War economics: Policies and performance

S.N. Eisenstadt pointed out in a recent essay that perhaps the greatest challenge facing small states was to create a standard of living comparable to that in larger countries, given that the domestic markets of small countries are neither large enough nor sufficiently diversified to produce all they need or to consume all they produce.[1] A small state must in consequence give paramount importance to developing and maintaining export competitiveness in world markets, and nowhere has this been done with more determination than in Finland. Indeed, a paucity of adequate domestic energy resources, limited raw materials and an inability to meet home requirements in investments and consumer goods have meant that export outlets have been essential to underpin imports and so raise the overall standard of living. In developing a prosperous open economy since the war, however, Finland's achievement has been notable. The export of goods and services accounts at the time of writing for about one-third of its GDP, while imports constitute a quarter of total supply. On the basis of GDP per head, Finland is one of the ten leading manufacturing countries in the world and, boasting a relatively high capital-output ratio, its industry has been highly competitive in international markets. Industrial productivity, moreover, has risen steadily since 1973. There was, for

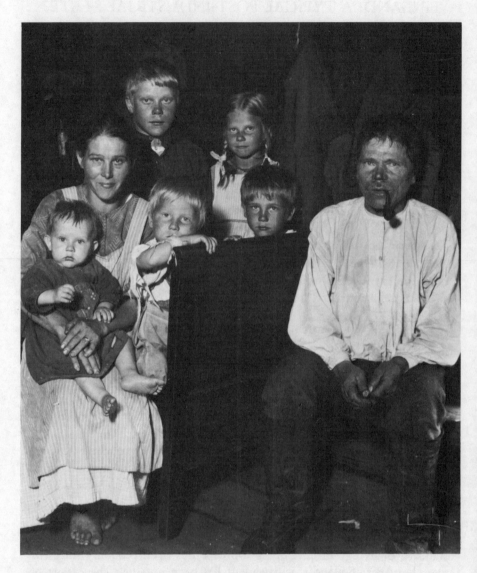

The Mykkänen family, photographed by Ahti Rytkönen in 1927. The sooty chimneyless cottages in which inpoverished families lived in the eastern backwoods are no more; large families are no longer common, either. *B*

example, a 6 per cent industrial growth rate in 1983–7, whereas in the same period industrial export prices rose by only 4 per cent and production costs by 5 per cent. Finland's macro-economic balance in the 1980s, in sum, has been remarkably healthy.

In achieving this situation, four factors have been of particular significance for Finland, when viewed comparatively. First, Keynesianism never really took hold there to the degree that it did in the other Scandinavian states. Instead, Finland took the road of export orientation sustained by devaluation cycles. A high investment strategy directed towards developing the domestic infrastructure and industry's export capacity was based on foreign borrowing, and balance of payments constraints therefore took primacy over fiscal activism. At its worst point in 1974–5, the foreign debt stood at 23 per cent of GDP. By 1978, however, this substantial deficit had been transformed into a balance of payments surplus, and the unstable economy of the first three post-war decades entered the 1980s as a remarkably stable one.

Secondly, there has been the counter-cyclical tendency of Finnish-Soviet trade — which has accounted for about one-fifth of Finland's trade since the 1940s — particularly during the recessionary period following the 1973 oil crisis. Distinctively for a Western nation, Finland has a clearing-house arrangement with the Soviet Union which had tended to buttress the economy against the vicissitudes of world markets. This has been especially important, since there have been wide fluctuations in demand for Finland's principal export sector — products of the forest industry. True, the drop in world oil prices dictated a concomitant decline in bilateral Finno-Soviet trade after 1986: the fall in the value of Soviet exports (primarily energy supplies) to Finland necessitated a comparable decline in the value of Finnish exports to Russia. However, this has largely been compensated for by a growth in Western markets, while at the same time Finland has been seeking to diversify the structure of its imports from the Soviet Union.

Thirdly, a highly durable incomes policy system emerged in the late 1960s. By minimising the incidence of disruptive strikes, it has contributed to sustaining industrial competitiveness and underpinning the effects of routine devaluations of the currency. In addition to 'bread and butter' questions relating to wages and prices, the bi-annual incomes packages have generally contained a number of ancillary social policy measures promoted or at least adopted by the government as a *sine qua non* of consensus-generation among the principal economic actors. The first incomes agreements were successful in curbing inflation — which after a general strike in 1956 had risen sharply — and following an inflationary spiral in the 1970s there has been a generally downward trend.

Finally, to prevent a rise in domestic prices negating the effects of devaluation, Finland instituted a package of innovative supply-side policies in the late 1970s designed *inter alia* to decrease the growth-rate in the public sector and stimulate the private sector through taxation. Some of the main lines of Thatcherism and Reaganomics therefore took shape in Finland before becoming so prominently associated with the British prime minister and American president.

## *Post-industrial society: Ideal-type and application*

By a process of extrapolation from the burgeoning literature, five conditions or features of a model post-industrial society can be delineated and their application to the Finnish case briefly examined.

A first condition of an ideal-type post-industrial society is that there should be substantial and continuing growth in the information and service sector relative to other branches of the economy. Tertiary growth is likely to be particularly evident in health care, leisure and education, and as a by-product of these developments there will be a growing demand for high-tech service systems. Expansion in the service sector will also permit the accommodation of a greater number of women on the labour market.

In the Finnish case, just over half of the workforce in the late 1980s is employed in the service sector, while the closed sector (including the public sector) constitutes about three-quarters of the economy. A Ministry of Labour working group which reported in December 1987 noted, moreover, that much of the increased demand for labour in the period 1987–95 would be in the service sector — food, accommodation and insurance — linked to the leading population centres. In business terms, Finland is predominantly a nation of small capitalists, i.e. firms employing under 100 persons. In 1984 86.5 per cent of all enterprises were small businesses and this represented just over a 2 per cent increase on the figure of ten years earlier. Significantly, however, the bulk of the small business growth has been in the service sector where in recent years there has been a heightened tendency towards the private production of public services (care of the elderly, medical services, cleaning services etc.). Privatisation has not been part of the rhetoric of public debate in Finland in the manner of Britain or Sweden, but in many ways a silent revolution has taken place in this area. Predictably, there has been opposition to this development from the public sector unions.

A second condition of post-industrial society is that there should be a relative decline in the contribution of traditional (secondary) industry as an employer of labour. Equally, this process of de-industrialisation will entail a sharp drop in the proportion of the economically active population engaged in large work-units. There will also be a marked specialisation of industrial production and a tendency for subsidiary services, previously undertaken by large firms, to be undertaken by specialised small businesses. As a corollary, the tendency will be for the importance of middle management in large firms to decline. Generally too there will be a diminution in stock levels as a consequence of more expeditious commercial transactions between manufacturers and customers both nationally and internationally.

In Finland the need to repay a substantial reparations debt to the Soviet Union, largely in kind, was the trigger to mobilising and modernising the

THE INDUSTRIAL STRUCTURE OF THE LABOUR FORCE, 1900–2000

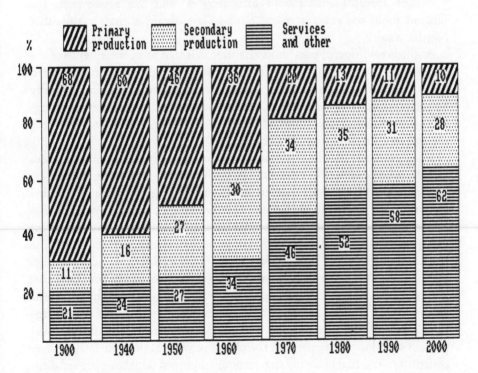

industrial wheels of the defeated nation. Indeed, although the impact of intensive industrialisation was felt relatively late in Finland, the transition from a predominantly agricultural to a predominantly industrial society was notably rapid. By the advent of the Second World War, only 200,000 workers (18 per cent of the economically active population) were engaged in manufacturing industry; this figure had doubled by the early 1960s and trebled to over 600,000 by the beginning of the 1980s. Nowadays, industry (excluding construction) employs a quarter of the economically active population, and industry and construction together generate two-fifths of the national product (see table). In contrast, agriculture and forestry employed under 9 per cent of the economically active population in the 1980s. The tardy onset of accelerated industrialisation meant that industrial machinery and equipment are unusually young, and in many sectors they remain technologically competitive. In a comparative perspective, moreover, Finnish industry is relatively labour-intensive. All of these factors have conspired to delay the process of de-industrialisation and the attendant absorption of labour into services, and this process affected Finland about ten years later and remains less advanced than in the other Nordic states.

A third condition of post-industrialisation is that as a consequence of the increasingly skilled (often high-tech) character of production and the need for vast re-training programmes among large sections of the economically active population, advanced societies are characterised by problems of long-term (structural) unemployment. There is, in short, a mismatch between the demand for labour and its supply.

It is significant that in a questionnaire survey of Finnish small businesses in 1986 which focused on the main obstacles to the development of firms, 16.9 per cent of respondents mentioned the shortage of a suitably skilled labour force.[2] Although high in the Nordic context, unemployment levels in Finland over the last two decades have been relatively low by West European standards. After a period of virtually full employment until the late 1960s, unemployment began to rise in the mid-1970s and in the late 1980s stood at 5.5 per cent (about 140,000 persons out of work). Lauri Korpelainen's illuminating analysis, however, demonstrates that in recent years numerically the largest single category of unemployed — perhaps two-thirds of the total — has comprised the (essentially middle-age) persons who lost their jobs over the recession years of the mid-1970s. They constitute a residual body of long-term unemployed who have proved difficult to re-accommodate in work as plant modernisation has demanded new skills and techniques. There has in short been a convergence of cyclical and structural unemployment.[3]

A fourth feature (rather than strictly a condition) of the arrival of post-industrial society is the emphasis given to fresh commercial ideas, stimulating new types of business venture and the generation of an 'enterprise culture'. This has been largely essayed through government taxation designed *inter alia* to reduce the range of payroll costs shouldered by employers. Yet while many traditional small businesses still complain of under-capitalisation, high interest rates and a heavy burden of taxation, several new high-tech enterprises have been established, especially in biotechnology, and in many cases sustained by the 'technological villages' which were founded in Finland during the early 1980s. Located in the vicinity of universities and technical high schools, the seven technological villages provide a range of facilities — office space, research assistance, marketing advice and finance — to small and medium-sized high-tech concerns in areas where a skilled workforce is most likely to be available. These and other developments have meant that an enterprise culture has developed in the 1980s, and business and the business spirit are favoured in a way they were not during the previous decade.

Even so, the structural ecology of entrepreneurialism exhibits pronounced regional contours. In many ways the transition to post-industrialism has served to consolidate the dualistic nature of the economy and the existence of two contrasting business cultures in Finland. Industry and services are heavily concentrated in the 'deep south' — the four southern provinces including the large towns of Helsinki and Tampere — where 70 per cent of the jobs are located. Northern Finland and Northern Karelia, on the other hand, are peripheral regions, still dominated by primary production (farming and forestry) which account for only about 10 per cent of the nation's jobs. Since the end of the 1960s, the government's regional policy has involved substantial expenditure aimed at invigorating and diversifying the infrastructure of these poor outlying regions and off-setting the 'blight spiral' in the many depressed rural communities within them.

A final feature of nascent post-industrialisation is a shift in the orientation of a section of the citizenry away from narrow acquisitive values towards considerations of the quality of life — that is, so-called post-materialist norms. These can embrace such evidently diverse areas as a re-appraisal of personal ethics (anti-secularism), a growing concern for the environment (opposition to nuclear energy, nuclear weapons etc.) and enhancing a sense of personal competence in the workplace (through industrial democracy) and society at large (regular use of referenda etc.).

Survey data in the late 1970s indicated that a massive majority of Finns favoured the mixed economy and opposed socialism, while there has been

equally overwhelming support for incomes policy as a means of maintaining living standards. The existence of an 'incomes policy culture'[4]
represents a powerful statement of the belief of most Finns in the continuing ability of the corporate sector to deliver the economic goods. The
enormous and relatively recent rise in living standards compared with
Sweden is an obviously important factor in this context. The Finns enjoyed
the fruits of affluence significantly later than their Nordic neighbours, and
among older people memories of harder times doubtless remain vivid.
Perhaps it is not surprising, therefore, that the challenge to the consensus
from the 'new left' came almost a decade later in Finland than in Sweden.
Yet during the 1980s broad-based opposition to the prevailing standards
has arisen especially among an educated younger generation. Chernobyl
stirred a wider conscience, but it appears that Finland became a post-industrial society so quickly that there has been insufficient time for a substantial
post-materialist backlash to develop.

### Politics in the 'Second Republic'

It has become fashionable to allude to the existence of a 'Second Republic'
in Finland, referring to the period from the 1944 armistice with the Soviet
Union onwards. Such a designation, however, disguises substantial
institutional continuities in the political sphere. An era of accelerating
economic change, in other words, has been contained within a framework
of basic political stability. Thus, unlike France in 1945, no new constitution was adopted, nor was the 1919 document amended; there were no
changes in the balance of power between the major policy-making structures of the state — the president, parliament and so on—and, with the
significant exception of the legalised Communist Party, the fundamentals
of the party system remained intact. What can be contended, however, is
that the changed geopolitical circumstances of the post-war period have
had an undoubted influence on the *de facto* institutional balance — the vital
need to maintain amicable Finno-Soviet relations, for example, elevated
the office of the presidency — while the party system was ultimately
obliged to respond to the imperatives of rapid socio-economic change.

　　Because of its exposed position as a frontier state on the ideological map
of Europe, Finland's role during the Second World War was distinctive. It
was a small, neutral, democratic state in which patriotic resistance was
directed not against Central European fascism — as, for example, in the
Low Countries and Denmark — but against the strategic demands and
territorial claims of neighbouring Soviet communism. However, two
defeats at the hands of the Red Army (in the Winter War of 1939–40 and

the Continuation War of 1941–4) meant that the Second Republic was born in adversity: land in Karelia was ceded, and the Soviet Union imposed a substantial reparations levy. It is against this backdrop that the main features of politics in the Second Republic must be viewed. Five in particular need emphasis.

First and foremost, there has been the paramount importance of foreign policy, which is defined in Finland by references to two former presidents — Paasikivi and Kekkonen.[5] The cornerstone of post-war Finnish foreign policy has been the 1948 Treaty of Friendship, Co-operation and Mutual Assistance (FCMA) with the Soviet Union, the text of which has remained unamended since its original drafting.

This treaty constitutes an unparalleled agreement between a small capitalist state and the communist superpower. True, article 1 contains a defensive commitment: Finland must defend the Soviet Union in the event of an attack (or the threat thereof) on the latter through Finland. But the Kremlin has all along recognised Finnish independence and neutrality (although, of course, it has its own definition of neutrality), and in recent decades has supported Finnish initiatives to further the process of international détente — the policy of what Kekkonen called 'active neutrality'. Moreover, there has been growing economic co-operation between the two states — originally envisaged by article 3 of the FCMA treaty — and this has meant that, particularly during periods of recession, Finnish capitalism has been buttressed by its trade links with command economy communism.

The Paasikivi-Kekkonen line has been a notably stable element in post-war Finnish policy and by the late 1970s it united all the major political parties from the communists to the conservative National Coalition. Acting within the inevitable constraints imposed by the dynamic nature of East-West relations (the FCMA treaty was signed at a time when the advent of the Cold War had left Finland isolated and pessimistic), the Paasikivi-Kekkonen line has contributed to developing generally amicable relations between Helsinki and Moscow. Certainly, there is evidence that for a period in the 1950s and early 1960s the Finnish leadership did not fully appreciate genuine Soviet apprehension about the possibility of renewed German militarism, and two short-lived crises in Fenno-Soviet relations resulted from this. Indeed, while Fenno-Soviet relations have remained very stable since Mauno Koivisto became president in 1982, this has been facilitated by a favourable climate of international relations and Mikhail Gorbachev's *glasnost*-style concern to improve relations with all West European states.

A second trait of politics in the Second Republic has been the way the

President Urho Kekkonen: *above*, relaxing after a sauna in the wintry wilds of Lapland, 1975; *below*, in more formal attire, sharing a joke with the British prime minister Harold Wilson at the signing ceremony during the European Security Conference. President Valéry Giscard d'Estaing of France seems less amused. G

Paasikivi-Kekkonen tradition of 'sauna' diplomacy (i.e. summitry) with the Kremlin has elevated the office of the presidency. This was particularly so during the long era of Urho Kekkonen, for the personal trust he enjoyed 'in high places' enabled him to build up an unchallengeable and unprecedented position of authority. In the late 1970s, comparisons were in order between what Duverger described as the 'all-powerful French presidency' and Kekkonen's role as head of state in Finland.[6] Between 1986 and 1988, of course, *cohabitation* imposed practical limitations on the powers of the French presidency, while in 1982 Finland entered a period of a type of voluntary cohabitation in which Kekkonen's successor, Mauno Koivisto, committed himself to 'living with' the prime minister and government of the day in the sense of restricting his own activities to the formal presidential preserve of foreign policy direction.

Thirdly, the Communist Party (operating as part of the umbrella Finnish People's Democratic League) became one of the largest of its kind in Eastern Europe in the post-armistice years and has participated in government coalitions far more frequently than its counterparts in any other pluralist democracy. Defections from the social democrats enabled the radical left to become the largest parliamentary force shortly after the 1945 general election and numerically the strongest element in a broad centre-left government. There were obvious parallels with the situation in contemporary Czechoslovakia, where following competitive elections in 1945 the communists gained dominance in the cabinet. However, a vigorous minority among the Finnish communists, the so-called 'rifle group', adopted a thoroughly combative approach to capitalism and parliamentary democracy during these so-called 'danger years'. Against the backdrop of recent rumours of a proposed communist coup, the 1948 general election became a 'bridgehead election' comparable to that in Italy the same summer. In Italy it was partly American funding that sustained the Christian Democratic Party's campaign against the communists while the West looked anxiously on. In Finland it was the two main bourgeois parties, the Agrarian Union and the National Coalition, which acted as the bridgehead against communism, and their stridently anti-communist propaganda successfully stemmed the radical leftist tide.

The communists thereafter entered a long period in the political wilderness, eventually broken by their incorporation into the broad-based popular front governments of 1966–70. The party became divided at this time into a majority wing, (which participated intermittently in government throughout the 1970s) and a minority abstentionist wing, and formally split in 1986. The division and electoral decline of Finnish communism has obvious parallels in France and Spain, and points up the wider strategic dilemma of communist parties in Western pluralist democracies. In the Finnish case, however, the re-emergence of a sizeable radical left in the post-war period had two important repercussions. First, in reducing the partisan cohesion of the blue-collar electorate it meant that the social democrats, although the largest party, could not dominate government in the manner of their celebrated Swedish counterpart. And secondly, the existence of a large communist party in the lee of the Soviet Union presented the non-communists in Finland (including the social democrats) with the twin challenge of achieving a *modus vivendi* with Soviet communism (at both the state and party levels) and accommodating the radical left within the domestic political mainstream. Ultimately, this would dictate the need for bridge-building rather than the bridgehead mentality of 1948.

A fourth characteristic of post-war Finnish politices has been an historic fragmentation of the bourgeois electorate, typical of the Nordic region, which has contributed to the fact that bourgeois majorities at the polls have not been translated into bourgeois domination of government. Throughout the years of independence, Finland has been predominantly 'White' in the sense that the non-socialists have gained a plurality of the vote. Only twice, in 1958 and 1966, have the left-wing parties won a majority of the popular ballot, and in 1987 the percentage discrepancy was as much as 62.1 to 37.9 in favour of the bourgeois parties. However, the pre-eminent electoral position of the bourgeois parties has not been converted into broad-based governments. There has been only one majority coalition (Virolainen 1964–6) in the post-war years made up exclusively of the bourgeois parties.

The particular configuration of bourgeois parties has been remarkably durable and impervious to the forces of integration. Traditionally the dominant element (for a quarter of a century after the armistice) was a large and powerful Agrarian Union, which changed its name to Centre Party in 1965. This it did, unlike its Swedish sister party, from a position of electoral strength. In 1965 it commanded the highest number of votes and seats of any of the parties, claimed the prime ministership and had easily outlived its fraternal parties in Norway and Sweden. The Agrarian-Centre has been a 'hinge group' in government-building.

Next there has been a historic and distinctive ethnic party, the centre-based Swedish People's Party, which is one of the oldest ethnic parties in democratic Europe and has represented the (slowly declining) national language minority as a perennial coalition partner. A third centre-based strand in the bourgeois bloc has comprised a succession of small and essentially town-based liberal groups which till 1979 enjoyed a regular governing role but since 1983 have lacked a parliamentary toehold.

Up till 1970 the right-wing National Coalition played second fiddle at the polls to the Agrarian-Centre. Unlike the British Conservatives or Icelandic Independence Party, the National Coalition has rested heavily on white-collar support (educated professional groups) and to a lesser extent on large farmers. The scale of working-class conservatism in Finland has been extremely small. The National Coalition's eligibility for government was not enhanced by the need to accommodate a sizeable radical left, the Agrarian-Centre's propensity to look left for allies and, above all, President Kekkonen's application of a law of anticipated reaction — the anticipation of, and desire to avoid, a possibly hostile reaction in the Kremlin to the National Coalition's participation in government.

A further element in reducing cohesion on the non-socialist side has been the numerous parties in the Poujadist tradition of radical rightist politics, led by politicians formerly in the bourgeois mainstream, which have trawled an essentially bourgeois electorate. As in France, a radical right has been a recurrent feature of Finnish electoral politics.

A final feature of politics in the Finnish Second Republic has been the way the multipolarity of the party system has been impossible to reconcile

Harri Holkeri, the National Coalition leader, presents his government team (which includes the former prime minister and social democratic leader, Kalevi Sorsa) to President Mauno Koivisto in 1987. G

with the application of the Westminster model of alternating government
and opposition. If there has been a rudimentary bipolarity in a crowded
multi-party market place, it might be argued that it has not differentiated
socialists and non-socialists but rather the social democrats and National
Coalition on the one hand and the Agrarian-Centre Party and Communist
Party on the other. Until the mid-1960s, the Social Democratic Party and
National Coalition found themselves frequently aligned together, and they
are at the time of writing the leading parties in a distinctive left-right coalition formed after the 1987 general election.

## Finland: A post-industrial state?

Finland has evolved rapidly towards a post-industrial stage of economic
development in the post-war era and accordingly manifests many of the
structural characteristics of post-industrial *society*. These include a drop in
the number employed in primary and secondary production, an expansion
in the service sector, the emergence of a vigorous culture of business and
enterprise and, of course, in the wake of these developments, the existence
of deep-seated problems of structural unemployment, particularly in the
peripheral economic regions. Have there been analogous developments in
the political arena which have transformed Finland into a typical post-
industrial *state*?

   While it has been argued that, throughout this period of accentuated
economic change, the basic nature of the institutions of government
and policy-making (the constitution, parliament, presidency, civil service
and so on) has remained stable, the nature of policy-making itself has
changed substantially. Finland became a welfare state in the 1960s —
rather later than the other Nordic countries — and in line with most
advanced technocratic democracies, governments have assumed a central
role in the management of the economy. The incomes policy system is a
good example of the regular consultation between the cabinet and the main
economic groups which has become indigenous to modern government.
However, it is perhaps at the join between state and society — that is the
party system — where the process of adaptation to the imperatives of
socio-economic change has been most visible. The traditionally class-based
Finnish party system has had to respond to three processes bearing on the
composition of the electorate which are closely bound up with the transition to a post-industrial society. De-industrialisation has betokened a
*relative* decline in the size of the blue-collar electorate; tertiary expansion
has meant a steady growth of the so-called 'new middle class'; and a conti-

nuing decline in primary production has caused a fall in the numbers employed in farm/forestry work.

In the mid-1960s the party system was predominantly class-based. Put in a somewhat simplified form, the majority of the rapidly expanding body of blue-collar workers that were a product of intensive industrialisation supported one of the parties of the left, the social democrats or communists, while the Swedish-speaking workers were split between the Swedish People's Party and the social democrats. The vast majority of the large body of farmers that were a legacy of relatively belated industrialisation backed the Agrarian Union, while elements among the small farmers in the north opted for the Communist Party and the large farmers in the south and west for the National Coalition. The Swedish-speaking farmers aligned themselves exclusively behind the Swedish People's Party. The bulk of the educated Finnish-speaking professional groups (the so-called 'old middle class') supported the political right, the National Coalition; a minority preferred the liberals, and of course the Swedish-speaking white-collar population backed the Swedish People's Party. These processes, however, have to a degree blurred the class contours of electoral and party politics.

These things have not been peculiar to Finland. Indeed, to some extent across much of Western Europe, the structural changes associated with advanced economies and in particular the rise of a new middle class have injected an element of volatility into the electorate. They have also meant that in pursuit of an increased body of floating voters, established parties have inclined towards the pursuit of catch-all strategies rather than sectional or class-based approaches. To a degree there is also evidence of a shift in the normative orientations of citizens and a disjunction between the values of the materialist-secularist mainstream and those of post-materialist reaction.

In Finland heightened electoral volatility has occurred within the context of a greater stability in government (at least in terms of the partisan continuity of cabinets) and widespread talk of consensus politics. Most evidently, there have been movements of voters between the main party of the left (social democrats) and right (National Coalition) in the tertiary-dominated constituencies in the southern third of the country where there has also been support for the once protest-based Finnish Rural Party. The incidence of abstentionism (non-voting) in Finland has been one of the highest in Western Europe in recent elections.

The best illustration of the explicit adoption of a catch-all strategy is the Centre Party, which adopted its new name precisely to attract a wider spectrum of support in the southern towns and so supplement its core constituency of farmers. Thus far it has been only moderately successful, and in fact none of the larger Finnish parties is catch-all in a regional sense. Instead, each appears to have its natural environment — the social democrats and the National Coalition in the south, the Centre Party and (to a lesser extent) communists in the north and east.

Parties of post-materialist reaction have included the small Christian League, which has gained a handful of parliamentary seats since its breakthrough election in 1970 (it polls well among low-church groups within the state Lutheran church and nonconformist denominations outside it), and the Greens who in 1983 became the first environmental group to gain a foothold in a Nordic parliament. In turn the established parties have become 'greener', and before the 1987 general election, with Chernobyl still fresh in voters' memories, they were united in their opposition to the development of a fifth nuclear reactor in Finland.

Finland in the late 1980s is a typical post-industrial society with the evolution to an advanced economy bringing significant changes in the social structure, particularly the development of a numerous class of service sector employees. Finland may also be viewed as a post-industrial state in the sense that the role of government has expanded to include not only the area of welfare provision but, vitally too, responsibility for supervising the economy to ensure maximum export competitiveness in world markets. New cleavage lines — such as the *economy* versus the *environment* and the *national culture* versus *mass international culture* — have indeed underpinned the party system, and it is the resolution of these conflicts which will largely determine whether Finland will take its place as a typical post-industrial member of the global village of nations.

During the Second Republic, Finland has become an ever more self-confident and outward-looking small state and, in contrast to the parochialism of the inter-war years, has generated a strongly internationalist perspective in both the political and economic arenas. It seeks to complement its trade links with Eastern and Western Europe by establishing stronger ties with the developing countries, and has applied for membership of the Council of Europe. Yet Finland remains a relatively young nation. Partly because of this, no doubt, it is becoming increasingly concerned not to sacrifice its distinctive identity on the altar of internationalism.

This was the basic message of the Centre Party candidate in the 1988 presidential election, Paavo Väyrynen, who argued with some success that Finland's inevitable integration into the wider international economic and cultural environment should not be at the expense of the country's own culture and economic independence. Finland, he seemed to be saying, should remain Finnish. Indeed, this 'new nationalism' is in many ways reminiscent of nineteenth-century cultural nationalism and Snellman's assertion in correspondence with J.J. Nervander in 1846 that while Finland had a *history*, it was not, in the absence of a literature in the majority Finnish language, a *nation*.[7] A crucial scenario in the twenty-first century may well involved striking the right balance between Finland's inevitably greater commitments on the international stage and the protection and promotion of the indigenous language(s) and cultural traditions that invest a state with its quality as a nation.

## NOTES

1. S.N. Eisenstadt, 'Reflections on Centre-Periphery Relations and Small European States' in Risto Alapuro, Matti Alestalo, Elina Haavio-Mannila and Raimo Väyrynen, *Small States in Comparative Perspective*, Oslo 1985, p. 44.
2. *Suomen Yrittäjäin Keskusliiton vuosikirja 1986*, p. 12.
3. Lauri Korpelainen, 'Työttömyyttä voidaan alentaa', *Työvoimakatsaus*, 2 (1987), pp. 3–12.
4. David Arter, *Politics and Policy-Making in Finland*, Brighton 1987, pp. 198–226.
5. Max Jakobson, 'Paasikiven-Kekkosen linjalla', *Suomen Kuvalehti*, 29 Jan. 1988, pp. 3–6.
6. David Arter, 'Kekkonen's Finland: Enlightened Despotism or Consensual Democracy?', *West European Politics*, 4, 3(1981), pp. 219–33.
7. Kauko Kare (*ed.*), *Näin puhui Snellman. Kirjoituksia, katkelmia, ydinlauseita*, Porvoo, Helsinki 1960, pp. 48–9.

# A NOTE ON BOOKS IN ENGLISH ON
# FINNISH HISTORY AND POLITICS

The following list is intended as a guide for readers with no knowledge of Finnish or Swedish. A more extensive bibliography of works in those languages is provided with the original articles, published in *Historisk Tidskrift för Finland*, vol. 3 (1987). The most recent and comprehensive bibliography for the anglophone reader is J. Screen, *Finland*, World Bibliographical Series, vol. 31, Oxford and Santa Barbara 1981.

There are a number of Scandinavian periodicals which regularly publish artricles on Finnish history and politics in English. These include the *Scandinavian Economic History Review* (*SEHR*), the *Scandinavian Journal of History* (*SJH*), and *Scandinavian Political Studies* (*SPS*).

Of the general histories of Finland, the most recent are J. Jutikkala and K. Pirinen, *A History of Finland*, new revised edition, London 1979: L. Puntila, *The Political History of Finland, 1809–1966*, Helsinki and London, 1974: and D. Kirby, *Finland in the Twentieth Century*, second impression, London 1984. A lively account of the extension of Catholicism into the eastern Baltic, including Finland, is provided by E. Christiansen, *The Northern Crusades: The Baltic and the Catholic Frontier 110–1525*, London 1980. See also S. Suvanto, 'Medieval Studies in Finland: A Survey', *JSH*, vol. 4 (1979). The chapter by S. E. Åström, 'The Swedish Economy and Sweden's role as a Great Power, 1632–1697' in M. Roberts (*ed.*), *Sweden's Age of Greatness, 1632–1718*, London 1973, places Finland within the context of Swedish expansion in the seventeenth century. E. Thaden, *Russia's Western Borderlands, 1710–1870*, Princeton 1984, and E. Thaden (*ed.*), *Russification in the Baltic Provinces and Finland, 1855–1914*, Princeton 1981, help place the grand duchy of Finland within the context of the Russian empire and its western borderlands in the nineteenth century.

A general survey of the achievements of the grand duchy, richly illustrated, is *Finland in the nineteenth century*, Helsingfors 1894. Of the travel accounts published in the nineteenth century, those of J. Acerbi, *Travels through Sweden, Finland, and Lapland, to the North Cape in the Years 1798 and 1799*, London 1802, and Mrs A. Tweedie, *Through Finland in Carts*, London 1897, are perhaps the most entertaining. J. Hampden Jackson, *Finland*, revised edition, London 1940, is a perceptive survey of the first two decades of the new republic.

The only comprehensive study of Finland's prehistory in English is by E. Kivikoski, *Finland*, London and New York 1967. A number of demographic studies have been published in the *Scandinavian Economic History Review*, including E. Jutikkala, 'The Great Finnish Famine in 1695–1697', *SEHR*, vol. 3 (1955), and O. Turpeinen, 'Regional Differentials in Finnish Mortality Rates 1806–65', *SEHR*, vol. 21 (1973). See also O. Turpeinen 'Fertility and Mortality in Finland since 1750', *Population Studies*, vol. 33, 1979.

The importance of the 'green gold' of the forests is emphasised in W. Mead, *An Economic Geography of the Scandinavian States and Finland*, London 1958. See also W. Mead and H. Smeds, *Winter in Finland*, London and New York 1967. The technique of burnbeating is described in A. Soininen, 'Burn-beating as a Technical Basis for Colonisation', *SEHR*, vol. 12, 1964.

Although several large-scale studies of the history of Ostrobothnia and Karelia have appeared in recent years, there is as yet little available in English. H. Ylikangas, 'Major Fluctuations in Crimes of Violence in Finland: A Historical Analysis', *SEHR*, vol. 1 (1976), examines some of the reasons why crimes of violence reached almost epidemic proportions in Ostrobothnia at the beginning of the nineteenth century. R. Alapuro, 'Regional Variations in Political Mobilization: On the Incorporation of the Agrarian Population into the State of Finland, 1907–1932', *SJH*, vol. 1 (1976), provides interesting insight into the history of Ostrobothnia. J. Hautala, *Finnish Folklore Research, 1828–1918*, Helsinki 1969, and W. Wilson, *Folklore and Nationalism in Modern Finland*, Bloomington 1976, throw light on the importance of Karelia in Finnish folklore, and M. Kuusi, K. Bosley and M. Branch (*comps*), *Finnish Folk Poetry — Epic: An Anthology in Finnish and English*, Helsinki 1977, offers a rich selection of the verses collected by folklorists and others. A detailed study in German of the East Karelian question in the aftermath of the First World War should be mentioned: J. Jääskeläinen, *Die ostkarelische Frage*, Porvoo 1961. M. Engman, 'Migration from Finland to Russia during the Nineteenth Century', *SJH*, vol. 3 (1978), is a brief summation of the author's major study of the influence of St Petersburg upon Finland.

J. Paasivirta, *Finland and Europe: International Crises during the Period of Autonomy, 1808–1914*, London and Minneapolis 1981, examines the position of the grand duchy of Finland in international affairs during the period of autonomy. R. Schweitzer, 'The Baltic parallel: reality or historiographical myth?', and E. Thaden, 'Finland and the Baltic provinces: élite roles and social and economic conditions and structures', *Journal of Baltic Studies*, vol. 15 (1984), consider parallels and differences in the status of the western borderlands of the Russian empire. A crucial period in modern

Finnish history is considered in O. Jussila, 'Nationalism and Revolution: Political Dividing Lines in the Grand Duchy of Finland during the Last Years of Russian Rule', *SJH*, vol. 2 (1977).

Finland's relations with the Western Allies at the end of the First World War is dealt with by E. Lyytinen, *Finland in British Politics in the First World War*, Helsinki 1980, and J. Paasivirta, *The Victors in World War I and Finland: Finland's Relations with the British, French and United States Governments in 1918–1919*, Helsinki 1965. See also the recent article by K. Hovi, 'The Winning of Finnish Independence as an Issue in International Relations', *SJH*, vol. 3 (1978).

There is an extensive foreign-language literature on the Finnish Winter War. The planned Allied intervention is the theme of J. Nevakivi, *The Appeal That Was Never Made: The Allies, Scandinavia and the Finnish Winter War, 1939–1940*, London 1976. A good general account of the war is A. Upton, *Finland, 1939–1940*, London 1974. Chapters in H. Nissen (*ed.*), *Scandinavia during the Second World War*, Oslo and Minneapolis 1983, place the Finnish experience of war in a broader context. The difficult postwar settlement is well described by T. Polvinen, *Between East and West: Finland in International Politics, 1944–1947*, Minneapolis, 1986. M. Jakobson, *Finnish Neutrality: A Study of Finnish Foreign Policy since the Second World War*. London 1968, is the work of one of post-war Finland's most experienced diplomats. See also R. Allison, *Finland's Relations with the Soviet Union, 1944–1984*, London 1985. There are many essays on post-war Finnish foreign policy in the *Yearbook of Finnish Foreign Policy*, published by the Finnish Institute of International Affairs since 1973.

An original and comparative interpretation of the development of the Finnish nationalist movement in the nineteenth century is to be found in M. Hroch, *Social Preconditions of National Revival in Europe*, Cambridge 1984, and may be compared with R. Alapuro, 'Nineteenth Century Nationalism in Finland: A Comparative Perspective', *SPS*, vol. 2 (1979). P. Hamalainen, *In Time of Storm: Revolution, Civil War and the Ethnolinguistic Issue in Finland*, Albany, NY 1979, looks at the tensions generated in 1917–18, while M. Rintala, *Three Generations: The Extreme Right Wing in Finnish Politics*, Bloomington 1962, examines the background of the Lapua movement. See also R. Alapuro and E. Allardt, 'The Lapua Movement: The Threat of a Rightist Takeover in Finland, 1930–1932' in J. Linz and A. Stepan (*eds*), *The Breakdown of Democratic Regimes in Europe*, Baltimore 1978. A brief history of the University of Helsinki is offered by M. Klinge, *University of Helsinki: A Short History*, Helsinki 1977.

A short summary of the main findings of her thesis (in Finnish) is offered

by I. Sulkunen, 'Temperance as a Civic Religion: The Cultural Foundation of the Finnish Working-Class Temperance Ideology', *Contemporary
Drug Problems*, vol. 11 (1983). The *Report of the Committee on the Position of
Women in Finnish Society*, Helsinki 1973, is informative on the contemporary scene.

The left in Finland has been covered by J. Hodgson, *Communism in
Finland: A History and an Interpretation*, Princeton, 1967, and A. Upton,
*Communism in Scandinavia and Finland: Politics of Opportunity*, New York
1973. See also D. Kirby, ' "The Workers' Cause": Rank-and-file
Attitudes in the Finnish Social Democratic Party, 1903–1918', *Past and
Present*, vol. 111 (1986). On the civil war of 1918, the most thorough
study is A. Upton, *The Finnish revolution, 1917–1918*, Minneapolis 1982.
See also O. Manninen, 'Red, White and Blue in Finland, 1918: A Survey
of Interpretations of the Civil War', *SJH*, vol. 3 (1978). E. Allardt, 'Social
Sources of Finnish Communism: Traditional and Emerging Radicalism',
*International Journal of Comparative Sociology*, vol. 5 (1964), looks at
'industrial' and 'backwoods' communism in Finland. D. Arter, 'Cat-and-
mouse Games in the Finnish Communist Party', *Journal of Communist
Studies*, vol. 1 (1985), is an up-to-date analysis of the problems of the left in
modern Finland.

A recent comparative study of the development of Finnish society is
provided in M. Alestalo and S. Kuhnle, 'The Scandinavian Route: Economic, Social and Political Developments in Denmark, Finland, Norway and
Sweden', in R. Erikson *et al.* (*eds*), *The Scandinavian Model: Welfare States
and Welfare Research*, London 1987. See also E. Allardt, 'The Civic
Conception of the Welfare State in Scandinavia' in R. Rose and R.
Shiratori (*eds*), *The Welfare State East and West*, Oxford 1986.

J. Nousiainen, *The Finnish Political System*, Cambridge, Mass. 1971, and
K. Törnudd, *The Electoral System of Finland*, London 1968, give compre-
hensive surveys. The early decades of the modern political party system in
Finland are covered in J. Mylly and M. Berry, *Political Parties in Finland*,
Turku 1984. Modern politics are well covered by D. Arter, *Politics and
Policy-Making in Finland*, London and New York 1987.

# INDEX